Colin Turing Campbell

British South Africa

A History of the Colony of the Cape of Good Hope, from its Conquest 1795...

Colin Turing Campbell

British South Africa
A History of the Colony of the Cape of Good Hope, from its Conquest 1795...

ISBN/EAN: 9783744756938

Printed in Europe, USA, Canada, Australia, Japan

Cover: Foto ©ninafisch / pixelio.de

More available books at **www.hansebooks.com**

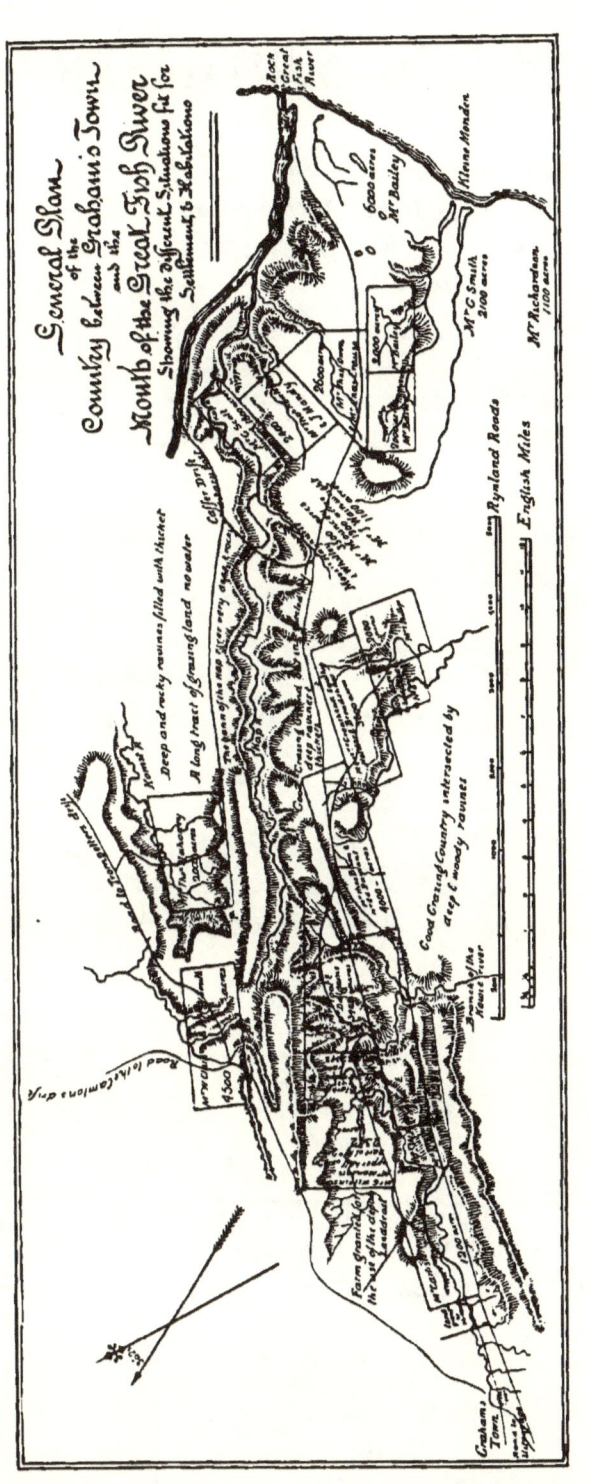

BRITISH SOUTH AFRICA

A History of the Colony of the Cape of Good Hope from its Conquest 1795 to the Settlement of Albany by the British Emigration of 1819 [A.D. 1795—A.D. 1825]

WITH NOTICES OF SOME OF THE BRITISH
SETTLERS OF 1820

BY

COLIN TURING CAMPBELL

[Resident at Graham's Town, 1848-1871]

WITH MAP OF THE ZUURVELD DIVIDED INTO LOCATIONS

JOHN HADDON & CO
6 BELL'S BUILDINGS, SALISBURY SQUARE, LONDON, E.C
J. C. JUTA & CO., CAPE TOWN, PORT ELIZABETH, JOHANNESBURG
1897
All Rights Reserved

PREFACE

THE following pages are the outcome of a long-cherished wish to contribute to the stock of information respecting the British Settlement in the Colony of the Cape of Good Hope. What little there is of this portion of the history of the Colony is now antiquated, and no writer has given particulars of the British Settlers themselves, their experiences after arrival, and their troubles and trials before the severe sufferings they had to endure by successive Kafir wars. The history of these wars is full enough, in which the British military forces figure prominently with distinction, while the ruin of the Settlers themselves is hardly alluded to.

Many circumstances prevented my attempting anything in this direction whilst resident in Graham's Town. It was not till quite the evening of my life, and retirement from the public service in Griqualand West, that sufficient freedom from the distractions of unceasing labour allowed of my making a commencement of the work, and it has been pursued under difficulties, amidst many cares and anxieties. The work, however, was one of interest to me, and the disadvantage of distance from Graham's Town and Cape Town—where ready access could be obtained to such works as it was necessary to read and consult by way of preparation for my task—was lightened by the numerous books on South Africa to be found on the shelves of the Kimberley Public Library within my reach. Kind friends also supplied me with the loan of such other publications relating to the Settler period which were not to be found in that excellent institution.

The opportunity also presented itself to me about three years ago to pay a short visit to Cape Town, where, by the kind permission of the authorities, the original records of the past preserved in the archives could be examined, and from which copious notes and extracts were made to serve my purpose. My grateful acknowledgments are hereby expressed for the kindness and encouragement received from the Rev. H. C. V. Liebbrandt, Keeper of the Archives, and G. M. Theal, Esq., LL.D., Colonial Historiographer, who cheerfully and readily assisted me in my search and lightened my labours by imparting their knowledge of documents, reports and parliamentary papers, and generously allowing me the use of printed works not generally accessible. Nor must I omit to mention J. Templer Horne, Esq., the Surveyor-General, who kindly supplied me with a tracing of the Survey of the Zuurveld into locations for the British Settlers.

My warm and grateful thanks are also due to the Hon. Sir J. Gordon Sprigg, K.C.M.G., Treasurer-General, who manifested a practical interest in my work by taking the trouble to peruse the manuscript and encouraging me to get it printed ; also to the many kind friends and correspondents all over the country who readily responded to my invitation for particulars respecting their families, which has made the "Short Notices of British Settlers of 1820" highly interesting.

It is to the period of the British Settlement of 1820 in the history of the Colony that its progress and development as a part of the British Empire is to be traced. Without this valuable addition to the population the Colony would have remained nominally British by virtue of its conquest; its inhabitants, of mixed European origin, drifting away from its boundaries and involving the Government in expenditure for the preservation of the lives of the more peaceable, who were content to remain under British protection and government. Imperfect as this attempt to compile a history of the early years of the past may be thought, it is hoped it will be found interesting to the general reader, and the new material—never before published, as far as I am aware—especially attractive to the descendants of that band of Colonists who have given the country of their adoption its English character, its English spirit of enterprise, and its English independence, love of freedom, and attachment to the throne of Great Britain.

COLIN T. CAMPBELL.

BARBRECK, KIMBERLEY, *April*, 1896.

CONTENTS

CHAPTER		PAGE
I.	CONQUEST OF THE CAPE, AND ITS OCCUPATION BY BRITISH FORCES, 1795-1803	1
II.	RESUMPTION OF THE COLONY BY THE BATAVIAN GOVERNMENT, 1803-1805	10
III.	THE CONQUEST OF THE COLONY, 1805-1806	14
IV.	STORMY DAYS	19
V.	THE ATTACK UPON GRAHAM'S TOWN	23
VI.	COLONAL GRAHAM	26
VII.	PROJECTED SETTLEMENT OF THE ZUNSVELD AND INTRODUCTION OF BRITISH IMMIGRANTS	29
VIII.	REGULATIONS INTRODUCING SETTLERS TO THE ZUNSVELD	35
IX.	THE ZUNSVELD	40
X.	PREPARATIONS FOR RECEPTION AND LOCATION OF THE SETTLERS	43
XI.	LANDING OF THE SETTLERS—JOURNEY TO, AND ARRIVAL AT, THE LOCATIONS	47
XII.	THE ACTING-GOVERNOR'S VISIT TO ALBANY	52
XIII.	BIOGRAPHY OF THE LEADERS	55
XIV.	WILLSON'S PARTY	59
XV.	PARKER'S PARTY	63
XVI.	SIR RUBANE DONKIN'S ADMINISTRATION	69
XVII.	THE KOWIE RIVER'S MOUTH	76
XVIII.	RELIGION AND EDUCATION AMONG THE SETTLERS	79
XIX.	ADDITIONAL EMIGRANTS	86
XX.	REVERSAL OF LORD CHARLES SOMERSET'S POLICY	89
XXI.	LORD CHARLES SOMERSET'S GOVERNMENT	92
XXII.	LORD CHARLES SOMERSET'S RE... THE SETTLERS	

CHAPTER		PAGE
XXIII.	ALTERATIONS IN THE LAWS AND ESTABLISHMENT OF A FREE PRESS	105
	BRITISH SETTLERS WHO ROSE TO DISTINCTION .	110

APPENDICES:

I.	CAPE PARLIAMENT	121
II.	EARL BATHURST'S DESPATCH, NO. 280	123
III.	LIST OF THE SETTLERS OF 1820 . . .	125
IV.	GENERAL CAMPBELL'S SETTLERS . .	183
V.	LETTERS FROM SETTLERS	184
IV.	BRITISH SETTLERS OF 1820	188

BRITISH SOUTH AFRICA

CHAPTER I

CONQUEST OF THE CAPE, AND ITS OCCUPATION BY BRITISH FORCES, 1795-1803

THE Settlement on the shores of Table Bay founded by Van Rubeck, as representing the Netherlands East India Company in 1652, intended as a trading station for the exclusive benefit of that mercantile association, remained under the direction of that body by a succession of Commanders until 1795, when the importance of Table Bay as the key to India and the East was considered paramount in the struggle for supremacy among the European powers; it was acquired by conquest by a British fleet, under Admiral Elphinstone, with 5,000 troops under command of General Craig. That was the death-blow of this grasping, mercenary, trading corporation, whose despotic government and rigorous monopoly of all produce raised by the settlers in the country had driven those living outside Cape Town into open rebellion. Apart from the advantage of disciplined troops, more than sufficient to conquer the paltry fort and town of Cape Town and reduce its inhabitants into complete submission, the moment of attack was favourable. Disaffection existed all over the territory claimed to belong to the Company; open rebellion had been declared against the Government by the Boers, who dwelt inland at remote distances about Swellendam and Graaff Reinet, and who had in fact set up a Government of their own, under their own officers and style of " Nationalists." Even in the extremity of immediate capture these Boers declined to come to the assistance of Sluysken, who had been left in command of the Settlement by the Commissioners Nederburg and Frykenius, although he was weak in mind and body, and endeavouring to oppose the landing and march to Cape Town of the British forces. There was no help for it but unconditional surrender, and the Cape of Good Hope passed into the possession and occupation of the King of Great Britain. The captured were treated with great leniency; their laws and customs were guaranteed to them, property was to be respected, no new taxes were to be levied, and the Dutch Reformed Church was to keep its rights and privileges. From this date—1795 till 1802—the Settlement at Cape Town and all the country beyond it acquired by the inhabitants owing allegiance to the Dutch East India Company, became subject to Great Britain, and the people British subjects.

The population at this time consisted of an upper class, comprising the Commandant of the Fort and the several officials employed by the Dutch East India Company as storekeepers and officials of Government, who all resided in Table Valley around the castle of Cape Town—a garrison of soldiers and sailors of mixed nationalities : the burgher class, who were small farmers about Cape Town and Stellenbosch, originally soldiers or sailors who had been allotted patches of land for cultivation under condition that they remained in the Settlement for ten years and cultivated the ground ; and the Boers, descendants of the Huguenot settlers, who occupied loan-places beyond the mountains, and held graziers' licenses. The total of all this heterogeneous population of European origin was under 20,000. There was besides an equally mixed gathering of persons of colour, held in bondage as slaves : Malays from Batavia, negroes from Madagascar, from the West Coast of Africa, and Hottentots and Bushmen captured in the country. The total of all these races was slightly in excess of the number of the Europeans. With all this variety of race there was naturally a confusion of tongues ; each had to learn from the other somewhat to make himself intelligible, and the subject races had to acquire as much Dutch as would make them serviceable to their taskmasters. From this diversity of tongues there grew into use that unique language popularly called Dutch, but which is unintelligible to Hollanders.

General Craig administered the Government of the Colony until a Governor was appointed by the home Government. His rule lasted nearly two years, during which time, while he did all he could to conciliate the inhabitants, he showed a firm disposition to maintain law and order. The Boers about Swellendam remained passive, if not altogether submissive and loyal, but those further off, at Graaff Reinet, had still an idea of a national Government apart from Cape Town under their own chosen leaders, and continued intractable and refractory. The better educated inhabitants about Cape Town—in Table Valley—soon discovered the value of the change in affairs, having now an open market in which to dispose of their produce, freedom from oppression, and security of their property. There was, however, an apprehension that France or Holland would make an effort to retake the Cape, consequently General Craig prepared for such an eventuality by strengthening the defences about Cape Town, and was on the alert for an attack. Such an attempt was made soon after the news of the capture of the Cape reached Europe. The two Republics combined to make an attempt to recover it. It was arranged that the Dutch fleet of nine ships, under Admiral Lucas, with 2,000 troops on board, should meet off the Cape a French squadron coming from the East, and the combined fleets were to recover the castle and town of Cape Town, which Sluysken had lost. The Dutch ships were badly fitted, and insufficiently provisioned, so that when off the Cape they were leaky, and the crews and soldiers half-starved. There being no sign of the French fleet, Admiral Lucas put into Saldanha Bay with the view of obtaining supplies of food, and in the vain hope of enlisting the colonists to aid him. In both expectations he was disappointed: he could not procure food, and the Boers would not assist him; and to make matters worse, the crews were mutinous and the soldiers discontented. News of the fleet at anchor in Saldanha Bay was not long in reaching Cape Town, nor was there delay on the part of the General in acting accordingly. The English ships in Simon's Bay, that had been long waiting for tidings of the assailants, proceeded to the encounter, and the General, leaving Major-General Doyle in command at Cape Town, proceeded overland with the same object. As the English ships appeared in the distance, Admiral Lucas's hopes revived, as not unnaturally it was thought they were the fleet expected for Java. The illusion was soon dispelled when the flag of England was made out. It was impossible to think of escaping; they were securely caught in a trap; all they could do was to surrender. On boarding the prizes the Dutch forces were found to be completely demoralized, and it was necessary to place a strong guard over the Dutch officers to prevent them from being maltreated by their own men. Provisions were almost exhausted, the men had been on short rations so long that they appeared half-starved. A large number of the mercenaries and conscripts volunteered to enter the British service, an offer which Admiral Elphinstone accepted as soon as he returned to Table Bay with his prizes, putting them on board some Indiamen, taking an equal number of able seamen in return. Thus the entire force of ships and men composing the expedition, which the Batavian Government expected would recover the Colony, fell into the hands of the English without a shot being fired or a drop of blood being spilt.

The Boers, who had made Swellendam their headquarters and had pushed their way on to Graaff Reinet, continued their opposition to the Government at Cape Town, and set the authorities at defiance. They refused to submit to Mr. Bresler, who had been appointed in 1796 Landdrost at Graaff Reinet, and had appointed their own nominee, Gerotz, in his place. General Craig was not disposed to overlook this deliberate act of insubordination, and immediately ordered a detachment of troops to proceed to the spot and quell the insurrection. Intimidated by this prompt action, the rebels sent a deputation to Cape Town praying that the troops might be recalled, and promising submission and obedience to the laws. Circumstances favoured the granting of this request, and the insurgents were informed that the past would be overlooked, and Mr. Gerotz allowed to act as provisional Landdrost until it would be convenient to send Mr. Bresler to resume that office.

The home Government appointed the Earl of Macartney, a civilian of high rank and character, as Governor of the Colony, and martial law under General Craig came to an end on his arrival. General Craig distinguished his short, temporary rule by putting an end to the barbarous practice of proceeding by torture against persons suspected of crimes which prevailed under Dutch law, and after conviction of the accused, breaking them under the wheel. According to that law, capital punishment, especially of slaves and natives, was carried out by the executioners, who, in terms of the sentence, had to see that the criminals were "bound to a cross and broken thereon alive, from under upwards with the *coup de grace*," or, "laid upon a wheel, or hung on the gallows, there to remain a prey to the air and the birds of the heavens." General Craig obtained reports from the Courts of Justice relative to this atrocious practice, and urged upon the home Government to authorize a stop being put to this inhuman procedure. In the commission issued to the Governor of the Colony, the king's command was given that this practice was to be discontinued, and the racks, wheels, and other instruments of torture were destroyed, and for the future the execution for capital crimes was to be the same as in England—by hanging.

Earl Macartney assumed the government, May, 1797. He was accompanied by Mr. Hercules Ross as paymaster of the forces, and by Mr., afterwards Sir, John Barrow as his private secretary. The oath of allegiance to the British Crown was renewed, and merchants and others were cautioned against giving any account of the circumstances of the Colony in their letters, and foreigners were prohibited from settling without a license. But his Lordship soon found that the state of the country was disorganized and demoralized, all classes were discontented, and Graaff Reinet virtually in open rebellion. One of his Excellency's first acts was to send for Mr. Bresler, the Landdrost, and the clergyman, Rev. Kicheren, whom the Boers had expelled from the district, and inform them that he had resolved to compel the Boers to receive them back and apologise for their rebellious conduct. Both officials objected to return, and the Governor asked Mr. Barrow to go with them, saying, "I think you will have no objection to accompany one or both these gentlemen to the presence of these savages, which may lead them to reflect that it must be out of tenderness to them that I have preferred to send them one of my own family rather than at once to bring them to their senses by a regiment of dragoons. Besides this I have another motive for wishing you to accompany them. We are shamefully ignorant even of the geography of the country. I neither know, nor can I learn, where this Graaff Reinet lies—whether it is five hundred or a thousand miles from Cape Town. I am further informed that the Kafirs, with their cattle, are in possession of the Zunsveld, the finest grazing ground in the Colony, and that these people and the Boers are perpetually fighting and mutually carrying off each other's cattle. These matters must no longer be tolerated." When the party, under the direction of Mr. Barrow and the Landdrost—the clergyman positively refusing to go—arrived at Graaff Reinet, a meeting of the inhabitants was called, to whom the commission of the magistrate was read, and the intentions of his Excellency explained. They all seemed much pleased, but some malcontents complained that when the Kafirs had invaded the district, the acting Landdrost had not given an answer to their requisition for a commander. To this Mr. Barrow replied "that his instructions were to accompany the Landdrost to the part of the district where the Kafirs had located themselves, and to endeavour to persuade them to retire across the boundary to their country, and it was hoped they would be prevailed upon to do so; that it was the decided determination of the Governor to put an end to those commandoes which had caused so much bloodshed and ill-feeling; and moreover that the general opinion of their countrymen at the Cape and in the southern districts was that the plunder of the Kafir's cattle was the main object of these hostile expeditions." Matters having been arranged as well as circumstances would permit, Mr. Barrow and the Landdrost set out on the expedition to Kafirland. Their tents were pitched on the banks of the Kareiga River, about the centre of the Zunsveld, amidst hundreds of Kafirs, who alleged they had come thither in pursuit of game. It was explained to them that the country had passed into the hands of Britain, that it was necessary the boundary should be respected, and that they must recross the Fish River. Proceeding to the place of the great chief Gaika, about 15 miles beyond the Keiskama River, a conference was held, at which Mr. Barrow fully explained the wishes of Government, and the reply was satisfactory. The petty chiefs who had been met on the Kareiga were invited to return into Kafirland, and Gaika promised to keep up a friendly intercourse with the Landdrost by sending annually one of his indunas (captains) to Graaff Reinet bearing a brass gorget with the arms of Britain engraved on it. Subsequently the Kafirs on the colonial side of the Fish River refused to move, and Mr. Barrow considered that they were encouraged in this determination by a set of adventurers, "chiefly soldiers or sailors, who had either deserted or had been discharged from the Dutch army and the Company's shipping." The expedition proceeded over the Snow Mountains to the Orange River, through the country of the Bushmen, with the object of bringing about a conversation with some of the chiefs of these poor people, to persuade them, if possible, to quit their wild and marauding life, on being assured that the Boers would not be allowed to molest them; at the same time to see the state of this portion of the Colony, and of the "Christian inhabitants," as the Boers designated themselves. The Boers about the Snow Mountains appeared to Mr. Barrow to be in general a better description of men than those towards the sea coast; a peaceable, obliging, and orderly people, a brave and hardy race of men. It was found impossible, however, even to confer with the Bushmen, much less to persuade them of the good intentions of the British Government. In 1787-8 a part of the Slumbic (Kafir) tribe migrated towards the Orange River, and, afterwards being driven back, settled about the neighbourhood of Praamberg and Schutfontein in the division of Beaufort. Mr. Barrow subsequently travelled into Namaqualand. On his return to Cape Town, Earl Macartney appointed him Auditor-General of the Colony.

On accepting the appointment of Governor of the Colony, Earl Macartney had made it a condition that if his health gave way he should be authorized to transfer the duties of his office to the officer in command of the forces. The emoluments of the office were £10,000 per annum, and an allowance of £2,000 per annum as table money, the home Government making up any deficiency in the cost of the establishments if the revenue was unequal to the expenditure. The Earl did not extend his stay in the Colony beyond twelve months. Before his departure the boundaries of the Colony were proclaimed: on the eastern frontier, the Fish River; on the north, the Sea Cow River, behind the Snow Mountain, and the Karie behind Camdeboo, and the Sack River. Batteries had been erected on Devil's Hill and Craig's Tower, Cape Town, as well as at Fort Frederick at Algoa Bay. He left the Colony in November, 1798, Lieut.-General Sir Francis Dundas assuming the government.

The Governor who succeeded the Earl of Macartney was Sir George Yonge, Bart., December 18th, 1799. He proved unsatisfactory in every way. One of his earliest proclamations (February 19th, 1800) was an infringement of the liberty of the subject. It required all clubs to render an exact account of their origin and the nature of their institution. This inquisitorial proclamation was subsequently relied upon by Lord Charles Somerset in his prosecution of Messrs. Fairbairn, Pillairs, and Dr. Philip for holding meetings to form a literary society. He had already, under pretence of putting the avenues in the Government gardens in repair, closed to the public the gardens, which in the height of summer were the accustomed resort of the citizens to enjoy the refreshing coolness of the shady walks. Besides these petty acts of tyranny he made appointment of his private secretary as an examiner or taster of wines, brandies and other liquors, with penalties for wines and brandies of improper quality; also farming out of licenses for retailing wine, etc., and regulations for bidding for wine licenses. But other and graver charges were made of participating in the property derived by his aide-de-camp, private secretary and others around the Governor for facilitating the affairs of individuals with the Government. The fact was established by a Commission of inquiry that the practice prevailed of taking douceurs or bribes for obtaining or granting certain privileges or contracts. An instance of the depravity and profligacy of those immediately connected with the representative of the sovereign was given in the case of an official who wanted one-half, but agreed to take one-third of the property on the importation of a cargo of slaves. A Mr. Hogan was one who "facilitated affairs" with the official in question. He had a vessel named the *Collector*, which he employed as a privateer, and which was remarkable for the number of prize slave cargoes which she brought into port, ostensibly captured off the coast of Madagascar. Whilst in harbour, the *Collector* was identified by a Danish ship, which had arrived in Table Bay, as a well-known slave trader, that the *Collector* had never captured any prize, but that the slaves were purchased and put on board the vessel at Mozambique. The case was investigated by the Court of Justice, and it was proved that the Court of Vice-Admiralty had been grossly imposed upon by false witnesses and false log-books, and Hogan appeared to have been the person who planned the whole of it. Sentence was given against the captain of the *Collector*, but he fled the Colony and was declared an outlaw. Sir George Yonge was exonerated of all knowledge of these disgraceful affairs, but recalled by a dispatch from Downing Street, 14th January, 1801, directing him to resign his Government into the hands of Lieut.-General Dundas, without waiting the arrival of Lord Glenlurvie, who was to succeed him. The latter however did not take up the appointment, but accepted that of Paymaster of the Forces instead. From the departure of Sir George Yonge the Government was administered by Lieut.-General Sir Francis Dundas till the Colony was restored to the Batavian Government in 1803.

From the moment that the departure of the Earl of Macartney for England was made known in the distant parts of the Colony, the ignorant and misguided Boers, excited by that party of mischievous and not less ignorant persons in Cape Town, who had long shown their hatred to good order, seemed to think that with his Lordship had departed all authority, and the means of bringing them to legal punishment. Their restless and turbulent minds, and above all their avaricious and iniquitous views about the harmless Kafirs, could no longer brook restraint ; and they determined at a select meeting, as one of them observed in a letter to a friend at Cape Town, "Now that the old lord was gone away, to prove themselves true patriots" by going on commando against the Kafirs. Their first proceeding was to rescue a prisoner who was being sent under escort to be tried at Cape Town.

The Court of Justice had issued a warrant for the apprehension of a Boer named Adrian van Jaarweld, a commandant, residing on a lower place at the foot of the Nieuwveld Mountains, on a charge of attempting to defraud the Government by falsifying a receipt for interest on money borrowed from the Orphan Chamber. He was arrested, and was being conveyed from Graaff Reinet to Cape Town in charge of the secretary to the Landdrost and four dragoons. A short distance from that town the prisoner was rescued by an armed body of Boers, who strengthened their numbers by summoning all the Boers between the Long Kloof and Bushman's River to join them, under threat of being considered "traitors to the country, who would be dealt with after the affair was over." The ringleaders and their followers took an oath to be faithful to each other to the last drop of their blood. The most prominent of these rebels were the Boers of Bunitjes Hooghte. This force marched on to Graaff Reinet, and encamped on the Sunday's River for about a month, where rules were prescribed how the Kafirs should be treated, and threatened to hang the Landdrost and exterminate the garrison, which consisted of a sergeant and seven dragoons. The new clergyman, Rev. Mr. Ballot, repeatedly interviewed the insurgents, and by his persuasions succeeded in retarding their plans and preventing acts of personal violence. Meanwhile, on the news of this revolt reaching Cape Town, General Dundas immediately dispatched two divisions of troops, one overland, the other by sea, to Algoa Bay. Major McNab, with a detachment of dragoons and Hottentots, proceeded overland, General Vandeleur in command of the troops, who landed at Algoa Bay. The former proceeded without opposition to Graaff Reinet, and found the rebels had retired to Bunitjes Hooghte, who sent two of their number applying for pardon. Vandeleur followed them to Bunitjes Hooghte, where they laid down their arms. The ringleaders, Prinslov, Van Jaarweld, and others, were sent to Cape Town to await their trial ; others were pardoned on payment of a fine of one or two horses for the cavalry, and a few who refused to surrender retired as fugitives into Kafirland.

The march of the troops overland through the Hottentot kraals caused considerable excitement amongst those natives. Some thought it was an army to exterminate them ; others, who were in service to Boers, of whose harsh treatment they complained, took the opportunity to leave their cruel taskmasters, and with others joined the Kafirs, who were occupying the bushy country between the Sunday's River and the Bushman's River, and who were already massing against the Boers in their neighbourhood. The Kafirs, reinforced by those people who were in possession of firearms and accustomed to their use, immediately set to ravaging the country as far as even to the westward of the Lang-kloof and Kuysua. The Boers were panic-struck at this unexpected insurrection of the Hottentots, who, with their allies, the Kafirs, numbered about 750, with more than 300 horses and 150 muskets. Resort was had to a commando under Tjait van der Walt, and a detachment of troops under Major Sherlock. The commando was unsuccessful, the Commandant Van der Walt being killed by a musket ball whilst penetrating the woods near the Gamtoos River. Whilst this state of things was going on, General Dundas sent for Mr. Magnier, the former Landdrost of Graaff Reinet, to use efforts for the restoration of peace. Magnier went unarmed to where the confederacy was assembled, between the Sunday's River and the Bushman's River. After much trouble he concluded a peace with the Hottentots, the terms of which were that "the Government should protect them against the ill-treatment of the Boers in the most efficacious manner, and should provide that when they served the Boers they should be well paid and well treated." He returned to the General with the chiefs of the confederacy, Sturman, Boazah, and Borelander, with whom the General ratified the peace. A similar plan was adopted with regard to the Kafirs, to whom presents were forwarded, and with whom the General also agreed on terms of peace. Magnier was the appointed resident Commissioner at Graaff Reinet to carry out regulations to give effect to the agreement, and to restore order in the district. He opened a register of the time, wages and other terms upon which the Hottentots entered into service of any European master, as a matter of reference in case of after disputes. He urged the Boers to return and re-occupy their farms as the only way of restoring confidence and tranquility. But mischievous reports were afloat that the Kafirs and Hottentots were preparing to extirpate the Boers in Bunitjes Hooghte. A number of Boers therefore assembled in arms at Swager's Hoek under command of Renshug and Field Cornet Erasmus. They marched to Graaff Reinet, and requested leave to go on commando and ammunition. They complained of the privileges granted to the Hottentots, especially of their being placed on an equal footing with themselves, and being allowed the use of the church, and finally demanded that those Hottentots who had murdered their relations should be delivered up to them. Many Hottentots, alarmed by the movement of the Boers, had sought refuge in the town, and were received and provided for by the Commissioner, lest they might form themselves into predatory bands, and renew the system of plunder and devastation. The Commissioner consented to keep them out of the church, under Mr. Van der Kemp, and that such of the Hottentots as were accused of murder should be arrested and tried according to law. A small body of dragoons, with four field-pieces, in addition to the Hottentots, were prepared to defend the town; the other inhabitants, laying down their arms, refused to use them against their countrymen. The insurgent Boers threatened to destroy the place if the Hottentots were not delivered up. This challenge was received with firmness, and after their refusal to lay down arms the Commissioner opened fire upon them. Van Renshug and his party returned the fire, but at length retired and dispersed to their farms without loss of life on either side.

Magnier continued his efforts to restore order, and to get the Hottentots to re-enter into service with the Boers, but his firmness made him unpopular with these people, who circulated reports to his injury, amongst others that he had connived at the murder of a Boer named Nandi in the Camdeboo by the Kafirs. The general disaffection at Graaff Reinet induced General Dundas to recall Magnier, and a Commission was appointed to inquire into the charges made against him. These were that he had delayed acquainting the Government with the turbulent state of the country; that he had obtained cattle from the Kafirs and Hottentots for beads and other trifles : that he had sent Europeans among the Hottentots to dissuade them from entering into service ; that he had refused to bring certain Hottentots to Graaff Reinet accused of murder, and permitted them to escape; injustice and cruelty in the matter of the murder of Nandi ; and also in delivering into the hands of the Boers a number of Hottentots who fled to him for protection. After a lengthened investigation, the Commission reported that Magnier was "entirely innocent of all and every one of the charges preferred against him, and that some of the evidence was such as to merit the most serious reprobation." Magnier was thereupon reappointed to office as a member of the Court of Justice. Meantime an intimation had been received that the Colony would probably be restored to the Dutch Government. General Dundas accordingly made arrangements to terminate his administration. He proposed to the Rev. Dr. van der Kemp to locate the Hottentots at Graaff Reinet who had refused to re-enter the service of their former masters on a lone place near Algoa Bay, where they would have the protection of the military stationed at Fort Frederick. The proposal was accepted, and Van der Kemp left Graaff Reinet with 300 Hottentots, men, women, and children, and founded the mission station of Bethelsdorp, which became an asylum for members of the race, who left their kraals, and hiding-places in the woods, and settled there as peaceful subjects.

The Boer prisoners who had surrendered to General van der Lear in 1799 remained in custody in the castle at Cape Town until their trial in 1800 before the Court of Justice, the members of which were De Wet, Fleck, Matthieson, H. Truter, Baumgardt, and J. A. Truter, secretary. The leaders, Prinslov and Van Jaarsveld, were condemned to death ; others were ordered " to be delivered to the executioner blindfolded, to kneel down upon a heap of sand, to have the sword waved over their heads for punishment, and then to be banished for the remainder of their lives from the Settlement!" Some were recommended to mercy and set at liberty. Owing to the disturbances in the country and change of governors, the sentence of the Court of Justice was delayed, and in December, 1801, Governor-General Dundas recommended modification of the capital sentence, if not a full remission, " thereby to demonstrate the mild spirit of the English, and the peaceable, forbearing system actuating the Government." On the evacuation of the Colony, February, 1803, the prisoners were free to leave the castle under the amnesty granted by the Batavian Commissioners. The last proclamation of General Dundas was to absolve all persons not being British subjects from the oath of allegiance to His Majesty George III.

CHAPTER II

RESUMPTION OF THE COLONY BY THE BATAVIAN GOVERNMENT, 1803-1805

A SHORT interval follows, a period of three years, when the Colony was again under the Government of the Dutch republic. The Colony of the Cape of Good Hope was considered by the Batavian Government a national possession, to be protected as the most important position in the great highway of Eastern commerce. Liberal views were entertained as to its Government, which was to be such as to admit of the greatest amount of freedom compatible with a dependency, and every facility was to be afforded for the development of its internal resources, and for the advancement of the prosperity of its inhabitants. To collect information upon the administration of the old East India Company, to suggest improvements and necessary alterations, a committee was appointed, who entrusted the drawing up of their report to a very able man, J. A. de Mist. The report coincided so perfectly with the views of the Batavian Government that de Mist was sent out as High Commissioner to receive the Colony from the English, and to invest the Governor, General Janssens, with his office, and to make such regulations as he might deem necessary. On the 21st February, 1803, the Batavian flag was hoisted on the Forts, and the Government transferred to the Dutch. Governor Janssens and Commissioner de Mist were received with great courtesy by General Dundas, who immediately resigned to them his residence within the Castle. Stores had been valued, and everything was ready for departure when despatches, received by an English frigate, commanded the Governor on no account to give up possession of the Cape until further orders. In this serious dilemma it was cordially agreed that the Dutch should remove into cantonments at Wynberg, in order to prevent any collision, and wait there till definite orders should be received from home. A period of anxious suspense followed, and some of the radical party in the town did their best to cause a rupture, hoping they would meet encouragement from de Mist, who was supposed to be a friend of Talleyrand; but, says Barrow, "they were deceived in him; he was an able, agreeable, and, I believe, an honest man."[1] Towards the close of the year counter orders were received from England, and the abandonment of the Colony was speedily effected. On March the 1st proclamation was made of

[1] Autobiography, p. 241.

the assumption of the Government by the Batavian republic, and in April Dutch copper coin was substituted for the English copper coin in circulation. It is noteworthy to remark that soon after de Mist's arrival, General Janssens, April 11th, 1803, prohibited the landing or importation of slaves. An authoritative census appears to have been desired, as in August the inhabitants of the towns and districts were summoned to appear before the proper officers to state the number of their families, the produce of their farms, etc., and this was renewed in December following. In September proclamation was made of the renewal of war between England and France, and all commerce with British ships was forbidden. In November all persons in the Colony from British territories were required to take the oath of allegiance to the Dutch Government.

Soon after his assumption of office, Governor-General Janssens proceeded to the eastern frontier with the view of restoring order there. He found the Kafirs in possession of the Zunweld, the country between the Sunday's River and the Fish River. The Boers who had survived the war were in great distress, and found a refuge with their friends and relatives in other parts of the Colony. Hostilities had ceased for about three years, except an occasional raid on either side; and in spite of the peace that had been concluded by the late Government, the Boers continued to regard the Kafirs as intruders and their enemies. In May the Governor had an interview with T'Slambie, and afterwards proceeded to the Kat River, where he met Gaika, with whom he made a treaty that the Kafirs were not to molest the Boers in future. Some of the Kafirs complained that they had received ill-treatment from certain Boers. The Governor issued a proclamation that any one molesting a Kafir should be severely punished, all Kafirs held in bondage should be immediately released, and after June 1 that no one should engage a Kafir as a servant. With regard to the Hottentots, a regulation was framed that they should only be engaged as servants upon a written contract. Some Boers, who had been guilty of cruelty and oppression to these people, were punished, and he induced Klaas Stundman and his followers to remove to a distance from his late allies to the little Gamtoos River, where they were allotted a tract of land, with liberty to live there without molestation. The Hottentots, who had been allowed by General Dundas to retire to and remain at Fort Frederick (Algoa Bay), under their instructor Dr. Van der Kemp,[2] feared that they would be harassed by the disaffected Boers when the British troops were withdrawn. The Fort at Algoa Bay was evacuated in September, 1802. They had grounds for their fears, as on the arrival of General Janssens he was applied to by these insurgents to seize and distribute the Hottentots as slaves amongst them. The proposal was rejected with scorn and indignation. They then urged that the missionaries of the London Society should be expelled from the Colony, on the ground that

---

[2] Although a former schoolfellow and intimate friend of General Janssens, while refusing to permit the persecution of the Hottentots, he did not feel justified in giving much support to the missionaries.

most of them were Englishmen and would instil into the minds of their converts a hatred of the Dutch. Van der Kemp proved so plainly that the missionaries were not political agents, that the Governor only suggested that they should correspond with the London Society through the Dutch Missionary Society, which was assented to at once. Van der Kemp was then permitted to select a site for a permanent mission, and obtained a grant of land near Port Elizabeth, known as Bethelsdorp, where other Hottentots scattered over the district joined him and formed a village, that for many years remained a head institution, with affiliated branches in different parts of the country. At Genadendal, Commissioner de Mist expressed great satisfaction with the work carried on there, and assisted the missionaries with grants of money from the treasury. He also guaranteed to them the rights of property in the station lands.

Governor-General Janssens visited Graaff Reinet, where he found affairs in the utmost confusion. Lichtenstein, who accompanied the Governor, says :—" The chest of the district was empty, the books of accounts were in the most lamentable disorder, the public buildings were destroyed, and presented nothing but a sad monument of crimes; the most important posts were filled by people wholly ignorant and devoid of capacity; the disorderly populace displayed a reciprocal, irreconcilable spirit of discord and enmity towards each other. Their wholly perverted ideas of right and wrong, their extravagant notions with regard to liberty, their total want of true religious feeling, though making much external profession of piety, their perfect ignorance, in short, of all the social virtues, had placed them in a most unfortunate situation, both for themselves and the Government. A large number of Boers had emigrated; many farms were desolate, while the Kafirs occupied a considerable portion of the division." The inhabitants had always manifested a turbulent spirit, while their ignorance and perverted ideas of liberty made it impossible to place matters on a satisfactory footing. He, however, did what he could—all that was possible under the circumstances. He appointed Mr. Stockenstrom, secretary of the Swellendam district, to be Landdrost, arranged the finances of the district, provided funds for the erection of a residence for the Landdrost, a court of justice, and a church, and, later on, as the district was too extensive for one jurisdiction, he divided it into two. February, 1804, the southern portion with a tract out of the Swellendam district was called Uitenhage,[3] and Captain Alberti, of the Jager Company of the 5th (Waldeck) Battalion of the Dutch regular army, commandant of the garrison at Algoa Bay, was appointed first Landdrost.

In the interval between the departure of the British garrison in 1803, and its occupation by the Dutch commandant, Alberti, a neighbouring Boer, named Ferreira, was left in charge of the fort. He speedily began to exercise a most atrocious tyranny upon the natives. He roasted a Kafir envoy alive, and cut slices out of a living Hottentot who had displeased him, besides other acts of cruelty and oppression. The arrival of the Dutch authorities put a stop to

[3] Probable derivation Uit-en-hage—" outside the harbour."

Ferreira's career. He was arrested and removed from Algoa Bay, but was not tried or convicted.

In 1804 the district of Tulbagh was formed out of the Northern part of the district of Stellenbosch, the residence of the Landdrost being fixed at the village of Roodezand, henceforth called Tulbagh. The first Landdrost was Henry van der Graaff, nephew of the former Governor, Cornelis van der Graaff. While the north-western parts of the district of Stellenbosch were under the jurisdiction of the Landdrost of that town, it was found impossible to control the inhabitants, who were continually disobedient to the Government, quarrelling among themselves, and treating their servants with harshness. It was hoped by the formation of this district to restrain and correct these evils, to repress the robberies of the Bushmen, and to compel the Boers to treat them justly.

In February, 1805, Commissioner de Mist left the Colony. This excellent man, during his residence, had travelled through a portion of the Colony, and had been unremitting in his efforts to improve its trade and resources. Although the imminent prospect of war greatly interfered with his designs, he was enabled to effect much more than could have been expected. He drew up a plan for the establishment of public schools, promulgated a church ordinance, and reformed the courts of Landdrost and Henneraden. He appointed a commission to collect information and report upon the best methods of encouraging and improving agriculture, and the breeding of stock.

CHAPTER III

THE CONQUEST OF THE COLONY, 1805-1806

THE Colony had hardly been transferred to the Dutch when war broke out again in Europe, England being ranged against France and Holland. One of the first acts of this war was the seizure of all Dutch ships in British ports, and it was certain that possession of the Cape would be attempted by the English. The Dutch attached supreme importance to the Island of Java, which they had acquired, and directed all their energies to retain it from capture by the British. Accordingly General Janssens was directed to retain 2,000 men in his garrison, and to send the rest to Batavia. The Governor complied with his instructions, and to prepare for an attack, armed and drilled the colonists, organized a battalion of Hottentots and a corps of Malay artillery. Magazines were also erected at Hottentots Holland, and stores collected, so that in the event of Cape Town falling into the hands of the enemy, supplies might be prevented reaching it, and the invaders compelled to retire. His plans, however, were wholly inadequate to resist the seizure of the Colony, which consisted of an army of between 5,000 and 6,000 men, under command of Sir David Baird, and a powerful fleet under Commodore Sir Hume Popham. Intelligence of this great fleet approaching was brought to Cape Town by an American vessel, Christmas, 1805, and on the evening of January 4, 1806, the fleet came to anchor between Seal Island and the coast. It consisted of sixty-three ships, the greater number of which were transports loaded with stores and Indiamen under convoy. No time was lost in effecting a landing on the beach near Blaauwberg, Blue Mountains, with the loss of thirty-six men of the 93rd regiment, who were drowned by the swamping of the boat, four soldiers wounded, and one killed by the fire of the Dutch sharpshooters, posted on a commanding height. On the morning of the 8th the army was formed into two brigades, and marched towards Cape Town. The sharpshooters were easily dislodged from their position, and the ascent of the Blaauwberg accomplished. General Janssens, on receiving authentic information as to when the English had landed, hastened to meet them. His army was about 5,000 strong; only a small portion, however, consisted of regular troops, the remainder comprising mounted burghers, and a battalion of French seamen and marines from the stranded vessels *Atalanta* and *Napoleon*. He had twenty-three pieces of cannon, the English only eight. The English commander extended his lines to prevent his flanks from being turned, the Highland brigade pressing steadily forward under a deadly fire, which the artillery were playing upon the advancing corps from another direction. The Dutch stood their ground bravely until the Highlanders charged them with the bayonet. They then broke and fled, leaving 700 dead and wounded on the battlefield. General Janssens attempted to rally the fugitives, without effect. So much confusion ensued that a hasty retreat had to be made. As the British troops were fatigued with a march of six hours over scorching sands, after having been cooped up on board ship for five months, they were in no condition to pursue the enemy, so that General Janssens was able to retire without difficulty, and fell back upon Hottentots Holland. He sent some troops to Cape Town to assist in its defence.[1] General Baird advanced some distance farther, and formed camp for the night. His army was almost destitute of provisions, and water could not be found. By the exertions of the seamen belonging to the fleet, supplies reached him in a few hours. When the roll was called, it was found that his loss amounted to 212 killed, wounded and missing. On the next morning (9th), the march was resumed towards Cape Town without opposition. Arrived at Salt River, free communication was obtained with the fleet, and preparations made for landing a battering ram and an ample supply of provisions. But Colonel von Prophalow, who had been entrusted with the defence of Cape Town, had resolved to surrender without a struggle. He sent a flag of truce, requesting a suspension of hostilities for forty-eight hours, in order to arrange terms of capitulation, which met the English at Porpendorp. General Baird would only grant thirty-six hours, and required immediate possession of the outworks, with the alternative of taking them by storm. His demand could not be refused, and that night the 59th Regiment of Foot was admitted into the outermost fort. Next day, at 4 p.m., January 10, 1806, articles of capitulation were signed, and the town placed in possession of the English, the garrison marching out with the honours of war before surrendering, laying down their arms and becoming prisoners of war. Such officers as were natives of the Colony, or married with natives, or in possession of sufficient landed property to become regularly and *bonâ-fide* domiciliated, were set at liberty to continue thus so long as they behaved themselves as good subjects and citizens, and allowed to proceed to Great Britain with regular transports, having previously passed their parole not to serve until regularly exchanged. All officers who went to Europe were provided passages at the expense of his Britannic Majesty, with leave to realize their property previous to their departure, and received the same pay as they did in their own service, till the day of their embarkation. The French subjects

---

[1] It must be borne in mind, in connection with the defence of the Colony, that the Cape Town fortifications had been previously restored by the British, who had received them in an almost ruinous state in 1795. They comprised a chain of redoubts, connected by a parapet, with banquettes, and a dry ditch, block-house, and open batteries, the whole mounted with 150 pieces of heavy ordnance and howitzers. The English Government had been informed that the militia and inhabitants generally looked with anxiety for the arrival of the British troops. The instructions of Lord Castlereagh, July 25, 1805, directed the General to lose no time, but to take the place by a vigorous and immediate attack.

who belonged to the stranded frigate *L'Atalanta* and the stranded privateer *Le Napoléon*, which were here casually, were comprehended in the capitulation, and were treated on the same footing as the garrison, but were compelled to embark for Europe, as well as every other French subject in the Colony. The inhabitants of the town who had borne arms were considered as belonging to the town, and were allowed immediately to return to their former occupations. The distinction, however, between burghers and other inhabitants was to remain the same, and to be subject to the same restrictions as under the Dutch law. All *bonâ-fide* property, whether belonging to the civil or military servants of the Government, to the burghers and inhabitants, to churches, and other public institutions of that kind, were to remain free and untouched. Public property of every description, whether consisting of treasure, or naval or military stores, buildings, estates, or merchandise, belonging to the Batavian Republic or the Government of France, were to be faithfully delivered up, and proper inventories given of them as soon as possible. The burghers and inhabitants were to reserve all their rights and privileges hitherto enjoyed, and public worship, as then in use, was also to be maintained without alteration. The paper money actually in circulation to continue current as heretofore until the pleasure of his Britannic Majesty was known. The lands and houses, the property of the Batavian Republic, which were to be delivered up in consesequence of the capitulation, remained as security for that part of the paper money not already secured by mortgages upon the estates of individuals by its having been lent to them. This, however, was without prejudice to the free use to be made of said lands and houses for public purposes. Prisoners of war comprehended in the capitulation were not to be pressed into service of his Britannic Majesty, or engaged against their own free will and consent. The inhabitants of Cape Town were exempted from having troops quartered on them. Two ships, which were sunk in Table Bay, to the great detriment of the roadstead, either after the Batavian Republic had sent out a flag of truce, or whilst it was in contemplation to do so, were to be raised again and delivered over in an entire state of repair. This having been done without the sanction of the commandant, the raising of these ships was incumbent on those who had sunk them. These conditions being mutually agreed upon, three days after, the villages of Stellenbosch and Pavol were occupied by the 59th and 72nd regiments,[2] and the following morning the 83rd regiment was sent by sea to Mussel Bay. General Janssens, who had retreated to Hottentots Holland with about 1,200 men of all arms and twenty-eight pieces of artillery, had no hope of holding out; the burghers could not be depended upon, and when they deserted he would be

---

[2] Capt. Carmichael, who wrote an account of Sir David Baird's expedition, says : " On our arrival on the Parade we found the people prodigiously civil. Every door was thrown open for our reception, and several of the inhabitants carried their kindness so far as to send even to the Parade to invite us to their houses. Some of our speculators ascribed this marked hospitality to fear, while others, inclined to judge more favourably of human nature, imputed it to general benevolence. Those who suspended their opinion on the subject had the laugh at the expense of both, when, on our departure next morning, the true motive was discovered in the amount of their bills."—Hooker's *Botanical Miscellany.*

left with only a few hundred men. There was no seaport open to him, consequently no means of escape—only the thinly inhabited interior to retire to. Sir David Baird proposed honourable terms of surrender to General Janssens, out of respect for him individually and the troops under his orders, and with the view to preserve the inhabitants from the miseries and horrors of a protracted war in the bosom of the Colony. On January 19, 1806, General Janssens, Governor and Commander-in-Chief of the Batavian forces of the Cape of Good Hope, proposed articles of capitulation to Brigadier-General Beresford, duly authorized by Major-General Sir David Baird, K.C., and Commodore Sir Hume Popham, K.M., commanding the military and naval forces of his Britannic Majesty. These articles, twelve in number, relating to the surrender of the Settlement, subsistence of Batavian troops until embarkation, and their transport to some port in Holland, attendance of the sick, the forwarding of a despatch by General Janssens to Holland, was agreed to at once. The others, relating to the marching of troops, the quartering of soldiers on the inhabitants, and the treatment of troops on board ship, were more formally and definitely expressed, viz., the Batavian troops were to march from their present camp within three days, or sooner if convenient, with their guns, arms, baggage, and with all the honours of war, to Simon's Town, to retain all private property, and the officers their swords and horses; but the arms, treasure, and all public property of every description, together with the cavalry and artillery horses, to be delivered up. In consideration of their gallant conduct the troops would be embarked and sent straight to Holland at the expense of the British Government, and not be considered as prisoners of war, they engaging not to serve against his Britannic Majesty, or his allies, until landed in Holland. The Hottentot soldiers were to march to Simon's Town with the other troops, after which they were to be allowed to return to their own country, or be engaged in the British service, as might be thought proper. Those military men who, being wounded, had not been able to follow their army, and had fallen into the hands of the British,—any decision respecting them belonged to the British Commander-in-chief. The inhabitants of the Colony who were comprehended in the capitulation of the 10th instant, were, it was proposed, to enjoy the same rights and privileges as had been granted to those in Cape Town, which was agreed to with the exception of not quartering troops, the country not having the same resources as the town, and this right having been always an appendage to the Batavian Government. The troops when embarked would be treated in every respect as British troops when on board transports. The article stating that Baron von Hogendorp had expended a great deal of money for the execution of agricultural plans, stipulated that he should be supported by the British Government in carrying his plans into execution, and that the British Government should grant him all such rights and privileges as from the public records it would appear the Batavian Government meant to have given him, was left entirely to the discretion of the future British governors or commanders. These articles were finally signed at Hottentots Holland by General Janssens and Brigadier-General Beresford on January 18, 1806, and duly ratified and confirmed in the Castle of Good Hope, on January 19, 1806, by Sir David Baird,

Major-General commanding-in-chief, and Commodore Hume Popham, commanding his Majesty's naval forces. Early in March following the Batavian troops were sent to Holland, and the transport *Bellona* placed at the disposal of General Janssens, on board which he embarked with his family, friends, and attendants. On August 13, 1814, a convention was signed by the plenipotentiaries of Great Britain and the Netherlands, whereby all the foreign possessions of Holland which had been seized by England during the European War were restored, except the Cape of Good Hope, Demerara, Essequibo, and Bubria. These colonies were then ceded to Great Britain for £6,000,000 sterling, with the stipulation that Dutch ships were to be allowed to obtain refreshments and effect repairs at Cape Town on the same conditions as English vessels, and that the colonists should not be debarred carrying on trade with Holland. Possession of the Colony was formally ratified to Great Britain by the Congress of Vienna, in 1815, and has remained from that time a British Colony without attempt at its recovery. From this time forward the inhabitants became British subjects, and have remained so ever since, notwithstanding that many, in large numbers, of the original settlers, from some cause or other, migrated beyond the borders of the Colony, into the Free State, Natal, the Transvaal, and beyond it, and have been allowed to establish themselves into independent States, with local government. Their allegiance to the British Crown has, however, never been formally absolved, and late events show clearly that they cannot escape from this obligation.

The benefit of the English occupation was soon felt at Cape Town and its immediate surroundings by the people who were no longer hampered by the mercenary restrictions of the Dutch East India Company. They could now sell their produce in the open market, and the large garrison of British soldiers gave them an opportunity of obtaining excellent prices for ready money in British currency which they had not before. Ships, too, began to come into port more frequently, and trade was brisk. During the seven years of British occupation, it is calculated that upwards of £1,500,000 was spent in the Colony. Visitors from India began to come to the Cape in search of health, some of whom acquired properties in the neighbourhood of Cape Town, and they, with the garrison of British troops, introduced a knowledge of the English language, which the better-educated class of Kaapnars, as they were called,—that is, residents in and about Cape Town,—began to acquire. Their prosperity dates from this period.

CHAPTER IV

STORMY DAYS

SIR DAVID BAIRD caused a corps of Hottentot infantry to be formed, who were afterwards named the "Cape Mounted Rifles," and appointed Mr. William Stephanus von Ryneveld to be Vice-president of the newly constituted Court of Justice, in addition to his being his Majesty's Fiscal and Attorney-General. The Chamber for regulating insolvent estates was also reformed on a reduced scale, and Mr Rhenius appointed Political Commissioner for Church affairs. Relays of Hottentot runners were stationed at the houses of Boers on great routes to convey the mail bags, and these primitive postal arrangements were placed under the direction of Mr. William Caldwell, deputy postmaster. In March, 1806, a severe public punishment was inflicted upon a man named Cornelius Maas, who had caused the greatest alarm by positively assuring the Governor that he himself had seen an enemy's fleet at Saldanha Bay, and even conversed with some of the officers. Upon this information being proved to be thoroughly false, Maas was flogged at the cart's tail round Cape Town, and banished from the Colony; while an order was issued by General Baird, intimating that in future false reports would be punished by death, or such other chastisement as a general court martial should award. Affairs having been placed in a comparative state of order, Sir David Baird left Cape Town in the transport *Paragon*, January 24, 1807, having delivered over the Government to Lieut.-General the Hon. H. G. Grey, Lieut.-Governor and Commander of the Forces, who held supreme command for a few months, until the arrival of the Earl of Caledon. In the addresses presented to his Excellency from the Court of Justice, Burgher Senate, and other public boards, Sir David Baird was assured "that by your wise and well-directed measures for our internal government, together with the unparalleled discipline of the troops under your Excellency's command, our rights have been guarded, and the whole Colony enjoys at this moment a state of tranquility and plenty seldom or never realized."

Earl Caledon only held the Governorship for a short term of years (1807-1811), and was succeeded by Sir J. F. Cradock (afterwards Lord Howden), who also was Governor for a brief period (1811-1813). Lord Charles Henry Somerset succeeded in 1814, and held office till 1825.

When the British Government recaptured the Cape Colony, the importance of Table Bay to the maritime trade of the kingdom was established. Commercial enterprise was beginning to penetrate to the newly-acquired possessions in India, and the value of the port as a place of call for ships eastward and homeward was recognised. To maintain the supremacy of British vessels in the shipping trade, and in case of war as a strategic point, it afforded facilities for intercepting and preventing attempts at seizure or interference with national vessels on the high seas. This was the primary motive for acquiring their Colony, though, in taking possession of it the British Government was aware that the territorial boundaries of the Colony extended far and wide. During the three years' temporary occupation of the Colony it was known that the inhabitants generally were disaffected and likely to prove troublesome. They were a mixed body of Europeans and natives in a semi-savage state. The settlers, who had been introduced by the Dutch, were truculent, turbulent, and impatient of restraint of any kind. Many of their descendants were tainted with slave blood, and inherited the bad qualities of an inferior race. They were cunning, deceitful, and unscrupulous. Having been accustomed to the use of slaves, and been constantly engaged in forays against the Hottentot races, whom they exterminated when they could not capture them, they inherited an inborn hatred of the coloured population, and regarded them as fit only to live on condition of lifelong servitude, and where it was impossible to acquire them by fair means or foul, their duty was to extirpate them. There was thus from this class of the occupiers of the distant parts of the Colony an element of danger to the peace and prosperity of the Settlement. The slave population, on the other hand, had been so barbarously and cruelly used by their taskmasters that they were ready at any time to make an attempt at escape from durance vile. The Hottentot races also had been so much harassed by the Boers that in self-defence, as they thought, bands of them formed alliances with the Kafirs, a race superior to themselves, occupied the country to the east of the Outeniqua mountains, and this combination of forces also became a source of danger and difficulty. General Dundas, when administering the Government after the first conquest of the Cape, had, as already mentioned, an experience of these latent causes of trouble, more particularly those that pressed most on the borders, and the difficulty in reaching those parts that were the scene of disturbances. There was no regular communication to or from the seat of Government, no bridges across the raging rivers when flooded, no made roads across the mountain barriers. Lastly, the language in use by the people was foreign to English ears; the Boers were illiterate and as ignorant almost as the native races, while those about the Castle of Cape Town were not far advanced in ordinary education. The superiority of the European section of the population consisted chiefly, if not entirely, in the use of fire-arms, and their being bound together by family ties and race distinction. In other respects they were on the same level as the aboriginal inhabitants. It thus became apparent that in acquiring the Colony, the prospect of its Government being peaceful and progressive, not hampered with special difficulties, or likely to entail unusual expense, was unlikely to be realized. The first occupation and the cost of its capture had already entailed an expenditure of £16,000,000. Its permanent conquest and retention was to involve further heavy cost to the public treasury, and it was to become the grave of many lives by premature and violent deaths.

These results, whether anticipated or not, have been characteristic of the occupation of the Colony from this time till late years.

On the borders of the Fish River peace had not been known for years. The Kafir clans were about evenly balanced with the Boers, and thefts and recaptures of cattle were constantly taking place in small parties, with loss of blood on either side. Besides this, the Boers exasperated the Kafir chief, Slambie, by intruding into his country on the pretext of hunting wherever they chose and destroying the game. Some of these Boers, who had cast longing eyes on the fertile and beautiful valleys of the Kat River, petitioned the Governor, Earl Caledon, that they might be allowed to take possession of that part of the country and divide it among themselves. They met with a stern and decided refusal, and were told that the British Government would neither sanction nor permit any attempt of the kind. They were ordered to keep to their own side of the river in terms of the treaty of 1793. Orders like this were, however, in vain; the Boers resolved to fight their own battles and act on their own judgment. A fresh irruption of Kafirs, under Slambie, complicated the state of anarchy and confusion which prevailed. The Boers were disheartened, and dared not trust Slambie, who promised not to molest them if they returned to their farms. If their lives were spared, they knew their flocks would be swept off. Government viewed the intruders as political refugees, and declined to send troops to aid in their expulsion. The Boers scattered to other parts and increased the difficulty. It was thus that Earl Caledon, then Governor of the Colony, sent Colonel Collins to examine into and report upon Frontier affairs. His report, dated August 6, 1809, recommended that the Kafirs should be expelled by force from the Colony, and that the Zunsveld should be allotted to British settlers in farms of 120 acres each, who ought to have for their defence a strong militia force, composed principally of Boers accustomed to border warfare. There was an internal feud between the Kafir chiefs Slambie and Huitza, in the country beyond the Fish River, who refused to recognise Gaika as paramount. This afforded a pretext for another raid upon them, and Colonel Brereton marched into Kafirland with a powerful force of military and burghers —3,352 men—to support Gaika, and was joined by him with 6,000 fighting men. The Kafirs were attacked in their kraals, plundered of their cattle, slaughtered or driven into the woods. Not less than 23,000 head of cattle were carried off, of which 9,000 were allotted to Gaika for his losses, the remainder partly distributed among the Boers and partly sold towards the expenses of the expedition. The effect of this invasion of Kafirland led, as might be expected, to a counter invasion by the Kafirs. No sooner had the invading force retired, and the burghers been disbanded, than the Kafirs poured across the Fish River in numerous bands, eager for plunder and revenge. The districts as far as Algoa Bay were overrun, several military posts were captured, Captain Gethin, Lieutenant Hunt, and numerous small parties and patrols of British troops were cut off. The Boers were driven from the Zunsveld, the mission station of Theopolis was repeatedly attacked with great fury, and saved only by the bravery of the Hottentots. Enon mission station was plundered and burned, and the cattle of the Boers along the Fish River and the adjoining districts were in many places carried off. Thus by the insidious introduction of Boers among the Kafir tribes,—first on sufferance, after a time their acquaintance with the tribe among whom they located themselves, and their knowledge of the wealth the Kafirs possessed in the shape of cattle,—these ruthless intruders gradually spoiled them of their property, reprisals took place, and finally, by the aid of commandoes, rapine and bloodshed ensued. The firearms of the Boers were superior to the assegai of the Kafirs, and the savage destruction of their kraals and crops forced these unfortunate barbarians further back, only there to bide their time and make a fresh attempt at regaining their former domains and as much of the cattle of the Boers as they could recover. From the time when the Boers of Swellendam began to trek across the boundary at the Gamtoos river, and under graziers' licenses temporarily to mix with the natives,—to these lawless wanderers are attributable all the outpouring of blood and devastation which ensued for years after.

As the depredations of the Kafirs increased, and they showed themselves obstinately determined to retain a portion of the Colony to which they had neither right nor title, in 1811 Governor Sir J. F. Cradock decided to drive the whole of the Kafirs beyond the Fish River. It was absolutely necessary to adopt strong measures for their expulsion. Mr. Stockenstrom, afterwards Lieut.-Governor, one of the ablest and most humane of the Frontier authorities, even recommended a seizure of land to the eastward of the Fish River. For this purpose a large force of military and burghers, under command of Colonel Graham, of the Cape Regiment, commandant of Simon's Town, was assembled. When the forces entered the Zunsveld in December, 1811, the right division was commanded by Major Cuyler, the centre by Captain Fraser, accompanied by the Chief-in-command, Colonel Graham, and the left by Landdrost Stockenstrom. On December 28 the last-named officer, desiring to confer with the Colonel, left his camp, crossed the mountains accompanied by forty men, and, relying on his influence with the natives, rode up to a large party with the hope of persuading them to leave the country. The conference proceeded amicably for some time, till a messenger arrived with intelligence that a portion of the British troops had attacked the Kafirs. An agitated discussion immediately arose amongst several natives who stood apart; the war-cry was raised, and the Landdrost, with fourteen of his companions, killed. The remainder owed their escape to the fleetness of their horses. This treacherous act provoked a terrible retribution. From that day all who resisted were shot, their crops destroyed, their kraals burnt down, and their cattle seized. No prisoners were made, and the wounded and infirm were left to perish. The chief, Congo, who was ill and unable to get away, was slain near the present village of Alexandria, where he had long resided. The murder of the Landdrost and his companions was fully avenged.

CHAPTER V

THE ATTACK UPON GRAHAM'S TOWN

AFTER the Kafirs had been driven across the Fish River in 1811, a prophet arose among them, named by the Boers Linksch, or left-handed, but whose native name was Makanna. He was originally of common rank, but by his talents he had gradually raised himself to distinction. Before the war of 1818 he had frequently visited the British headquarters at Graham's Town, and evinced an insatiable curiosity and an acute intellect on the subjects that came under his observation. He talked of war and the mechanical arts with the military officers, and delighted especially to converse with Rev. Van der Lingen, the chaplain, on the doctrines of Christianity, puzzling the reverend gentleman with metaphysical subtleties or mystical ravings. Of the knowledge thus acquired he made extraordinary use, framed an extravagant medley, and boldly announced himself as a prophet and teacher inspired from heaven. His appearance was imposing, and his influence over the chiefs and common people was surprising. By degrees he gained complete control over all the principal chiefs except Gaika, who feared and hated him. It was under his directions that the confederated chiefs turned their arms against Gaika, though roused by their own immediate wrongs. After Colonel Brereton's devastating inroad, by which his followers, in common with the other confederated clans, had suffered most cruelly, he was bent on avenging the aggressions of the Boers and emancipating his country from their domination. By his spirit-rousing predictions of complete success, if only they would follow his counsels, he persuaded the great majority of Amokosa clans to unite their forces for a simultaneous attack upon Graham's Town. He told them he was sent by Uhlonga, the great spirit, to avenge this wrong, that he had power to call up from the grave the spirits of their ancestors to assist them in battle against the Amanglazi (English), whom they would drive across the Zwaarbkops River into the ocean, and then, he said, "we will sit down and eat honey." Having called out the warriors from the various clans, Makanna and Dushani, son of Slambie, mustered their armies in the forests of the Fish River, and found themselves at the head of between 9,000 and 10,000 men. There, in conformity with a custom in repute among Kafir heroes, they sent a message of defiance to Colonel Willshire, the British commandant, that "they would breakfast with him next morning." At day dawn the warriors were arranged for battle on the hills around Graham's Town, and before they were led to the assault Makanna harangued them in an animated speech, assuring them of supernatural aid in the conflict which would turn the hailstorm of the firearms into water. The British were completely astonished and taken by surprise when the Kafirs appeared soon after sunrise marching rapidly over the heights which environ Graham's Town, the commandant having treated Makanna's message as a piece of bravado.

To resist this attacking force the garrison at Graham's Town consisted of a company of the 38th Foot, a detachment of the Royal African Corps, at together 350 Europeans and a small corps of Hottentots, and two six pounders. Colonel Graham's military headquarters were first at the Nantoo, now known as Table Farm, about six miles distant from Graham's Town. Much had been done here under Captain McNeal; but after inspection of the vicinity, at the suggestion of Captain, afterwards Sir, A. Stockenstrom, who knew the country well, the headquarters were removed to the loan place lately occupied by a Boer named Lukus Meyer on a grazing license, at the source of the Kowie River, in a basin not unlike what is called a Dutch oven. Meyer had abandoned the place because of the insufficiency of water and pasture for his small flock of Cape sheep. The ruins of Meyer's dwelling, close to a tree near what is now the centre of Graham's Town, were covered in for the officers' mess, and it was directed by an official despatch, dated 14th August, 1812, that the headquarters encampment in the Zunsveld should be designated and acknowledged by the name of Graham's Town, in testimony of his Excellency the Governor Sir John Francis Cradock's respect for the services of Colonel Graham, through whose able exertions the Kafirs were expelled from the territory. The ancient citizen used to point to a spot in the High Street where stood a large mimosa tree on which Colonel Graham, on his first encampment, drove a nail whereon he hung his sword. The locale of the encampment was a tongue of land extending from the foot of the ridge on the west, with a slope to a rivulet on the south, to another rivulet on the north, with its front to the Kowie ravine below on the east. One of the field pieces was placed on a semi-circular sod bank to the right, and the other in a similiar structure to the left. In after days this spot was called Fort England, in lieu of the East Barracks, after Colonel England, 75th regiment, who laid it out more extensively to suit the requirements of the officers and men who were stationed there. On a similar tongue of land on the north side of the basin the cavalry barracks were placed, and the spot is still known as the Cape Corps Barracks. The ravines from the top of the flats to the basin were thickly lined with trees and bushes. The entry into the basin was by track ways along these ravines, and for wagons across the hill tops.

The attack was made on the 22nd April, 1819. When the Kafirs made their appearance, Colonel Willshire was at a distance from the encampment inspecting the cavalry troops. According to another account, he had gone with an escort of ten men to observe the position of the invader, upon whom he came suddenly while resting in a ravine skirting what is now known as the racecourse. He was recognised by the Kafirs, who rushed at and pursued him. The fleetness of his charger, Blucher, enabled him to reach his camp in a few minutes before the assailants. The engagement began at once. The field pieces, loaded with Shrapnell shells, and the destructive fire of the musketry, opened spaces like streets in the dense masses courageously advancing with their wild war cries. They were literally mowed down, their assegais falling short and ineffective. At a critical moment a Hottentot captain, Boezak, with 130 of his people, rushed intrepidly forward along the banks of the streamlet from the Cape Corps Barracks, and, being excellent marksmen, as well as knowing many of the Kafir chiefs and head men, in a few minutes killed a number of the most distinguished warriors. Panic and route ensued. In this brief conflict about 2,000 Kafirs strewed the battlefield, while many perished of their wounds along and in the rivulet down to the East Barracks.

Colonel Graham's plan of operations was to occupy the Fish River Bush, and thereby prevent access to the Zunsveld. The Kafirs were not prepared for this system of attack, which gave them no opportunity for an encounter *en masse*, the constant patrols from camp to camp effectually accomplishing this with comparatively small loss. It was not till they had found their way through the bush in detached parties on to the flats around Graham's Town, and there collected together to make an attack upon the headquarters camp, that they had full scope for the use of their native weapon, the assegai, and which they found to their cost was of no avail against the musketry and guns of their opponents.

CHAPTER VI

COLONEL GRAHAM

JOHN GRAHAM, second son of Robert Graham, of Fintry, County Forfar, Scotland, born at Dundee, April 24, 1778, was educated principally by Professor John Fairplay. He was a great favourite with the Duke and Duchess of Athol, and often at Athol house, and shared his studies there with their son, the Marquis of Tullibardine, under Mr. Josiah Walker. The friendship between the two boys lasted until the young Marquis went to Eton College.

In 1794, John Graham was gazetted ensign in the 85th Regiment of Foot, which, however, he did not join, as, having in the same year helped to procure men for the Perthshire Volunteers, or 90th Regiment, which his cousin, Thomas Graham, afterwards Lord Lyndoch, raised, he was promoted to a lieutenancy in that corps, and in July, 1795, went with it at the head of a company to Ile d'Yeu, on the coast of France. In 1796 Captain Graham was compelled by ill-health to return to England, where he remained until the following year, when he obtained permission from the Duke of York to join the Austrian army, where Colonel Graham of Balgowan was then serving. While with his regiment in Italy, he was present at the actions of the 26th March on the Adiju, of 30th March at Verona, and of 5th April at Villa Franca. In 1799, Captain Graham heard of the death of his eldest brother Robert, a civilian in the service of the East India Company, who was treacherously assassinated at Benares by command of Vizier Ali, a native chief who had made himself Nabob and whom the Governor was trying to depose. Soon afterwards John Graham became aide-de-camp to Lord Chatham, returning to England in June. In September he went to Holland, where he remained until the evacuation of that country.

In February, 1800, he obtained leave to raise men for a majority, and continued recruiting until August of that year. In October, Major Graham went with his regiment to Guernsey, where he remained until it was ordered to Ireland in 1803. Here he was appointed to receive the reserve, and in August to the command of a battalion of light infantry militia. He was subsequently made Assistant Quartermaster-General, which important office he held until the regiment was ordered on secret foreign service in August, 1805. They were ignorant of their destination until after leaving San Salvador, when the sealed instructions were opened, and Major Graham had the honour of commanding the light infantry battalion at the taking of the Cape in the action of the 6th January, 1806.

Immediately after the final capitulation of the Cape, Major Graham was ordered by Sir David Baird to raise and discipline a corps of Hottentots, to the command of which he was appointed, January 26, 1806, and was soon afterwards despatched to the frontier with full civil and military authority. Colonel Graham found the boundary agreed upon by l'Slambie had been disregarded, and the whole of the Zunsveld overrun by the Kafirs. In 1809 it was determined to expel the Kafirs beyond the Fish River, and to partition the country into farms and locate British immigrants on them. Vigorous measures were accordingly taken for the expulsion of l'Slambie, and Congo, and in 1811 a large force of burghers was called out, who, with the military stationed on the frontier, were placed under the command of Colonel Graham. In December, 1811, Colonel Graham took the field—the right division of his force under command of Major Cuyler, the left under Mr. Andrew Stockenstrom, Landdrost of Graaff Reinet, and the centre under Captain Fraser, Colonel Graham accompanying the centre division in chief command. The treacherous massacre of Landdrost Stockenstrom strengthened the resolve to drive the Kafirs out of the Zunsveld, their kraals were burnt, their crops destroyed, their cattle captured in large numbers, and to the number of 20,000 were driven across the Fish River. The forces were in the field till 1815. Having carried out the orders of Government, after a careful survey of the country, he fixed the headquarters of the Cape regiment on the site of the present city of Graham's Town. On the 14th August, 1812, it was recorded in official despatches that "the headquarters encampment in the Zunsveld shall be designated and acknowledged by the name of Graham's Town, in testimony of his Excellency the Governor Sir John Francis Cradock's respect for the services of Colonel Graham, through whose able exertions the Kafirs were expelled from the territory."

On 24th July, 1812, Colonel Graham married the daughter of Mr. Rudolf Cloete, of Great Westerford, near Cape Town, and his health having suffered from his long and arduous services on the Frontier, he obtained leave from Sir J. F. Cradock to visit England. He and Mrs. Graham embarked in H.M.S. *Galatea* in September, and arrived in England on November 15, having narrowly escaped capture by two large American frigates. He remained with his father until October, 1813, when Lord Lyndoch, then Sir Thomas Graham, was appointed to the command of the British troops in Holland. Colonel Graham could not resist the opportunity of serving again under his old commander; and having asked and obtained permission of the Government, and being promised by them that his going to Holland would in no way affect his interests at the Cape, he received the appointment of military secretary and first aide-de-camp to Sir Thomas Graham, and was with him at the battle of Marsem, near Antwerp, the attack on Bergen-op-Zoom, and the other minor actions in that country, returning to England on the abdication of Napoleon and his banishment to Elba. In June, 1814, he was gazetted full colonel, and his visit to his native country being brought to an end by the sudden death of his father in January, 1815, he returned to the Cape in the same year. Many changes had occurred after the departure of Sir J. F. Cradock and the arrival of Lord Charles Somerset. The appointment he had held on the Frontier had been abolished, in spite of the assurances of the Government before he left the Cape that it would be kept open for him until his return,[1] and arrangements were in process for turning the corps of Hottentot sharp-shooters he had raised into a regiment of cavalry to be commanded by a son of Lord Charles Somerset. Under the circumstances he thought it best to decline any active employment, and accepted the commandership of Simon's Town, which he held until his death. In 1820 Colonel Graham received a letter from Sir Outram Donkin, then Acting-Governor, requesting him to go to Algoa Bay, as representing the Government, to put in good working order the extensive immigration schemes which were then begun. But his health had become so bad that he was obliged to decline the honourable position offered to him, and he died 17th March, 1821, in the forty-third year of his age. The disease from which he died was brought on by the great and continued exertions not only of the campaign against the Kafirs, but also from the severe and trying hurried journeys on horseback at all seasons between the Frontier and Cape Town.

[1] The appointment alluded to was that of Commandant of the Frontier, which the Acting-Governor, Donkin, conferred on Major Jones, R.A., but which, on the return of the Governor, Lord Charles Somerset, was, with the other appointments of General Donkin, cancelled by him, and the commandership of the Frontier abolished.

CHAPTER VII

PROJECTED SETTLEMENT OF THE ZUNSVELD AND INTRODUCTION OF BRITISH IMMIGRANTS

IN June, 1812, proclamation was made by Governor Sir J. F. Cradock, annulling all loan places in the Zunsveld, and inhabitants from all parts of the country were invited to settle on the Frontier, not fewer than four families to be located in one spot, to each of whom a grant of land, 2,000 morgen in extent would be made on perpetual quitrent. The plan, however, failed, and the Governor recalled his proclamation, and proposed that any Boer who was desirous to obtain the 2,000 morgen of land might go and fix on a place in order to establish himself there. Among the difficulties to which the Boers who attempted to settle in the Zunsveld were subjected were the following : they were unable to provide herds for the protection of their cattle from the attacks of the Kafirs, being too poor to purchase slaves, and there being in the country no Hottentots except those of Bethelsdorp, whose circumstances were better than they would have been in the service of these indigent Boers. To remove in part this difficulty, Government gave orders that soldiers should be employed to protect the cattle of such Boers as resided in the vicinity of military ports. In 1813 the inhabitants of Bethelsdorp being much straitened for pasture ground for their cattle, it was proposed to form another missionary institution, and Governor Sir J. F. Cradock being at the time on the Frontier, Theopolis was fixed upon at the entrance of the Karuja Bush, therefore favourable for keeping the Kafirs in check in that quarter. A grant was made, supposed to contain 6,000 acres, and the Hottentots who removed from Bethelsdorp were put in possession of extensive pasturage, while the opportunity of fishing at the mouth of the Kasonga River, and by burning lime from shells collected on the sea-shore, they were enabled to carry on trade.

Government having failed in their previous attempts to people the Zunsveld, issued another proclamation, 28th January, 1814, offering further favourable conditions, and confined the offer to the first fifty applicants. The Boers objected to the grants of 2,000 morgen as being too small, and little progress was made in peopling and civilizing the Zunsveld. In 1817, Lord Charles Somerset, who had succeeded Sir J. F. Cradock as Governor, being on the spot, made a fresh attempt to effect occupation of the Zunsveld, and by advertisement dated 29th March confirmed the advantages offered in preceding proclamations, with other favourable conditions.

In 1817, whilst on the Frontier, his Excellency Governor Lord Charles Somerset was favourably impressed with the appearance of the unoccupied country between the Sunday's River and the Fish River, which he had vainly endeavoured to get occupied by Boers on favourable conditions. He therefore expressed the wish to the home Government that it might be settled by those in England whom it was understood were willing to emigrate, and the Government would assist. His lordship's despatch ran : " Here is indeed a very fine country upon which to employ and maintain a multitude of settlers. This tract, particularly healthy for every description of cattle and sheep, well-wooded, and having very fine springs in it, is nearly uninhabited. The paucity of borderers has been such that they have never been able to settle in quiet. The Kafirs, whose territory is on the east side of the great Fish River, and whose propensity to thieving is similar to that of most other savages, have continually viewed the occupation of this fine country by the colonists with jealousy, and have molested them so systematically by constant depredations upon their lands, that insulated settlers have imbibed a great dread of occupying land in the vicinity of these artful marauders. It was found necessary in 1812 to drive them back by military measures, as your Lordship is aware, and since that period to keep a military force on the Frontier to check further inroad, and to give time for settlers to establish themselves in such strength and numbers as shall supersede the necessity of keeping a military force for their protection. This, then, is the situation of that part of the country which I would wish to draw your Lordship's attention to the settlement thereof as a measure of Government, fairly stating to your Lordship the disadvantages to which settlers would be at first exposed, and not disguising from you that I am much swayed in recommending the plan by a strong wish to be able eventually to withdraw the military detachments from that quarter, for many reasons which are not at this moment the subject of discussion. It is just that settlers should be aware that their property will be in some measure exposed, in the first instance to be plundered by their restless neighbours, unless their own vigilance and courage shall considerably aid in protecting it ; but it is at the same time proper to tell them that vigilance and courage will have the effect of giving their property efficient protection ; that the Kafirs do not molest those hamlets where six or seven families unite in case of attack. We have several instances of associations of this nature living in perfect security quite on the border of the Fish River, not one hundred yards from the Kafir country. The Kafirs are constantly on the watch, and commit their thefts when they discover our settlers to be off their guard. The herds of these families are tended in common by armed watchmen. Should these be indolent or negligent, they are the victims of their supineness by the loss of their property, and sometimes the sleeping herdsmen lose their lives. It is obvious that increase of population will remedy this evil, and that the Kafirs cannot, from their not using firearms, be any match for Europeans who have such to oppose to them. Having thus stated the disadvantages to which settlers would be liable in the country we have to offer them, it is now necessary to advert to the more favourable side of the picture, and to say that their reward is to be found in the cultivation of a most fertile soil in the most healthy and temperate climate in the universe, where cold is never so piercing as to congeal water, and where the rays of the sun are never so powerful as to render exposure to them injurious, or to impede the usual labours of the field. Upon a most fruitful soil, the same species of cultivation which affords food to man in our country is most likely to be successful here ; added to which that when the immediate wants of the new settlers are supplied, no country yields finer wool than may be here reared; that the corn of this country has brought in the London market the highest price known there ; that tobacco is an article which might be advantageously cultivated and prepared, so as to equal the best American produce ; and that experiments upon the cotton plant have proved that it may be cultivated here to the greatest advantage."

The drawbacks as well as the attractions of the Frontier were thus clearly and candidly placed before the Government, who, moreover, must have been fully aware of the state of things on the borders by the events that happened between 1809 and 1817, and the difficulties immigrants would have to encounter. It is surprising, therefore, that no reference was made to these in the speech of the Chancellor of the Exchequer when he submitted to the House of Commons a vote of £50,000 for the encouragement of emigration to the Cape. The record of that proposal given by Hansard is glowing in its description of the climate, fertility and natural beauty of the country. It is as follows :—

"HOUSE OF COMMONS,
"*Monday, July* 12, 1819.
" EMIGRATION TO THE CAPE OF GOOD HOPE.

"The Chancellor of the Exchequer, Right Hon. Nicholas Vansittart, said he had to propose a grant for the purpose of enabling her Majesty's Government to assist unemployed workmen of this country in removing to one of our colonies. It had been the wish of Her Majesty's Government first to try an experiment on a small scale, how far it might be possible to employ the surplus population of this country in one of our colonies in such a manner as might be advantageous to the people removed and beneficial to the country. From the satisfactory result of this experiment it was that the Government were now desirous of trying the experiment on a larger scale. The Colony selected was that of the Cape of Good Hope. The greater part of the persons disposed to emigrate from this country rather wished to go to the United States of North America, where the Government could give them no direct encouragement, or to the British Colonies of North America. But with respect to the latter, Her Majesty's Government, considering the inconvenience to which these persons would be subjected on their arrival in America, had selected the Cape of Good Hope as the Colony to which emigration might be most advantageously directed. From the mildness of the climate, and the fertility of the soil in some parts, a rapid and abundant return might reasonably be expected. That Colony was also highly favourable to the multiplication of stock. The particular part of the Colony selected was the south-east coast of Africa. It was at some distance from Cape Town. A small town was already built there. It was proposed to pay the expense of the passage, and at the same time to secure to the settler the means of employing his industry to advantage on his landing at the destined spot. But a small advance of money would be required from each settler before embarking, to be repaid him in necessaries at the Cape, by which means, and by the assistance given him by the Government, he would have sufficient to procure him a comfortable subsistence till he got in his crops, which in that climate were of rapid growth. The Cape was suited to most of the productions both of temperate and warm climates,—to the olive, the mulberry, the vine, as well as most sorts of culmiferous and leguminous plants. The persons emigrating to this settlement would soon find themselves comfortable. The right hon. gentleman concluded with moving the grant of a sum not exceeding £50,000, to be issued from time to time, for the purpose of enabling the Government to assist persons disposed to settle in Her Majesty's Colony of the Cape of Good Hope.

"Mr. Hume said he was sorry ministers had not gone further. Parishes having able-bodied men willing to work chargeable on them ought to be called on to subscribe sums towards removing a part of them to this or some other Settlement, where their industry might provide them with a comfortable subsistence. He thought that if men under such circumstances were unwilling to emigrate, it might even be advisable to transport them without their consent. If the parishes would but contribute the money they were forced to pay to those persons for one or two years, from the excellent climate of the Cape, and the fertility of the soil, the greatest advantages could not fail to be the result.

"The Chancellor of the Exchequer said it was a part of the plan that parishes should have the power of sending out persons who might be desirous of emigrating ; but there ought to be nothing compulsory. When the parishes and the individuals chargeable on them were desirous, an opportunity would be afforded.

"Mr. Alderman Wood was surprised that labourers should be removed from this country, when there was so much waste land in it that might be cultivated to advantage. There were about 80,000 acres of waste land on which both corn and flax might be grown.

"Mr. Hutchinson approved of the grant. The right hon. gentleman had said that persons wishing to settle in the Colony must make a deposit in this country ; he wished to ask him if such people as the distressed manufacturers and labourers of Cork, who had not the means of making any deposit, might not be exempted from this regulation? If the Government would give a loan to such persons, and afford them protection till they came to the Colony, there could be little doubt, from the glowing language in which the right hon. gentleman had described that country, that they would soon be able to repay the sums aforesaid.

"Mr. Williams was convinced that this country possessed within itself the means of employment for all its inhabitants, and that nothing more was necessary than to cultivate those lands which at present were waste.

"The motion was agreed to."—*Hansard's Parliamentary Debates*, vol. from 3rd May to 13th July, 1819, p. 1549, *et seq.*

In June, 1817, Mr. Benjamin Moodie, Laird of Milsetter, Orkney Islands, at two different periods brought 200 settlers to the Colony. They were of the common sort, who placed themselves under his guidance, and entered into regular indentures, by which, in return for the expense of their exportation and outfit, they bound themselves to work for Mr. Moodie on a certain fixed rate of wages, during a certain number of years after their arrival ; or to buy up their indentures at a reasonable rate, also fixed and determined beforehand. The people selected were from the neighbourhood of Edinburgh, closely allied to each other, over whom he had no special influence. They had not long been in the Colony when the great majority of his people broke all their contracts, abandoned him for ever, and scattered themselves over the country wherever they could get good wages, without the least regard to his interests, and in such a manner as to baffle him and his agents most completely. To the success which many of them individually met with, may, in a great measure, be attributed the attention and interest which the British public gave to the capabilities of the Cape. Many of Mr. Moodie's people were established in Cape Town and throughout the Colony in respectable trades. They were principally mechanics of the most valuable description. They were to have been settled upon a grant of land promised to Mr. Moodie by Government. Ever since his arrival the country bordering on Kafirland, where only he could expect a suitable grant, had been so much disturbed by the incursions of the Kafirs, that it would have been injurious to the interests of the public, as well as inconsistent with his duty to his followers, to have exposed their lives to danger by settling them on the borders at that period. He preferred purchasing, on account of the locality, in the district of Swellendam, near the confluence of the Buffalo-hunt (Buffeljagt) and Broad (Breed) Rivers. Mr. Moodie was induced to relinquish his intention of claiming a grant of land for the moment by the discovery that the demand for labour was so great in the Colony that his people were employed much more profitably to the public in the service of others than they could have been in his own, with the limited colonial experience he then possessed. He was the first person who attempted to direct emigration from the mother country to the Colony. When grants were being given to settlers in the Zunsveld, Mr. Moodie memorialized the Acting-Governor, representing the loss it had been to him not being able to occupy the grant originally intended for him owing to the disturbed state of the country, that twenty of his people had deserted from him, and that out of the remaining 180 in the country, he could now only carry to the Zunsveld seventy-one persons, the others being more usefully employed to the community than they could be on the Frontier. The Acting-Governor, Sir R. S. Donkin, recognised the value of the introduction by Mr. Moodie of British-born subjects, and recommended his memorial to the favourable consideration of the home Government, who directed that on his conveying himself and the specified number of able-bodied individuals to the Zuurveld, he should receive a grant of land in the proportion of 100 acres to each individual who should be located on such land, the grant itself to be made out at the expiration of three years from the date of location in the form and on the conditions directed by Her Majesty's Government for persons emigrating to the Colony. Unfortunately for Mr. Moodie, the grant which he obtained was on the Gualana River, near Fredericksburg, in a part which Lord Charles Somerset, on his return to the Colony, found was within the neutral territory, and that it was a breach of treaty-faith to occupy it. Mr. Moodie's and all other grants were consequently cancelled. Disgusted and disheartened by his ill-success in South Africa, he sold out all he had and migrated to Upper Canada, where he died at Belleville in 1868.

In 1817 an addition to the 200 introduced by Mr. Moodie was made to the British population of the settlement by allowing the discharge of 700 or 800 time-expired soldiers and sailors, who also found ready employment.

In 1819 another Scotch gentleman, Mr. Peter Tait, endeavoured to follow Mr. Moodie's plan of introducing settlers; but he was not so fortunate, as it was not till April, 1820, that he sent out sixteen men, three women, and six children: viz., Andrew Marshall, Robert Robson, Edward Wake, George Harvey, Henry Aitchison, Thomas Hill, John Douglas, James Donaldson, James Stevenson, James Grier, Joseph McDougall, James Foord, George Ogilvie, Isaac Tait, his wife and four children, William Tait (aged fourteen years), William Foord, his wife and two children, and Margaret Harvey.

CHAPTER VIII

REGULATIONS INTRODUCING SETTLERS TO THE ZUNSVELD

NO time was lost after the House of Commons had passed the Vote for emigration applied for by the Chancellor of the Exchequer in issuing circulars stating the terms and conditions upon which passages would be given to those applicants who were approved. They are dated eight days after the Vote had been taken, and were sent to the Governor at Cape Town. These circulars were as follows, being also the only official documents published on the subject :—

No. I.

Government Circular.

"DOWNING STREET, LONDON, 1819.

"I have to acquaint you, in reply to your letter of the ———, that the following are the conditions under which it is proposed to give encouragement to emigration to the Cape of Good Hope.

"The sufferings to which many individuals have been exposed, who have emigrated to his Majesty's foreign possessions, unconnected and unprovided with any capital or even the means of support, having been very afflicting to themselves, and equally burdensome to the Colonies to which they have proceeded, the Government have determined to confine the application of the money recently voted by Address in the House of Commons to those persons who, possessing the means, will engage to carry out, at the least, ten able-bodied individuals above eighteen years of age, with or without families, the Government always reserving to itself the right of selecting from the several offers made to them, those which may prove, upon examination, to be most eligible.

"In order to give some security to the Government that the persons undertaking to make these establishments have the means of doing so, every person engaging to take out the above-mentioned number of persons or families shall deposit at the rate of ten pounds (to be repaid as hereinafter mentioned) for every family so taken out, provided that the family does not consist of more than one man, one woman, and two children under fourteen years of age. All children above the number of two will have to be paid for, in addition to the deposit above mentioned, in the proportion of five pounds for every two children under fourteen years of age, and five pounds for every person between the ages of fourteen and eighteen.

"In consideration of this deposit, a passage shall be provided at the expense of the Government for the settlers, who shall also be victualled from the time of their embarkation until the time of their landing in the Colony.

"A grant of land, under the conditions hereinafter specified, shall be made to him at the rate of one hundred acres for every such person or family whom he so takes out; one-third of the sum advanced to Government on the outset shall be repaid on landing, when the victualling at the expense of the Government shall cease. A further proportion of one-third shall be repaid as soon as it shall be certified to the Governor of the Colony that the settlers, under the direction of the person taking them out, are actually located upon the land assigned them; and the remainder at the expiration of three months from the date of their location.

"If any parishes in which there may be a redundancy of population shall unite in selecting an intelligent individual to proceed to the Cape, with settlers under his direction not less in number, and of the description above mentioned, and shall advance money in the proportion above mentioned, the Government will grant land to such an individual at the rate of one hundred acres for every head of a family, leaving the parish at liberty to make such conditions with the individual, or the settlers, as may be calculated to prevent the parish becoming again chargeable with the maintenance of such settlers in the event of their return to this country.

"But no offers of this kind will be accepted unless it shall be clear that the persons proposing to become settlers shall have distinctly given their consent, and the head of each family is not infirm or incapable of work.

"It is further proposed that in any case in which one hundred families proceed together, and apply for leave to carry out with them a minister of their own persuasion, Government will, upon their being actually located, assign a salary to the minister whom they may have selected to accompany them, if he shall be approved by the Secretary of State.

"The lands will be granted at a quit-rent to be fixed, which rent, however, will be remitted for the first ten years; and at the expiration of three years (during which the party and a number of families, in the proportion of one for every hundred acres, must have resided on the estate) the land shall be measured at the expense of the Government, and the holder shall obtain, without fee, his title thereto, on a perpetual quit-rent not exceeding in any case two pounds sterling for every hundred acres; subject, however, to this clause beyond the usual reservations,[1] that the land shall become forfeited to Government in case the party shall abandon the estate, or not bring it into cultivation within a given number of years.

"I am, your most obedient and humble servant.

"P.S.—In order to insure the arrival of the settlers at the Cape at the beginning of the planting season, the transports will not leave this country till the month of November."

---

[1] The usual reservations are the right of the Crown to mines of precious stones, of gold and silver, and to make such roads as may be necessary for the convenience of the Colony.

No. II.

The following regulations as to the mode of apportioning the land are said to have been contained in a memorandum from the Secretary of State to several gentlemen, friends of the emigration to the Cape :—

"1. Parties wishing for grants in the district appointed by the Government [2] will not be necessitated to make a direct application to his Excellency the Governor, as in other cases, but it will be sufficient for them to address the Landdrost, pointing out where they propose to settle, and the authority of the Landdrost shall be sufficient warrant to the party of the intention of His Majesty's Government in his regard.

"2. The Landdrost is, however, to be particularly cautious in the distribution of the ground, so as to preserve waters, that the most extensive accommodation possible may be afforded in that regard to future settlers; the necessity of which must be obvious from the supposed scarcity of springs in the districts in question.

"3. In order likewise to obtain the most accurate information possible with respect to springs in the whole of this district, the Landdrost is called upon to give the greatest publicity to the proclamation issued, offering rewards for the discovery of springs proportioned to their strength.

"4. The Landdrost will communicate to the Colonial Secretary, quarterly, a list of persons taking lands under this invitation, and describing as accurately as possible the situation of the occupancies."

No. III.

"DOWNING STREET, LONDON.

"SIR,—In reply to your letter of the ——, I am directed by Earl Bathurst to acquaint you that as the circular letter distinctly specifies the nature and extent of the assistance which will be granted to individuals who may be allowed to proceed as settlers to the Cape of Good Hope, together with the conditions under which alone that assistance can be given to them, it is only necessary to refer you to that document, and to add that no proposal can be accepted which is not framed in conformity with the offer of His Majesty's Government.

"With reference to your particular inquiries respecting the mode in which the views of the settler may be attained, I have to acquaint you that it is not in Earl Bathurst's power to communicate to you that species of information which can most properly be afforded by the practical agriculturist, or obtained on the spot.

"The settlers will be located in the interior of the Colony, not far from the coast; and in allotting to them the lands which Government have agreed to grant them, their interests and their wishes will be consulted and attended to, as far as may be consistent with the public interests of the Colony.

"The settlers will be enabled to purchase a limited quantity of agricultural implements in the Colony at prime cost, although they are not debarred from

---

[2] This has been exactly pointed out. A paragraph in the *Courier* states that it is to be in Zuure Veld, or the neighbourhood, and that the settlers are to be landed in Algoa Bay.

taking with them a moderate supply of these articles as well as necessaries; and they will find no difficulty in purchasing seed corn in the Colony.

" The settlers will not find habitations ready for their reception.

" The person under whose direction a party of settlers proceeds is at liberty to secure their services by any legal agreement into which they may think proper to enter.

" The new Settlement will, of course, be governed according to the laws in force in the Colony.

"In conclusion, I beg to observe that it must be left to the persons taking out settlers to form their own opinions as to the amount of the pecuniary means with which they should be provided in order to support the persons placed under their directions, and ensure the success of their undertaking.

" I am, sir, your most obedient servant."

The applications under this scheme were far more than could be granted. It is said they amounted to 90,000, but upon what information this is arrived at is not clear, and is probably a figure of speech to denote the numbers who were ready to transfer themselves to an El Dorado. It is difficult to understand how the selection of 5,000 was made out of such numbers, as approved and accepted, without supposing that private influence and political considerations operated largely to determine the decision. This supposition would account for the number of half-pay officers of the united service, having little knowledge of agricultural pursuits, who were recognised as heads of parties who would employ labourers in the cultivation of the soil. The whole number to be embarked as future settlers of this *terra incognita* comprised all sorts and conditions of men : farmers, artisans, fishermen, and labourers, most of them from England, some from Wales, some from Scotland, and some from Ireland.[3] Twenty-six vessels, brig-rigged, were chartered to convey these individuals, their wives, families, luggage, and stores. In order that they should arrive at their destination about the planting season, the embarkation was delayed till November, 1819. In five months from the passing of the vote in the House of Commons all was in readiness, and the ships sailed from Gravesend, each being in charge of a lieutenant of the Royal Navy. The first vessel to sail was the *Nautilus*, which left on December 3 ; the others followed in quick succession.[4] The voyage to Table Bay occupied 104 days, and the disappointment of the emigrants at not being allowed to land, after such a lengthened passage, may be imagined. The vessels were placed in quarantine owing to the epidemic at the Mauritius and the small-pox at Bourbon, besides owing to whooping-cough and measles which had broken out on board ship, from which complaints several deaths had occurred.

At that time a general order existed prohibiting any one from landing without permission from the Governor, from whatever part of the world they might come. To obtain this permission, the process was to present a memorial to his Excellency the Governor, praying for permission to disembark, and for a

[3] Appendix for list of (1) parties, and (2) of individuals.
[4] For names of vessels, the dates of their sailing and arrival, see Appendix.

passport whilst on shore, supported by references. The memorial required to be stamped, and being in order, was referred to the Fiscal, who endorsed it to the effect that, upon due inquiry in his office, nothing was known to the disparagement of memorialist, and the referees bound themselves as sureties for the good conduct of applicant. Thereupon the memorialist was granted permission to remain in the Settlement so long as he conducted himself in a quiet and orderly manner. It was not only individuals that required this permit, but batches of persons also. Thus David Thomas Nightingale, agent of John Leigh, junr., & Co., of London, merchants, who had been sent out at the head of eighteen men, eight women, and fifteen children by that firm to establish and conduct a commercial concern and superintend a whale fishery, and to engage in agricultural pursuits, not being supported by the firm, had to ask and obtain permission for said persons to remain in the Colony. A small trade was carried on between Cape Town and Mauritius and St. Helena, and to export to those places a permit was required to be obtained likewise by memorial, stating particulars of the intended shipment. The difference in regard to the emigrants by the *Nautilus* and succeeding transports was, that they were sent with the knowledge and by the direction of the home Government, and ought not to have been required to go through this humiliating process, which, however, the heads of parties and others had to do, to enable them to land and make arrangements about their half-pay and other monetary matters. Persons from abroad, *e.g.* Watermeyer from Hamburg, who wished to visit or reside at the Cape, had to procure from the Colonial Secretary in London a permission to do so, granted upon certificate of the British or foreign consul of the place they came from that they were peaceable and respectable individuals, and the permit so obtained was subject to the further approval of the Governor on their arrival.

A further disappointment was experienced by the new comers. The detention at Table Bay and the voyage thence to Algoa Bay occupied twenty-three days, and the *Nautilus* and her consort, the *Chapman*, who had arrived in Table Bay the same day as the *Nautilus*, both arrived at their destination on the same day also. On landing, the emigrants were told they were to be sent to the "interior," at some distance off. Memorials to the Acting-Governor had been addressed to His Excellency by William Howard, John Henry Dixon, and Nathanael Morgan, whilst on board the transport *Ocean* in Table Bay, dated 2nd April, 1820, stating in earnest terms that they had been told they and their parties would be located on the sea coast, praying that, if sent inland, the instalment of deposit-money lodged in England before their departure should not be applied to defray the expense of their conveyance to the spot selected for their location. Others thought they might engage in commercial pursuits, as did Mr. William Parker, of the Irish party. Others that they were to be located about the Kuysua. Altogether the settlers felt discouraged. Their expectations were not justified, as the designation of the locality given in England was the "Zunsveld," and the grants of land to be made were intended for cultivation. It was the idea of going beyond the Settlement at Cape Town, into an unknown region at a considerable distance from the coast which, not unnaturally, seemed so terrible.

CHAPTER IX

THE ZUNSVELD

THE tract of country called the Zunsveld was that which lay between the Sunday's River on the south and the Fish River on the north, having the coast line for its boundary on the east, and the Sour-grass (Zuurbergen) Mountains on the west. It was so called by the Boers to distinguish it from other parts, such as the Karroo (a native word signifying barren, or bare), Gebroken, or Droken (mixed), Zoetveld (sweet), and Zuurveld, meaning "sour grass," fit for cattle grazing only. It had been occupied by Kafirs of a mixed race, as already related, whose predatory habits kept them in constant strife with the Boers occupying loan places in the adjacent country, as well as with those who had ventured into this region. The frequent reprisals and loss of life in these encounters determined the authorities to drive the aboriginal occupants out of this tract of country, and restrict them to the other side of the Fish River. There was no hope of peaceful occupation in this and the adjoining parts of the Swellendam district for the Boers except by this process, which was that which had been adopted in the successive expansions of colonial territory. At whatever cost, and by whatever means, the savages must be driven further away, and such of them only as were required for domestic and predial service amongst the invading Boers were allowed to exist in a state of perpetual slavery amongst them. After the expulsion of the Kafirs from the Zunsveld by Colonel Graham, in 1811, as previously related, it was placed under the jurisdiction of the deputy Landdrost of Uitenhage, August 14, 1812. The efforts of Lord Charles Somerset to induce the Boers to settle in this tract of country by the promise of extensive grants of land on favourable terms,[1] proved unavailing; and after his personal inspection of the Frontier line in 1817, as previously mentioned, the only way of establishing a permanent barrier against future Kafir incursions appeared to him to be by the introduction of British immigrants. The description of the country contained in his Lordship's despatch to the home authorities on this suggestion, quoted *ante*, was not exaggerated. It was a fertile land, watered by numerous streams, the most important being the Bushman's River,

---

[1] Several parts of the Zunsveld were occupied by Boers, whose names are preserved to this day in the spots they lived on; *e.g.*, Brookhuysen's Poort, Grobbelaar's Kloof, Howitson's Poort, Woest Hill, etc., etc. They had vacated these loan places before the settlers arrived, who in many cases were glad to avail themselves of the rude houses which the Boers had left partially standing for temporary occupation.

was well timbered and grassy, in places presenting a park-like sight—just the appearance to gratify the eye of an English settler, and is still such. It was bordered on the north by the almost impenetrable Fish River Bush, and on the south-west side by a similar natural barrier—the Kouri Bush. Both were of considerable length, and could only be traversed by the Kafirs on foot, who were acquainted with the paths made by wild animals. It was through these natural passes that the Kafirs penetrated single file into the grassy plains of the Zunsveld, spoiled the dwellers therein, and safely retreated through the same channels to their kraals in Kafirland. It is impossible to give a description that would convey an idea of the density of this bush, which at the period of the settlers' arrival was more impenetrable than it is at the present day. An idea may be formed of the dense character of this growth of underwood peculiar to the country, known generally by colonists as "bush," and the difficulty of penetrating it, by recalling the misadventure that occurred so late as 1867 to the curate of the English Church at Southwell. The reverend gentleman left Graham's Town in the afternoon on horseback, and thought to reach his home through the Kouri Bush, but lost the path, and remained self-immured in it the whole night. Fortunately it was summer time, and happily next morning a cattle-herd found him in an exhausted condition, and put him in the right track, whereby he was enabled to reach his home, to the relief of his wife and family, who could not account for his absence, and had no idea of his perilous adventure.[2] The settlers were exposed to insidious attacks through these channels in their front and on their flank, and it was a wise and strategic move of Lord Charles Somerset to abandon Bathurst in its incipient stage of existence, and remove the civil headquarters from thence to the military cantonment at Graham's Town, as affording a more central and convenient point to check intrusion. Bathurst was situated with the Kouri Bush immediately behind it, where the bush was more dense than elsewhere, and could easily have been destroyed by a small force of ruthless savages, who knew where to retreat in perfect security in case of need. A small fort at Kafir Drift, near the mouth of the Fish River, through which fort the Kafirs drove the large herds they succeeded in plundering, was deemed sufficient protection in that direction. The part of Albany that now constitutes the division of Bathurst was called Lower Albany, and is still so spoken of. The whole Zunsveld is now divided into the divisions of Bathurst and Albany, and a part falls into the division of Alexandria. The area of this home of the British settlers is estimated at 1,730 square miles. In this remote and extensive region they were deposited to com-

[2] On his early journeys through the locations Mr. Shaw relates: "I frequently missed my way, and was at times benighted in the woods, which at that period were infested with various kinds of ferocious animals. I could not always obtain a horse, and hence I had frequently to walk over considerable distances, through rugged districts, upon unformed paths, and not seldom having to wade through the unbridged streams that intersect the district. Indeed, several years subsequent to this period my missionary colleagues, before they became familiar with the country, often missed their way; and occasionally it happened that a missionary had to solace himself at night in the midst of a bush, by seeking such security and repose as could be obtained from climbing a tree and secreting himself in its branches."—*Story of my Mission*, p. 90.

bat occupation first of all with the wild animals that abounded : the elephant, the buffalo, the leopard, wolf, etc., and in after years the more formidable opponents to peaceful habitation : the Kafirs, who claimed to be the original possessors of the country. It is a marvel that with these serious obstacles to overcome, as well as the drawbacks of new comers in a strange land, with seasons opposite to those they had been accustomed to in the land of their birth, they should have overcome difficulties and conquered their enemies, and so prevented the emigration from Britain in 1819 being recorded as an absolute failure.

CHAPTER X

PREPARATIONS FOR RECEPTION AND LOCATION OF THE SETTLERS

IN the month of November, 1819, Lord Charles Somerset, the Governor of the Colony, received the first intimation of the intended emigration from England. No time was lost in directing preparatory arrangements. On the 12th November his Excellency addressed a letter to Lieut.-Colonel Cuyler,[1] Landdrost of Uitenhage, enclosing copy of Earl Bathurst's despatch on the subject, which pointed out the encouragement and assistance contemplated by the home Government. The Governor's letter emphasized the importance to the Colony of making this scheme of the home Government successful, and that much depended in that direction on the exertion of the local magistrates. It was pointed out that the old line of military posts between Graham s Town and the mouth of the Fish River presented a country of great fertility and promise, capable of maintaining with industry a large population. The advantage to the Colony and to the individuals themselves from this portion of the ground being early settled was urged. His Excellency wished to see the abandoned farms nearest to Graham's Town first occupied ; and in those so occupied the settlers were to be encouraged in agricultural pursuits, rather than in the maintenance of large herds of cattle, as had heretofore been the practice of the insulated Boers, who at different periods had occupied lands in the extensive district of Albany.

The Landdrost of Uitenhage was directed to instruct Mr. Knobel, land surveyor, as soon as possible to make a minute survey of the unoccupied places in the immediate vicinity of the limits of the land attached to Graham's Town, and in his report to specify not only the quantity of land calculated for garden ground, for the plough, and for pasture, but to describe accurately the different springs or other water which such places contained or commanded. Next after this he was to survey the Blauw Kraus (blue wreaths) and any situations in that vicinity where the settlers could be advantageously placed. From thence the surveyor was to take the direction of Waai-plaatz (the Windy Vale)

---

[1] Afterwards General Cuyler, an American loyalist. The family of this gentleman preserve with great care an interesting relic—the portraits of their grandparents, painted by the unfortunate Major André, who was executed as a spy by General Washington in 1780, and while he was a prisoner at New York, of which city Colonel Cuyler's father had been mayor.— Chase's *Annals*, p. 274.

to the lower Kafir Drift post, where it was believed that great facilities would be found for a very considerable proportion of the settlers, who were to be allowed in the first instance to avail themselves of the hutting which had been occupied by the troops. The spot called the Palmist Fontein (Rush Fountain), in the immediate vicinity of the mouth of the Fish River, was also pointed out as eligible, and upon these spots, at the intervening ground, it was thought that a greater number of persons and families could be placed than would be expected for a considerable time from England.

When the line thus chalked out was occupied, all the eligible ground which intervenes between it and the mouth of the Bushman's River, including those fertile tracts watered by the Kouri, the Karonga, and the Kareiga, was next to be filled in.

Having disposed of the locality to which the expected arrivals were to be sent, his Excellency directed the Landdrost's attention to Earl Bathurst's despatch directing that the emigrants were to be provided with the means of transporting their baggage to the places of their destination; the cost of which he was authorized to defray from his district chest, keeping a separate account thereof, in order that the amount might be subsequently refunded to him, either from the public funds of the local Government, or from the individuals.

The Landdrost was further instructed as to any stores which might have been embarked in the ships with the emigrants, and which might be public property, that they were to be safely landed and stored at Algoa Bay, taking an inventory of them, and noting the condition in which they were landed. He was further advised that the Governor would give particular directions to the Deputy-Assistant Commissary-General as to their subsequent issue, and as to provisioning the new comers from the moment of their arrival at Algoa Bay till that of their arrival at Graham's Town, and the subsequent necessary aid for their subsistence until the settlers should have had time to provide by their own exertions for themselves. These were admirable arrangements, showing clearly what was in the mind of the Governor. Placing a large number of the settlers on the extreme border of Albany, with the Fish River Bush just beyond, a natural entrance for incursions, would afford a living wall of defence, supported by the after settlement of other parties below them down to the Bushman's River. This plan would also strengthen and support the military headquarters at Graham's Town, as that cantonment would in turn inspire confidence among the settlers thus within easy reach of assistance if needed. At the time of giving these instructions and laying down the plan of settlement determined upon, Lord Charles Somerset had no idea of the number of emigrants who would be poured in upon the country, nor how rapidly they would arrive. Happy for the settlers would it have been if he had remained in office to personally carry out his plans, but he left the Colony on 13th January, 1820, on leave of absence, to arrange family affairs, his wife having died a few years previously. Lieut.-General Sir R. S. Donkin was appointed Acting-Governor. He had recently come to the Cape from India in search of health, which was impaired by his service in India and the recent loss of his wife. He would seem to have been of a kindly disposition, but of not much capacity for the responsibility of office, and acted upon his own judgment instead of carrying out the policy of the Governor for whom he acted.

After the attack on Graham's Town in 1819, the country had been cleared and left vacant. The British occupiers then became the advanced guard of the Colony, and dearly they paid in after years for the post of honour allotted to them. I need not describe the country, picturesque and beautiful as many portions of it are. It then abounded with game of various kinds. Springbucks bounded in thousands over the plains. Rheabucks and klipspringers were plentiful among the mountains. Bushbucks, duikers, grysbucks, and others, were numerous in the woods and thickets, while in the larger forests of the Kouri, Fish River, and Addo, herds of elephants and buffaloes challenged the courage of the more adventurous sportsmen. Not were beasts of prey wanting. The lion indeed was seldom met with in the coast country, but there were plenty of them in the Winter mountain ranges. The deep bass of the African tiger was a frequent sound in the wooded kloofs by day as well as by night. The hideous laugh and yell of the hyena frightened the little children in their beds, and the horned cattle and young horses suffered terribly from them. Packs of wild dogs were waiting ready for the ration sheep, and jackals disturbed the rest of those who were not used to their night cries. Whole colonies of baboons migrated from region to region, and very fond were they of young lambs and mealie fields.[2]

However, the first survey directed to be made was finished before the arrival of any of the settlers,[3] and in February, 1820, the Acting-Governor, General Sir R. S. Donkin, addressed the Landdrost of Uitenhage to provide camp equipage and provisions for those who should arrive, up to that time being ignorant of the number to be expected. Camp equipage, however, for 1,500 persons and rations for one month for 2,000 were ordered to be provided, and conveyances ready to the places of destination. The Landdrost was also directed to ascertain, with as much accuracy as possible, what aid the district would want, if any, for the supply of an influx of population calculated at 5,000 souls for six months. The importance of these measures can only be appreciated by those who know how difficult it is, in a country so thinly populated and at a distance of 600 miles from the only market, and that merely calculated for the limited population of its environs, to procure provisions for so great an influx of people upon such very short notice, and to collect the great number of wagons requisite for so extensive a conveyance as that necessary for 5,000 persons, with stores and agricultural implements. In March following, the Landdrost of Uitenhage was informed of the arrival in Table Bay of the transports *Chapman* and *Nautilus* with a proportion of the settlers to be located in the Zunsveld. These settlers were under seven directors, with whom only the local Government had communication, and to whom only grants were to be given, the directors subsequently giving titles to such as would locate in their respective allotments. These seven directors were :—

[2] Dugmore's *Reminiscences*, p. 202.
[3] See Map.

	Men.	Women.	Above 14 years.	Under 14.	Total.
Mr. G. Scott	14	9	4	10 =	37
Lieut. Crause	12	9	1	22 =	44
Mr. T. Rowles	11	11	4	26 =	52
Mr. T. Owen	10	5	—	12 =	27
Mr. J. Mundy	11	10	—	23 =	44
Mr. J. Carlisle	11	—	—	4 =	15
Mr. J. Bailie	96	63	13	116 =	288

A total of 507

These seven directors and their dependents were all to be located on the line surveyed by Mr. Knobel, Mr. Bailie's grant being 10,000 acres; Crause and Owen, 2,600, to be equally divided; Rowles and Mundy, 2,300, to be equally divided; Scott, 1,800; and Carlisle, 1,200. There being some few cases of whooping-cough among the children, it was deemed prudent not to direct the march of the settlers through the town of Uitenhage, but to take the lower road by Jager's Drift, as also a shorter route to the place of their location. The Landdrost was again reminded that from the moment of their coming ashore the Government ceased to be at any charge for the directors or their settlers. The Commissary-General, however, had directions that should they require it, rations should be issued to them, the cost of which would be charged against the funds they had deposited.

CHAPTER XI

LANDING OF THE SETTLERS—JOURNEY TO, AND ARRIVAL AT, THE LOCATIONS

AT the time of the arrival of the fleet, with the British immigrants on board,[1] the shore of Algoa Bay was inaccessible except through the surf in small boats, and at great risk. The landing of the settlers was thus a work of time and difficulty. They were all, however, safely landed, Captain Fairfax Moresby, R.N., in command of the *Menai* warship, superintending and directing, for which service, as well as having accompanied them from Table Bay to Algoa Bay, Earl Bathurst directed that his sense of Captain Moresby's zealous co-operation should be conveyed to him as having been fully appreciated. The arrangements which had been made for the landing and reception of the settlers were altogether so complete and satisfactory that they were entirely approved by the home Government.[2] Tents had been pitched in parallel rows, and the several parties were assigned these each distinct from the other. The first view of Algoa Bay on arrival is thus described by Rev. W. Shaw from on board the *Aurora*, one of the last transports to arrive :—

"Next morning, as soon as the day dawned, most of the people came on deck [of the *Aurora*] to view the land of their future residence. As the sun rose over the wide expanse of ocean towards the east, and gilded with his light the hills and shores of the bay towards the west and north, a gloom gradually spread itself over the countenances of the people. As far as the eye could sweep, from the south-west to the north-east, the margin of the sea appeared to be one continued range of low, white sand hills. Wherever any breach in these hills afforded a peep into the country immediately behind this fringe of sand the ground seemed sterile and the bushes stunted. Immediately above the landing place the land rose abruptly into hills of considerable elevation, which had a craggy and stony appearance, and were relieved by little verdure. Two or three whitewashed and thatched cottages, and Fort Frederick—a small fortification crowning the height, and by its few cannon commanding the anchorage—were all that arrested the eye in the first view of Algoa Bay, with the exception of the tents of the British settlers,

---

[1] See Mr. John Mundy's interesting letters descriptive of the voyage, and arrival at Cape Town and Algoa Bay (Appendix).
[2] Despatch 317 ; July, 1820.

many of whom had already disembarked and formed a camp half a mile to the right of the landing-place. The scene was at once dull and disappointing. It produced a very discouraging effect on the minds of the people, not a few of whom began to contrast this waste wilderness with the beautiful shores of old England, and to express fears that they had foolishly allowed themselves to be lured away by false representations to a country which seemed to offer no promise of reward to its cultivators. However, the needful preparations for landing, and the anxiety to be relieved from the discomforts and monotony of their long confinement on board ship, changed the current of their thoughts, and thereby afforded some relief to their gloomy forebodings."[3]

The Commandant of Fort Frederick, Captain Francis Evett, formerly of the 21st Light Dragoons, waded through the surf, and landed with his own hands the greater number of the women and children. His kindness and cordial welcome to the arrivals did not end there. His quarters and table were open to all whose character and conduct deserved the attention. Sir Rubane Donkin, the Acting-Governor, arrived soon after the landing of the first comers to locate the immigrants. He ordered the building of a small pyramidal cenotaph[4] in memory of his lately-deceased wife, and named the village he there founded Port Elizabeth, as a perpetual token of respect to her memory. At this time the only buildings were Fort Frederick[5] (which had been built by the English in 1795, and named after the Duke of York), a small barrack, a mess-house, the Commandant's quarters, three indifferent houses, and a few mud and straw-built huts, besides the original farmhouse belonging to a Boer

[3] *Story of my Mission*, p. 30.
[4] On the east side, looking down upon the town, there is the following inscription :—
"To the memory of one of the most perfect of human beings, who has given her name to the town below."

On the west side it bears the following inscription :—

"ELIZABETH FRANCES LADY DONKIN,
Eldest daughter of Dr. George Markham, Dean of York.
Died at Merat, in Upper Hindostan, after seven days' illness,
On 20th August, 1818, aged 28 years.
She left an infant in her seventh month, too young to know
the irreparable loss she had sustained, and a husband
whose heart is still wrung by undiminished grief.
He erected this Pyramid, August, 1820."

[5] "On the last hill which goes down to the shore stands Fort Frederick, built by the English in 1799. Eight guns, twelve-pounders, command the shore, and protect the buildings lying near, and the barracks, guard-houses, etc. Westward of the hill on which the Fort stands, comes from a deep gulley, a little stream called Baaken's (Beacon's) River. At the ford of the river, which is concealed between the hills that rise on each side of it, is another wooden block-house, which, under the English Government, was prepared in Cape Town, and sent in parts by sea to the Bay. It serves at once as a prison and as a guard house. Between the block-houses lie extensive barracks for soldiers, a magazine for provisions, and another for military stores and field equipages, a smith's shop, a bakehouse, a carpenter's workshop, and other small buildings. A strong powder magazine, which will contain about 2,000 lbs. of powder, is within the Fort itself. Some small houses have been run up in the neighbourhood for the officers, among which the house of the commandant is the most distinguished."—*Lichtenstein's Travels*, vol. i., p. 232.

named Hartmann. The population was about thirty-five souls. The work of locating the parties proceeded as rapidly as circumstances would allow. Lord Charles Somerset, prior to his departure, had anticipated the arrival of the settlers, and made arrangements accordingly for their reception. The commissariat department had everything in readiness, the Boers in the neighbourhood having been requisitioned to supply wagons for the conveyance of the settlers, their wives and families, their stores and farming implements. The first to leave Algoa Bay—April 18, 1820—were the seven parties specified in the previous chapter, together numbering 507 souls, for whom ninety-six wagons were provided. Earl Bathurst had directed that the spots to particular settlers should be assigned, so that they might on landing at once proceed to the places which they were permanently to occupy. His Lordship added that he was aware, from experience of what had taken place in forming settlements of this kind in North America, that the settlers would for some time after their arrival require much superintendence and direction; therefore that to each party of settlers some intelligent soldiers or non-commissioned officers should be attached for the purpose of instructing them as to hutting, or otherwise providing the necessary covering for themselves and their families, and that some officers should have the general command and direction of persons so selected.

Journey and Arrival at the Locations.

The new comers were glad to leave the inhospitable-looking shore of Algoa Bay, with the prospect of shortly reaching the locality they were to occupy. The journey was a novel experience to them, as well as the cumbrous wagon drawn by oxen with Dutch-speaking drivers and native leaders of the teams. The journey was propitious. Splendid rains had fallen a few months before, the rivers were overflowing, pasturage luxuriantly rich. Game was abundant—the hartebeest, springbok, quagga, ostrich. The route taken was *via* Jagersdrift, on the Bushman's River, instead of through the district town of Uitenhage, and thence across the Sunday's River at Addo Drift. It was feared the strangers might infect the townspeople of Uitenhage with measles or whooping-cough, of which complaints there had been some cases on board ship, if they travelled that route; so the train of wagons were directed to take the lower road. There were ninety-six wagons altogether, and the wagon-paths were almost inaccessible. Small forests had to be penetrated, and rivers crossed through "drifts," as there were no bridges. The monotony of the journey was broken by the sight of wild animals new to them, and by the frequent "outspans" at halting times. The distance was at last accomplished without accident. On the 26th the party with great ease crossed in their wagons the Kouri River mouth, and on the evening of the 28th the wagons in turn deposited their loads of human beings, together with their goods and chattels, on the bare veld, at a deserted farm called Kornplace, under the mud-walls of a house not long before consumed by the Kafirs. Here the immigrants decided to settle down permanently, and called the embryo village "Cuylerville," in compliment to Colonel Cuyler, whose attentions and kindly manners during the time he accompanied them on their long and fatiguing journey were unremitting. After inspecting the mouth of the Fish River, on the 3rd May Colonel Cuyler took his leave with this ominous caution : "Gentlemen, when you go out to plough, never leave your guns at home."[6] What an experience for persons brought from Britain, many of whom had not been used to anything approaching the discomfort and rough and trying life suddenly forced upon them, and others who had been brought up in a town ! " It is not easy to describe our feelings at the moment when we arrived," writes the Rev. W. Shaw. " Our Dutch wagon driver intimating that we had at length reached our location, we took our boxes out of the wagon, and placed them on the ground. He then bade us 'goeden dag' (good-day), cracked his whip, and drove away, leaving us to our reflections. My wife sat down on one box and I on another. The beautiful sky was above us, and the green grass beneath our feet. We looked at each other for a few moments, indulged in some reflections, and, perhaps, exchanged a few sentences. But it was no time for sentiment, and hence we were soon engaged in pitching our tent ; and when that was accomplished, we removed into it our trunks, bedding, etc." All were not so philosophically disposed as this Methodist minister and his wife ; all have not the virtue of resignation to circumstances which are unavoidable, and which they cannot change. Thus another Wesleyan minister, Mr. W. Sargeant, writes : " The settlers were put down and left by their Dutch drivers, strangers in an African wilderness. Some were disposed for a time to sit down upon their baggage and indulge in a reverie, or to philosophize on their novel circumstances ; but they were soon aroused from all such sentimental speculations by the realization of their true matter-of-fact position."[7] They were now a hundred miles inland, without the possibility, however much they might wish it, or however piteously they might pray for it, of returning to the land of their birth. There was no help for it What they had to do now was to make the best of the arrangement, and settle down to *bonâ-fide* occupation. Koorn-plaatz, subsequently named Cuylerville, was forty miles distant from Graham's Town, and about seven miles from the military outpost at Kafir's Drift, near the mouth of the Fish River. By the time of the Acting-Governor's visit, a month afterwards, they were spread over the tract marked out for them by the surveyor for their occupation, and had fixed the sites of their future dwellings, and prepared spots for cultivation. Subsequent experience showed that they had made mistakes in this respect —not unnatural in new comers, unacquainted with the nature of the climate— and in consequence had the mortification to find their primitive dwellings swept down by the raging torrents that flowed through the streamlets along- side of which they had erected them, and their cultivated lands on the slopes of these rivulets washed away by the floods. They bore these adversities manfully and cheerfully, one asking another whether he had seen anything of his house floating down the stream ![8] and, profiting by this dearly-bought

[6] Chase, p. 275.
[7] Sheffield's *Story of the Settlement*, p. 152.
[8] " Another incident of my early settler life was not forgotten by one of the family. Sup- plies had fallen short, and we had not a day's food left. My father set off on foot, to a place

experience, began again to put themselves in situations less exposed to such calamities, and to cultivate their lands beyond the water mark.

about twelve miles distant, to buy as much meal as he could carry home on his back. We had literally 'a dinner of herbs' in his absence, and waited anxiously for his return. Night set in, but no father made his appearance. Meantime a heavy rain flooded the river, which would have to be crossed at his own door. About ten o'clock at night my father's usual signal was heard on the other side, and we hurried to the drift, only to find it impassable except by swimming. My father at first tried to wade with his load on his head. The water was up to his shoulders before he reached the middle, and he had to turn back to the farther side. The situation was not a pleasant one. The mother, with her hungry children, in the dead of night, on the one side; the father, with his supply of food, on the other, but unreachable, though only some half-dozen yards divided them. My father at length resolved on the desperate expedient of finding the narrowest part of the river, where the stream ran between two deep banks, and trying if he could not throw his twenty pound bag of meal over. Painful suspense followed on the part of the little ones while the preparations were being made, followed by a cry of despair when a heavy splash told that the bag had fallen short, and was lost in the stream. Nothing was left but for my father to swim through at the drift, and the family to go to bed supperless, as they had been dinnerless. A forlorn hope took us to the riverside early in the morning, when to our amazement there hung the little bag of lost provisions caught by the overhanging branches of the trees that bordered the river, and saved from either sinking or being carried away. A shout of a very different character from that of the midnight cry hailed the welcome sight. The bag was speedily disentangled from the hands of its preservers, with its contents little or nothing the worse for a slight external wetting which had scarcely penetrated below the surface, and a sorrowful night was followed by a joyous and thankful morning."—Dugmore's *Reminiscences*, p. 217.

CHAPTER XII

THE ACTING-GOVERNOR'S VISIT TO ALBANY

AFTER the campaign of 1819 Lord Charles Somerset obtained leave of absence, his wife—a daughter of the second Viscount Courtenay, having died September 11, 1815,—and proceeded to England. In his absence the Government was entrusted to Major-General Sir Rubane Shawe Donkin, an officer who had seen much active service in Europe and in India. While employed against the Mahrattas in 1817-18, he had the misfortune to lose his wife, who died at Meerut, at the age of twenty-eight, on 21st August, 1818, leaving him with an infant son, much shattered in health, bodily and mentally. He was invalided to the Cape, his name being retained on the Bengal establishment whilst acting for the Governor. Upon him fell the responsibility of receiving and locating the British settlers. He took a great interest in the welfare of the immigrants, and did all he could to forward them to their destination, and to put them in occupation of their grants of land. Very shortly after their arrival at Algoa Bay he proceeded to give such directions as might be needed, and founded the future Liverpool of the Colony under the name of Port Elizabeth, after his late wife. Thereafter he proceeded to Graham's Town, 14th May, 1820 ; and it being of the utmost importance that every facility should be given to the obtaining immediate shelter for the different families located in the district, he was pleased, by notice to the different parties of British settlers, to declare that wood and thatch for purposes of building, were from that date, for the space of twelve calendar months, matters of common use, and that no claim of trespass would be entertained against persons acting according to that notice. Similarly, that water for drinking, as well of man as of beast, should be used in common, provided that that privilege was exercised without injury to any cultivated ground. His Excellency's personal visit among the settlers led to his addressing a letter to Captain Trappes, on May 23, whom he appointed provisional magistrate, for his guidance so far as the then undefined state of the measure in progress would allow. The object of the instructions was the administration of the more pressing exigencies of municipal law among the settlers. Captain Trapper's duties would embrace the preservation of the peace, and as far as regards civil proceeding, the settlement of disputes likely to arise between individuals placed in such novel circumstances of social relation. Upon this head, it was pointed out that it would be necessary that he should be apprised of the nature of the engagements subsisting between the heads and the individuals composing the different parties. These were to proceed upon two principles, the one of joint labour and equality of allotment of land, the other of personal service for a certain time upon fixed conditions. The ordinary process of law did not, in the event of discussion, at once reach agreements of this description, and the course hitherto adopted had been to induce a return to union and mutual assistance by refusing permission to individuals so circumstanced to quit their location. The colonial law, which considered all persons travelling without a pass as vagrants, afforded a ready mode of carrying this object into effect. No difficulty presented itself to the arrangement of disputes where the case was that of personal service, the colonial law compelling the performance of reciprocal duties of master and apprentice. Admonition, it was thought, would in general be sufficient to enforce good conduct on the part of the master; otherwise the threat of dismissal from the Colony would be used, and it could scarcely be expected that both would prove ineffectual. Similar admonition, accompanied by threats of imprisonment, and in cases of positive refractoriness and violence imprisonment itself, might be applied to apprentices. But in general the exhibition of the power of control and punishment, rather than the actual exercise, was what was most contemplated. The instructions received from Earl Bathurst provided for the separation of mechanics and artificers from their parties with the consent of the respective heads. But so much caprice had been manifested by the settlers generally in this respect, that Captain Trappes was not authorized to grant any such permission without specific authority from the Colonial Office, it being considered of the utmost importance that positive establishment should take place on the lands assigned, the only exception allowed being in the case of artificers required for public works.

These instructions to Captain Trappes were followed by a circular, dated the same day, addressed "to the different parties of British settlers established in the district of Albany." It recited that the Acting-Governor having observed the capricious manner in which permission to quit the respective parties and to proceed to Graham's Town had been given to individuals, by which the peace of that town and military cantonment was endangered, and the practice of vagabondizing, in direct violation of colonial law, much encouraged, directed that thereafter, in the event of any individual proceeding to Graham's Town for any reasonable occasion, he must immediately, if not a head of a party, produce a permission to quit the party before a magistrate, who would exercise his discretion as to allowing him to remain. The only difference with respect to the head of a party was, that he required no pass for quitting the location, but he must obtain a town pass. Further, the Acting-Governor directed that applications for permission permanently to quit the party must in the first instance be signed by the head of the party, then transmitted to the provisional magistrate, by whom the same would be forwarded to the Colonial Office, from whence the permanent permission, either for residence in the district or the Colony generally, as the case might be, would be issued. Permissions of separation for a period not exceeding one month might be granted by the Landdrost for the district at large; for the deputy Drostdy, by the deputy Landdrost at Graham's

Town; and for the locations in the district of Albany, by the provisional magistrate. These instructions show that some of the settlers were cross-grained, and that there was a good deal of disaffection amongst them generally. To maintain law and order, Sir R. S. Donkin appointed Major James Jones, R.A., provisional Landdrost of Albany, Captain Trappes, 73rd Regiment, provisional magistrate of Bathurst. He also appointed Dr. Daniel O'Flynn, provisional district surgeon of Bathurst. Prior to his departure for Cape Town, he received the following address :—

"CUYLER TOWN, June 30, 1820.

"We beg leave to express our gratitude for the kind, liberal and considerate manner with which our Government have attended to and provided for ourselves and the comforts of our families in this distant and almost uninhabited region. Also to make known to the Government at home, and our countrymen through your medium, the care that has been taken of us since our departure from England. At the same time, we cannot help expressing our satisfaction, and returning our sincere thanks thus publicly, to your Excellency and the resident authorities for the able, humane and energetic manner with which you and they have attended our steps under every difficulty : of passing almost inaccessible roads, woods and rivers ; caused the supply of provisions to be brought to us from distant parts, and seen our necessities supplied, confiding in our industry and gratitude for a return and payment. Thus supported and assisted in one of the finest countries of the world, with pleasure we toil and look forward to the day when we shall be enabled to repay our country, and convince the heads of the departments that their confidence in our exertions has not been misplaced, and that we have been deserving of the maternal solicitude with which the Government at home and here have attended us.

"Wishing your Excellency every happiness and honour your noble exertions merit, we remain very respectfully, Thomas Price Adams, Thomas Griffin, William Blair, John Walker (surgeon), William Seymour, James Hoole, William Harrison, William Hart, William Foster, George Stokes, William Harding, George Fulgou."

By this time all the transports with emigrants had arrived at Algoa Bay, the number landed between the middle of April and end of June, 1820, being given as 3,659. Eighty families had been sent to Clanwilliam, where, according to the best informed accounts, eight could scarcely have found scope for their industry, while positions were tendered to other settlers on the Endless River, which upon inspection were declined, or upon trial were relinquished.

CHAPTER XIII

BIOGRAPHY OF THE LEADERS

OF the fifty-six parties that were sent out under Government regulations, four only were numerically strong. These were Bailie's party, Willson's party, Sephton's or the Salem party, and Parker's or the Irish party. They severally exceeded 100 families in number. The first to arrive was Bailie's party, to whom was assigned the post of danger, namely, the fringe of the northern border of the Zunsveld, immediately next to the Fish River Bush, with an established pathway through the bush into Albany across the location upon which Bailie's party were settled. Of this dangerous situation the unfortunate settlers had no idea when they were deposited upon their grants of land, and there was nothing to strangers unacquainted with Kafirs and their predatory habits to lead them to suspect they might be called upon to defend their lives and property by force of arms. This fate they cruelly experienced when the Kafirs, after frequent incursions in small parties, had succeeded in despoiling the settlers of their cattle, finally broke out into open general irruption and laid the country waste, murdering the defenceless settlers, burning their habitations and plundering them of their cattle. A short account of the fortunes of the heads of these parties will suffice to exemplify to a certain extent that which befell many of those who had accompanied their leaders to Albany and exerted their best efforts to establish themselves in the land of their adoption.

BAILIE'S PARTY.

John Bailie, son of Colonel Thomas Bailie, of Inishargy, County Down, Ireland, and Anne Hope, daughter of Archibald Hope, of Dumfries, Scotland, was born at Angola, Carnatic, 5th July, 1788. In 1793 Colonel Bailie returned to England and John Bailie and his brother Thomas Manborary Bailie went to France and were educated at the Polytechnique. In 1803 John Bailie entered the Royal Navy, and during his service in the navy visited the Cape. In 1809 he retired from the navy and entered the Foreign Office. He married Amelia Crause, daughter of Mr. William Crause, of Pembury, Kent. After Waterloo he was secretary for foreign claims in France, his duties being in connection with indemnities to be paid to allied subjects for losses and damages in France during the war. In 1817 he returned to the Foreign Office in London and worked out his pet scheme of settling the Cape with British settlers. He led the first, or Bailie's, party in 1819 on board the *Chapman*, which arrived in

Algoa Bay in 1820. Chase, Godlonton, Stringfellow, Major Hope and some of the Crause family were of this party. He held a dormant commission as Lieutenant-Governor for the new Settlement, which he resigned very soon after landing, because "the Whigs were in," and settled with his sons Charles Theodore, Archibald Hope, Thomas Cockburn and John Amelius, on the two farms, the Hope and Harewood, at the mouth of the Fish river in Albany. He and his sons served, during all the wars and disturbances, the expedition against the Fetcani, etc., until the Kafir war of 1835 broke out. Charles Theodore, the eldest son, was appointed Lieutenant in the first provisional battalion, and met with his death at the hands of the Kafirs, June 26, 1835, at Intaba-Ka-'Ndoba, near the abandoned Pirie mission station, the spot being to this day marked and known as Bailie's grave. He was, says Moodie,[1] an officer of the most cautious, though enterprising character, bold and undaunted, discreet and judicious, possessing every qualification to render him one of the highest ornaments of his profession. He had more experience in this desultory warfare than almost any other officer, and had frequently distinguished himself in his rencontres with the enemy. Being at the moment compelled from the nature of the ground to separate from his party, the whole, with the exception of their gallant officer, fell pierced with innumerable wounds. He did not fire with his men on their making their final effort, but sprang into a small thicket near the spot, where with matchless heroism he met his fate. Three of the enemy rushed upon him, two of whom were shot dead by a discharge from both barrels of his gun ; one of these was a chief, Tchalusay ; but having no further means of defence, he was instantly overpowered and slain. The spot was subsequently visited by the father of this gallant and amiable young man, who collected the remains of the brave men who fell, and consigned them to one common grave on a spot which is now marked by a heap of stones. The Rev. Mr. Chalmers, of the Glasgow mission, was present on the occasion, and offered up, with the little party who had assembled, a most impressive prayer. The large and expensive residence which the father erected on his farm was burned to the ground and the whole estate laid waste, and his son's young widow, who had been obliged to flee from it for her life, was left so destitute that the only property she had in the world beyond her personal attire was a Bible found in her dead husband's belt and forwarded to her.

In 1824-5 John Bailie made surveys of the coast from Port Elizabeth to East London, and was mainly instrumental in getting Government to land stores at Waterloo Bay, Peddie district. Indeed, to convince Government of the practicability of landing stores at East London during war time, he chartered the first ship that entered the Buffalo River mouth and took it in at his own cost.

For some years after the war of '35 Mr. Bailie and his son Thomas lived on his farm, the Hope, and in Graham's Town, and went trading across the Orange river. During one of their absences from their station the license expired, and Du Plooy, the Field Cornet, seized and sold everything. On his return, July 8, 1845, Mr. Bailie, hearing what had happened, went with his son Thomas to demand restitution. Du Plooy refused to refund, and he and Bailie had words

[1] I. 317.

about it. Du Plooy seized his gun, his wife shrieking to him to shoot the —— Englishman. Bailie closed with him, and in the struggle that followed Du Plooy was shot. Mr. Bailie always declared the gun went off accidentally. He had no arms, and was a calm-tempered man, not likely to do anything revengefully. The report of the gun brought his son Thomas from outside the door where he was talking to some of Du Plooy's friends. On his entering the room, his father said to him, " Look to your pistols." At the trial, the witnesses swore that Thomas Bailie had fired at Du Ploy and helped his father in the struggle. The Dutch were all most embittered against them, and having no sense of honour, or regard for truth, did their utmost to prove them guilty, while the Bailies had no counsel and only one witness out of ten whom they requested to be summoned in their defence. After Du Plooy was shot, Bailie went to Colesberg and gave himself up to the authorities. On the report of Du Plooy's friends his son Thomas was apprehended. The accused, owing to the influence exerted by friends and the Press, were removed to Uitenhage for trial. In spite of all efforts, the jury, who were in deliberation all night, found them guilty, but accompanied their verdict with a strong recommendation to mercy, and Chief Justice Wylde sentenced them to death, April, 1846. While awaiting this, a number of prisoners endeavoured to escape. Thomas Bailie helped the gaoler to recapture them, which stood him in good stead. The death sentence was commuted to imprisonment for life, and some months later, additional evidence was given by Du Plooy's widow, which showed that the act had been committed in self-defence, which had all along been maintained by the elder prisoner. In December, 1847, they received a " free pardon," that being the legal manner of release from confinement. They remained for some time after this in Port Elizabeth, where Mr. Bailie was connected with the harbour works. Thomas returned to the Free State, where he spent many years in hunting and trading.

In 1848 Mr. Bailie went to Natal and established a trading station at Durban. In 1852, after having made surveys of the coast from Durban to East London in his yacht called the *Haidee*, he commenced a coast trade between Port Natal and the mouth of the St. John's River and the Umgasi River. When returning on Tuesday, 27th July, 1852, from one of these trips, the *Haidee* observed a barque in distress between the Umtwalimi and Umzintu Rivers. This proved to be the *Hector*, 600 tons, Captain Brooks, from Batavia to Bremen, laden with rice and sugar. Mr. Bailie at once went on board the *Hector* with three of his men, leaving only Captain Sorrel and one man on board the *Haidee*, to render what assistance he could. On Wednesday, at 2 a.m., a breeze sprang up, and the *Haidee* had to stand off from the *Hector* and come on to Port Natal. After doing all he could to save the ship, the boat left for the shore, having on board the first and second mates and two seamen. On nearing the shore the boat capsized in the surf and was rendered incapable of again returning to the wreck. All managed to reach the land on spars except Mr. Bailie and Benjamin Hoar, a West Indian, about fifteen years of age, son of one of the owners of the vessel. Bailie had only the use of one hand, the other had been injured. Those on shore watched him climb into the rigging, cling there for hours, then, losing his hold, drop into the raging sea. Throughout he had evinced the greatest coolness, firmness, and presence of mind. He thus died at the age of sixty-three years, just when he had pioneered the way to a new opening of coasting commerce, and while in the act of rendering his generous assistance to fellow-creatures in distress. Of Mr. Bailie's children, (1) Charles Theodore, as already mentioned, was killed by Kafirs in 1835, leaving one son, Henry John, who settled and still lives in the Queen's Town district ; (2) Archibald Hope, died in Port Elizabeth in June, 1850, from injuries received during the war of 1846-7, leaving a daughter, who married Mr. G. G. Wright, attorney-at-law, in practice at Graham's Town, and two sons, Archibald Hope, who settled in the Free State, and Alexander Cumming, who was entrusted with several responsible and delicate duties on the northern border, which he discharged with much sagacity, namely, making a peace between the Bakwena and Bakhabla, who were at war ; prevented a Boer attack on Khama, chief of the Bamangwato ; arranged with Khama and Sicheli for their countries to be handed over, and submitted offers to the Administrator of Griqualand West ; arranged with Lobengula to receive a British resident ; made a route map from Kimberley to Buluwayo ; and later (1881), at urgent request of Government, proceeded to Basutuland as a Magistrate, and after serving in that country till 1884, received a letter of thanks from the Cape Government and H.M. Commissioner, three months' pay, and promise of re-employment ; now living in the Harrismith district ; (3) Thomas Cockburn, who died in 1876, leaving two sons, Charles Campbell (Major Bailie), who died in 1883, and John Crause, who has settled in the Transvaal ; (4) John Amelius took orders and died at Cape Town in 1883, after a long missionary career principally in Namaqualand and Damaraland. The daughter, Isabella Bennett, married Mr. C. H. Huntley, Civil Commissioner and Resident Magistrate of Graham's Town.

CHAPTER XIV

WILLSON'S PARTY

WILLSON'S party arrived three months after Bailie's party, and they were located at some distance from Bailie's people, in a more central position, between the plain called Waai Plaats and the Kowie Bush, a situation, however, fraught with danger in case of Kafir disturbances. Mr. Thomas Willson, the head of this party, hailed from London. At one time he had been in the office of H.R.H. the Duke of York, and when his offer was accepted to bring out a hundred families, was connected with the Chelsea waterworks. It is from thence he dated his circular explaining his plans and the position he would occupy towards those who came out under his protection, which shows he had given full consideration to the project and its responsibilities. His circular was as follows :—

He proposed, "first, that ten gentlemen unite an equal proportion of funds and form themselves into a committee of management of their own immediate concerns, and that each provide or take out five able-bodied men for the purposes of tillage and other requisite employments, with a sufficient store of implements, seeds, and the several necessaries of life, so as to enable them to cultivate immediately after their location a proportion of land equal at least to one acre per family, and to erect a sufficient number of cottages of the simplest and cheapest character for the whole of their party before the rainy season sets in, and that until such covering is obtained a provision of tents shall be made as a temporary resort. As this arrangement is merely designed for the above society, it is submitted only as a principle upon which other societies of the whole party may be formed upon a rational proceeding.

"Second, that duly considering the feelings of a party of British subjects leaving their native country to take the benefit of the advantages held out by Her Majesty's Government, it will be my first care to make the most liberal provision and distribution of the lands with which I am to be invested by a grant from the Crown, in order that such subjects, who so well understand the nature and value of rational liberty, may enjoy an undoubted right, and be enabled fairly to prosecute those objects of my improvement by agricultural pursuits and the formation of a well-organized state of society as may be consistent with my individual rights as Lord of the Manor, the general good, the order, harmony, and welfare of the Settlement, with the reservations, laws, and public views of Her Majesty's Government.

"Third, for the better regulation and management of so large a party, I propose one individual shall be selected as a director to represent such party, which will create a division of time and labour that is well calculated for the interests of individuals, and will be a ready and direct channel for communication for the redress of grievances, at the same time that it insures a mutual support and protection.

"Fourth, if any doubt should exist as to the purity of my intentions in confirming to individuals who may become entitled to a grant of land, such individuals may have a guarantee under my hand more particularly specifying my intention of making such grant by paying a stipulated sum towards the Fund of Indemnity in liquidation of the expenses incurred in the formation of this Settlement; and though at all times I shall be happy to assist others with my counsel or advice in maturing their several projects, it is not to be expected that I could devote my time and services in aid of individual interests or the maintenance of general order without adequate pecuniary support to enable me to dispense such important objects of utility.

"Fifth, that there shall be no abuse of liberty which at all times it will be my glory to maintain in a pure state, consistent with the laws of the Colony, by sound principles of justice, humanity, and moral decorum. I invite the cordial support of every director of each ten of this party to unite with me in the dispensation of those benefits which I propose to all who confide in me their personal welfare and property, to protect them as far as I may be invested with power and authority from acts of aggression, illegal or improper conduct. And in all cases of difference or matters of dispute, more particularly as to the division and partition of land, I recommend an immediate recourse to the decision of a disinterested person, whose judgment shall be final and conclusive, reserving to myself the powers of interposing in cases where such judgment is not effective to dispossess both parties from the lands in dispute, and to assign to them a portion of land in such other situation as may be deemed consistent with the peace and general welfare of the Settlement.

"Sixth, in consideration of the heavy responsibility, severe anxiety, and great burden of expense, which naturally occurs in organizing a Settlement that combines individual benefit with objects of national importance, it is an indispensable part of the system upon which the settlers who are to participate in the advantages of a grant of land, that they also participate in the due proportion of expense for indemnification of what has been incurred, or what may hereafter accrue, in carrying into effect objects of general interest, and what may be considered necessary or important on public grounds.

"Lastly, it is essential for the convenience and accommodation of the Settlement that a communication should be held with the mother country to facilitate a return of cash payments for the produce of the Colony. I have therefore opened an account with a London banker of the highest respectability, which will afford a safe and honourable medium for all money transactions, and I shall likewise open an account with the Government Bank at Cape Town to give more immediate effect to the views of the Colony; and I conclude by recommending the establishment of a savings bank at the Settlement, as soon as circumstances will admit, as a security for the returns of honest industry and a stimulus to the exercise of the natural powers and energies of the mind."

Willson and his party were, like the other settlers, dismayed at the general order prohibiting landing on their arrival in Simon's Bay. Several gentlemen — among them, Lieut. Alexander Bisset, half-pay R.N., Mr. Walter Currie, purser, half-pay R.N., Thomas Randall, James Collis, Thomas Cock, and James and Benjamin Wilmott, who had each brought their own servants and dependents — asked permission to land to attend to their private affairs; and Willson himself, on behalf of the rest on board, writes to the Colonial Secretary from the ship at Simon's Town, May 20: "The several persons of my party who receive half pay or pensions expect me to answer them. The clergyman looks up to me with his large family, to satisfy his *pressing wants*, his *hopes*, his *fears*! Several of the respectable part of the settlers, who have the means to return to England at their own expense, prefer, and have proposed, to adopt that course. Will you permit them, and furnish me with your permission, to have them landed with their goods at Simon's Town for that purpose? I really think it would be advisable. The enclosed letter is from a very respectable gentleman, who, I am persuaded, from his feeble state, will never reach our destined station alive. May he be permitted to land? In fact," he continues, "the whole party, from disappointed hope in the *unexpected distance* which they will have to travel at their own expense, appear exasperated and dismayed. They desire everything from me which they conceive themselves entitled to, and I have nothing to expect from them but murmur and disaffection and revenge! Yet under all these difficulties and disadvantages, feeling that my honour is in a manner pledged to Government, I will never shrink from this my disastrous agreement as long as I meet with due support from the Executive." He applied for a moderate grant of useful land in the neighbourhood of Wynberg in lieu of 10,000 acres near Bathurst, which, however, he was told could not be entertained. Willson was more reasonable than Parker, and ready to acknowledge the efforts of Government to make things as comfortable and hopeful to them as could be expected. Thus, on arriving at Algoa Bay, eight days after the foregoing letter, he writes to the Colonial Secretary, May 28: "On my arrival here, I find the paternal care of the Colonial Government is conspicuous in every arrangement which has been made for our reception and welfare. I shall therefore feel it my duty, and cannot fail to exert myself in carrying into effect the plans of his Excellency the Governor; and it will afford me the highest satisfaction to be able to report to our friends in England and to the Government at home the advantages and comforts which the settlers have derived from so excellent an appreciation of the local means, both as to victualling and transport, and the superior wisdom and humanity which is displayed in every branch of the service."

Government not only provided conveyance for them to their destination without charge, but also supplied them with rations while *en route*, and for some time after their location. They had nothing to complain of. Having seen his party to their destination, Willson does not seem to have been enamoured of his prospects, as so early as August 10 we find him writing to Government imploring to be sent back to England; and finally, December 11, 1820, he embarked at Port Elizabeth, not, however, without an appeal by Mr. James Collis to the authorities for his detention till the claims of his party were adjusted.

CHAPTER XV

PARKER'S PARTY

THE Irish party was another instance of the mixture of elements not easily contented. It comprised five smaller parties under Mr. William Scanlen, Mr. Robert Woodcock, Captain Thomas Butler, of the Dublin Militia, Captain Walter Synnot, and Mr. John Ingram, besides the party under Mr. William Parker, who had once been Mayor of Cork. They were conveyed in the two transports, the *East Indian* and the *Fanny*. Quarrelling began soon after embarkation among those on board the first-named vessel, which contained Parker, his wife, and six children. The day after arrival in Simon's Bay Parker brought charges against the Rev. Francis McCleland, "that immediately on embarking in the *East Indian* he grossly insulted the wife of Dr. Holditch, the surgeon; and on the night of Sunday, January 30, in Cork Harbour, he vilified the English, saying he would get sixteen Irish who would flog any thirty English. He was so violent and insulting that he was threatened to be horsewhipped by John George Newson, Esq., an alderman of the city of Cork and a magistrate of the county; also by Thomas Parsons Boland and Edward Newson, Esqs., and Lieutenant Wentworth, R.N." His animosity to McCleland continued, as December 17, 1820, he memorialized Government against his appointment to Clanwilliam: "hearing that he is to be located at Klein Vallei, Clanwilliam, he earnestly entreated not to permit said McCleland to be established, as he has by his unremitted and scandalous ill-behaviour made himself generally despised, and forfeited by a continual course of drunken, immoral, profane, and irreligious conduct all the respect and veneration to which his sacred functions would otherwise have entitled him." With such a beginning at first start it is not surprising that others besides this excitable clergyman should be involved in disturbances whilst on the passage, and charges were preferred by Parker against two others as being insubordinate and ill-behaved, viz., Thomas Seton, late Captain Madras establishment, and Matthew Nelson, a lawyer. As no cognizance could be taken in the colonial courts of what had passed at sea, each party was recommended to forget or stifle their animosities or wrongs and join heartily in the endeavours for which they had left their country, as without unanimity, they were told, success could not be anticipated. Seton, applying for permission to land with his wife and Miss E. Coyle, her companion, mentions that E. Coyle was inserted on Parker's list as Mrs. Taylor to make up the number required, and to save a separate deposit for her and John Taylor. Other instances of a similar practice on the list are mentioned, viz., Cavenagh and Bridget, his supposed wife. Miss Coyle herself petitioned the Acting-Governor "that she should be given into the hands of the Church missionaries." Her petition recited that "she was the daughter of an old servant of Government, in the Ordnance department in Ireland, that she came out with the determination of attending to the religious and moral education of the female children of the settlers coming out in the ship with Mr. William Parker, under the idea and with the promise from the said William Parker that she should receive the same protection and treatment as his own children." That promise of protection had, however, she alleged, been cruelly and unjustifiably violated by said Parker.

Before proceeding to the frontier, Lieut.-General Sir R. S. Donkin, Acting-Governor, decided not to confine the location of the emigrants from England to the Zunsveld, but to place parties in several eligible situations throughout the Colony. This is another instance of Sir R. Donkin's not obeying instructions. The immigrants were to occupy the Zunsveld and not other situations in the Colony, however eligible. He gave instructions for locating the settlers from Cork when they should arrive in that subdivision of the district of Tulbugh, on the west coast, called Clanwilliam. This situation, the residence of a Deputy Landdrost, had been very favourably spoken of to his Excellency by a magistrate who had long resided there. Well watered, it had the Elephant's River running through it, which, at a distance of only twenty miles, becomes navigable to the sea, when it is supposed not to be obstructed by a bar, as the rivers of the Colony mostly are. Subsequently to Sir R. Donkin's departure for the Frontier, the *East Indian* and the *Fanny* transports from Cork arrived in Simon's Bay. Parker came to Cape Town and saw Colonel Bird, the Colonial Secretary, and was informed of the destination of the settlers under his direction. He appeared disappointed, and alleged that he had been assured he should be allowed a choice of situation, and that he had come out with the full pursuasion that he should be settled on the Kuyua. He was informed that the lands there were private property, and that there was no alternative but to order the transports to Saldanha Bay, where the emigrants would be disembarked and where every preparation had been made for their subsistence and conveyance to their ulterior destination. Parker begged to go to the place of location by land, and to join his party on their arrival at Saldanha Bay. Facilities were afforded him for this object, and letters of introduction to the authorities at Clanwilliam were given to him by the Colonial Secretary. Parker proceeded to Clanwilliam and sent the transports to Saldanha Bay, where the Landdrost of the Cape district, to whom had been entrusted all the arrangements for the transport and maintenance of the several parties, awaited him. The parties under Messrs. Ingram, Synnot, and Butler set out for their destination in the most orderly manner and in good spirits. Parker, however, informed the Landdrost he might dismiss the waggons collected for his party, as he was determined not to proceed so far from the seashore. His views were commercial and not agricultural, and the situation and soil of Clanwilliam were not calculated for his purposes in any degree. The place assigned to Parker's party was the well-watered loan place, called Klein Vallei. But Parker had an idea that he could found a new city of Cork at Saldanha Bay. He drew up an elaborate statement of what was possible and what he could do in this new-found place, covering several pages of foolscap closely written, which he submitted to the Colonial Secretary. He lost no time in requisitioning for various articles, such as tents, ploughs, etc., for the use of his settlers to be forwarded him first opportunity, and then applied to have the Deputy Landdrost removed and himself placed in the magistrate's chair. On examination of the neighbourhood of Saldanha Bay, he found all the water-springs were on the property of a Mr. Watney, which he requested Government to acquire by purchase at a cost of £5,000. With these strange demands, incidental aids and advantages for his new city of Cork, he contemplated the establishment of a fishery, and projected great commercial speculations without the remotest view to agricultural pursuits. He asked for the right to graze sheep on certain islands in the Bay, also for a certain portion of the seashore as a landing-place for the purposes of trade and building stores, which were granted to him. When he was told that the transports could not be detained longer at Saldanha Bay and that his party would be located with the great mass of the settlers in the Zunsveld, Parker changed his mind, and begged to be furnished with the means of going to Clanwilliam, which, being supplied, the party set forward and took possession of the location assigned them, Parker, his family and servants remaining in Mr. Watney's house at Saldanha Bay. Some of the settlers sent to Klein Vallei found it unsuitable to marine pursuits to which they had been accustomed. Seventy-six heads of families from the *East Indian* and forty-five from the *Fanny* required, by the stipulations of Government, 1,200 or 1,300 acres, but the whole of the land fit for cultivation in the neighbourhood, including the Drostdy, only measured 1,162 acres. It was represented that ten families in the neighbourhood of Klein Vallei might be a desirable object for the purpose of establishing a place for farmers from the more northern regions partaking of refreshments on their way to Cape Town and Saldanha Bay; but the poverty of the adjacent country totally precluded the possibility of establishing an inland trade. Mr. Seton and his family and servants petitioned to be allowed to move on to Clanwilliam or elsewhere on the banks of the Elephant's River. Most of those by the *East Indian* and the *Fanny* proceeded to Clanwilliam and its neighbourhood; but the prospects were not cheerful to any of them. Thus Parker writes to Viscount Ennismore, July 15: "A sad and dismal disappointment to me and my large family that I was not particularly mentioned by Earl Bathurst for Government employ. The land at present assigned to me would not support twenty families, instead of the seventy-six that I brought with me. But I do not despair. My substance, however, will be wasted by unprofitably supporting my people, who most keenly feel my vast disappointment." Mr. Robert Woodcock also wrote, July 16: "that unless something be speedily done for them by Government they must be compelled to abandon the Settlement altogether and seek from the Boers a subsistence in return for their menial services, thus being fated to rank in the Colony exactly levelled with the Hottentot population. The party arrived in the Colony on April 30, and most arrived here (Klein Vallei) on June 10, and now, after a lapse of exactly eleven weeks, most of these settlers find themselves as unsettled as when they landed, without land, without implements, and generally without money." Mr. Ingram also, who brought sixty-seven settlers under him from Cork, dating from Partridge Valley, Clanwilliam, July 17 : " I should but ill discharge my duty by those people who have come out under my protection were I not to make an immediate representation of their situation, in order that my silence on the subject may not be construed into a tacit acceptance of the lands which have been allotted to me. Out of 2,700 acres, the most that can be cultivated is about 24 acres. Relying on H.M. Government that we should receive our full quantity of arable land as promised me by Lord Bathurst in presence of my friend and relation, Sir Benjamin Bloomfield." Yet one who describes the colony in 1822 gives a different version of the Clanwilliam settlement. "The growth of prosperity at Clanwilliam appears to have exceeded anything displayed by Albany. On that which has been under-rated, time and experience frequently affix a just value, and in the history of the locations, no estates have, as yet, attained a celebrity in the Cape newspaper equal to those of Clanwilliam." Which statement is supported by quoting the following advertisement : "John Ingram offers for sale by private contract the whole of his estates adjoining the deputy Drostdy of Clanwilliam, consisting of about 5,000 morgen of corn and excellent pasture land, in such lots as may be agreed upon ; also two pieces of land at the Klein Vallei, one consisting of 100 morgen, the other about 166 morgen ; and an erf, let to J. H. Niewouldt, at the Taaybosch Kraal, at the yearly rent of 20 mirds of wheat, payable on the 1st of January, every year, for ever. "The whole of the above lands, if not disposed of by the 11th of June next, will be positively sold by public auction at Patryze Vallei on that and the following day, 11th and 12th June, when a sale will be held, without reserve, of all his farming stock and implements, consisting of about 100 draught oxen, European (Vaderland) cows, horses, sheep, goats, ploughs, waggons, etc., etc. ; also household furniture, carpenters' and smiths' tools, and a great variety of merchandise too numerous to insert. Terms : one-third of the purchase-money of the estates to be paid in cash within one month ; the two-thirds may remain at interest for one or two years on mortgage of estate. Good farmers' fare, lots of wine, and a fiddle." And another advertisement. "To be let in a new town proposed to be built immediately opposite the Drostdy of Clanwilliam, several lots for building, containing two acres of highly fertile land. The subscriber will give to each person, to build a house, agreeable to a plan beforehand laid down by him, 100 Rs. worth of timber, and not to commence rent for three years, or any such other time as may be agreed upon. There is a constant supply of excellent water all the year, commanding every lot, and offers to industrious tradesmen the greatest prospect of success. A fair is proposed to be held on the lands every 1st of September, when the proprietor will give the following premiums : to the person who shall sell the greatest number of oxen, not being less than fifty, six dollars, 20; to the person who shall sell the next greatest number of oxen, not being less than thirty, six dollars, 10. Similar premiums for cows; similar premiums for sheep and goats, having sold, first-class premium, 400 and upwards; second, 300 and upwards; third, 200 and upwards. Similar premiums for Spanish sheep, first class, 200; second, 150; third, 100. Similar premiums for horses, having sold twenty. Apply to John Hugnam, Bloomfield Lodge, October 4, 1821." It may be inferred from the foregoing that the sale in June was not a success, and that the experiment detailed was tried in October following with similar result. Ingram and his party left this unsuitable locality and were located in Albany. Captain Thomas Butler and eleven others were assigned Tyber's Kraal, which consisted of five or six acres of land, a part even of which small quantity the Field-cornet claimed. Neither this, he alleges, nor ten times as much, would produce sufficient to feed his people. "Can it be possible," he asks, "that my country, which I served faithfully for twenty-four years, has sent me into the desert to starve, to be laughed at by the wealthy Dutch, many of whom tried this place before and gave it up as good for nothing? It cost me £1,000 to bring me here and what I have, and what I have not, and what has been destroyed."[1] From these descriptions of the locality to which they had been sent, it can hardly be said they were "eligible." Subsequently at their request the five parties were removed to the Zunsveld, and there located amongst the rest of the settlers. As for Mr. Parker, on Lord Charles Somerset's return to the Colony, he was received at Government House as an injured man, and his memorial, and particularly a letter to the king, were corrected by the Governor himself.[2] But his days of favour were not of long duration; his presence was inconvenient in many ways, and Lord Charles Somerset determined to send him to England to enlighten the Colonial Office on the oppression and indefensible measures pursued towards him by Sir R. S. Donkin and Colonel Bird. This he did at an expense to the public treasury of £450.

It may here be added that besides the Irish parties who were sent to other parts of the Colony instead of Albany by Sir R. Donkin, those of Messrs. Charles and Valentine Griffith and Captain Duncan Campbell were located on the Zender (Endless) End River, in the neighbourhood of the Moravian mission station, called Genadendal. They did not find the situation eligible, and remained there but a short time, finding the land not of a quality to afford

---

[1] George Thompson, in his travels, visited this locality. He writes: "We passed through the earlier location of the Irish party of settlers, a little dale called Klein Vallei. Found only one settler, of the name of Shaw, remaining, out of the whole original party of 350 souls, the rest having been partly removed to Albany (Tybus), and partly scattered in various parts of the Colony. It is indeed a most extraordinary circumstance that such a number of people should have been set down in this place, which is barely sufficient for the competent subsistence of two Boer families. There did not appear to me to be above 40 acres of land fit for cultivation in the whole place. The foundation of a house began by the eccentric and speculative Mr. Parker, the original head of the Irish emigrants, was a melancholy memorial of the entire failure and dispersion of this party."—Vol. ii. p. 101.

[2] Sir R. Donkin said he had proof of this ready whenever called for. *Vide* his letter to Earl Bathurst, p. 112.

employment for them as agriculturists. The Griffiths tried the experiment of renting a small farm, called Roode Bloem, near Cape Town ; but that did not answer their expectations. They all were removed at their own request to the Zunsveld, where they obtained grants of land and formed a substantial and influential addition to the numbers already occupying that territory.

CHAPTER XVI

SIR RUBANE DONKIN'S ADMINISTRATION

UPON Sir R. Donkin's return to Cape Town several subjects of importance connected with the settlers engaged his attention. His Excellency found it necessary to address the Provisional Magistrate of Bathurst, September 8, 1820, on the subject of the third instalment of the deposits of the settlers, Assistant-Deputy Commissary Johnstone having reported that the amount thereof had been expended in rations issued for their subsistence. It was conceded that it would be impossible to discontinue the aid of rations as hitherto made to the settlers until after the ensuing harvest, when each party should have reaped the fruit of his exertions. But it could not be expected that the charge of this supply should be ultimately borne by the public, therefore the Commissary was directed to apprise each head of a party that he would be debited with the amount of whatever might be drawn in the shape of rations, and that at the termination of the harvest he would be called upon to give a bond for the value of what he had received up to that period, and that these bonds would be secured in the nature of a mortgage upon and first claim against the lands, with all they might contain of the respective holders, to the defrayment of which the subsequent grants would be made subject. At the same time his Excellency directed that, as soon as the period of the harvest should have arrived, an accurate return should be made to him of the produce raised upon each location, and of the means the heads of parties possessed for the approvisionment of the respective individuals of their several parties. From this document he would be able to decide in what manner, to what persons, and to what extent the aid of the public stores should be continued subsequent to the period in question, so that from that moment the furnishing daily rations should stop, and the several heads of parties be only supplied from time to time according to their numbers and means with what, upon the lowest scale of calculation, should be absolutely requisite to the support of the people. As, however, it was thought that many of the settlers might relax in their exertions, were they aware that it was in contemplation to continue to support them in any shape, Captain Trappes was cautioned not to make any of this communication public that was not immediately necessary to be acted upon.

A week later, September 15, 1820, it became necessary to officially promulgate Captain Trappes's appointment as Provisional Magistrate of Bathurst, as then it was expedient to establish a court for matrimonial affairs. The proclamation on this head of same date recited that whereas the increased population, consequent on the recent location of the settlers who had arrived in the Colony from the United Kingdom, rendered it expedient to establish in the sub-drostdies in which they were located courts for the registration of marriages, and for the cognisance of criminal and civil cases, to obviate the inconvenience to which the inhabitants would be exposed from the necessity they would be otherwise under of resorting to the courts of the chief place in each province of the Colony in which they were settled, it was directed that the Deputy-Landdrost of the sub-drostdies of Clanwilliam and Graham's Town should assemble a court of Deputy-Landdrost and heimraden, the number of heimraden competent to constitute such court, with the Deputy-Landdrost, not to be less than two, on the first Monday of every month, at which court all the inhabitants of the proportion of the districts of Tulbagh and Uitenhage, then included in the subdivision of Clanwilliam and Albany, should be at liberty to have their marriages registered as customary in the Colony. Further, that the said Deputy-Landdrosts, with the number of heimraden aforesaid, at least, should constitute a court at the same time and place for the trial of such criminal cases as were cognisable by the courts of landdrosts and heimraden under the proclamation of 18th July, 1817, and of such civil cases as were of the competence of those courts to decide. The Landdrost of Uitenhage, Colonel Cuyler, was formally informed of the proposed change, the Acting-Governor having had under his consideration the state of that part of his district in which the emigrants from England had been lately located, and having perceived that it was desirable for the convenience of the inhabitants, and for the quiet and good order of the district, that certain further regulations should be promulgated on those heads, his Excellency had determined that there should be a monthly court for matrimonial affairs and petty cases at Graham's Town, at which the Deputy-Landdrost should as usual preside, with at least two heimraden, acting under the same instructions as the courts of landdrosts and heimraden are guided by in like matters at the chief places of the several provinces. As, however, the number of settlers and their distance in many instances from the sub-drostdy might make it inconvenient for them in very minute cases to go to Graham's Town, either for the purpose of procuring redress in such cases or giving information to the magistrates on more grave subjects, the Provisional Magistrate at Bathurst was empowered to take cognisance of certain matters defined in a proclamation issued for the guidance of special heimraden to be appointed, and the limits of his jurisdiction were defined, so that all collision between that officer and the magistrate at Graham's Town might be avoided. This jurisdiction embraced all the locations seaward of a line drawn from the north-west side of Mahoney's Settlement to Jager's Drift on the Bushman's River, and numbered altogether fifty-two locations, which henceforth belonged to the jurisdiction of Bathurst. The Acting-Governor did not overlook the difference of language which might be of considerable embarrassment in cases where the British settlers were concerned; he therefore decided to appoint two additional heimraden for the Graham's Town jurisdiction in addition to the heimraden already considered as belonging to the sub-drostdy, and directed

Colonel Cuyler to instruct the Deputy-Landdrost not to take cognisance in his court of any case either criminal or civil unless one of the said additional heimraden whom his Excellency would select from-among the British settlers residing in the jurisdiction aforesaid, was present when the cause in which such British subject was concerned should come on, matrimonial cases excepted, in which the usual and necessary queries might be put to the parties without its being necessary that an English member of the court be present, provided the deputy-landdrost himself was so. These additional heimraden were not, however, to be furnished with the special warrant alluded to in the proclamation ; but as it was essential to provide for the possible absence or illness of the Provisional Magistrate at Bathurst, the Acting-Governor had decided upon appointing a heimraad in that jurisdiction, with powers to act under such circumstances, according to the powers vested in such by the proclamation. This heimraad might or might not be called to the sitting of the court of Deputy-Landdrost and heimraden of Graham's Town, according as it might appear advisable to Colonel Cuyler or the deputy-landdrost. To carry out these instructions Messrs. Pigot & Campbell, of Botha's farm, were appointed Heimraden in the Graham's Town jurisdiction, and Mr. Phillipps for that of Bathurst. As arising out of these instructions, it appeared to be immediately necessary to provide a place of confinement for prisoners at Bathurst, Colonel Cuyler was to agree with Captain Trappes upon a plan for a goal accordingly, and to induce some of the heads of parties, or principal settlers, to tender for the work, and to submit such plan and tenders for his Excellency's approval.

Subsequently it came to the knowledge of the Acting-Governor that some of the heads of parties had in various instances stopped the issue of the rations to the men of their parties which had been directed to be delivered to them, under the pretext that such men had been refractory or had not worked properly. A circular was sent, December 14, 1820, to the Landdrost of Uitenhage, the Deputy-Landdrost of Graham's Town, to the Deputy-Landdrost of Clanwilliam, and to the Provisional Magistrate at Bathurst, signifying that his Excellency did not approve of the line the heads of parties had adopted in these cases, though he agreed in principle that if men would not work, they should not be fed by their employers. If the heads of parties had any just complaints against their people on this point, upon their laying them before these officials, they were authorized to sanction the withholding the number of rations according to circumstances, the number of which, however, was not to be drawn from the public stores, which it was necessary on every account to economize as much as possible. By this time rust had made its appearance in the crops sown by the settlers, and further circulars were, December 21, 1820, sent to the Deputy-Landdrost, Graham's Town, and the Provisional Magistrate, Bathurst, intimating his Excellency's intention that arrangements should now be made as should lay the foundation for the future supply of the settlers from means which should be independent of the local Government or Commissariat. These circulars stated that his Excellency was quite aware of the calamity of blight which had blasted the hopes of so many of the most industrious of the settlers, and that he would use every effort in his power to avert the consequences which withdrawing the Government supplies altogether would at such a period occasion. The entire stoppage of the Commissariat issues must therefore be still a prospective measure. But the circumstances of the country generally, in consequence of the great failure in all its districts by blight, and the welfare of the settlers themselves, which depended so much on their exertions for their own support, necessitated a strict economy in the issues. These official gentlemen were directed, by consultation on the subject with subordinate officials and by personal inspection, to ascertain from the heads of parties what resources from vegetables or otherwise the settlers could depend upon, so that each should draw no more from public stores than was absolutely indispensable. Independent of the consideration of economizing the supplies, it was necessary that some steps should be taken, which should have the effect of constraining the able-bodied to labour, which it was assumed they would not be inclined to do, while too much facility in procuring subsistence without labour was afforded them. On the same date, a circular was addressed to the heads of parties themselves, informing them that the Commissariat officers had been directed to close the accounts against the several parties up to the end of the year, charging them with the amount of stores, provisions, and wagon hire debited against them, with the view of discontinuing the issue of provisions by Government, as soon as that would be practicable, subsequent to the housing of the present harvest. It was admitted that circumstances had occurred which would probably prevent many of the settlers from being yet in a position to maintain themselves from the produce of their respective locations. Those circumstances arose from the late period of the season at which the transports had arrived at Algoa Bay, and from the want of ploughs and agricultural implements which unfortunately did not reach Cape Town till long subsequent to the arrival of the settlers, and finally from the unprecedented calamity of the blight which had cut off so much of the first expectations of the industrious. His Excellency therefore was induced, contrary to his original intention, to continue to authorize the Commissariat to provide in some degree for the failure of private resources, and to continue to issue upon payment or undoubted security such proportion of provisions as the respective parties might not have it in their power to procure from other sources in a country destitute of markets. Rations for a greater number of prisoners than actually on the locations at the time of drawing them would not be made, and only at Graham's Town and Bathurst. The heads of parties were informed that the demand against them for wagon hire from Port Elizabeth to Albany was very great, and they were reminded that it had been clearly stipulated that the home Government should be at no expense with respect to the settlers subsequent to their landing. His Excellency, whilst unable to release their accounts from that charge, unless under fresh instructions, stated that he had referred the question for consideration to the home authorities.

In May, 1821, the Acting-Governor found it expedient and advisable that a full and permanent seat of magistracy should be established in the district of Albany, in order that the inhabitants of that district, including the new locations of the settlers from England, should have the full benefit of easy access to a provincial court, and be visited annually by the regular commission of circuit from the worshipful the Court of Justice. A proclamation was accordingly published giving notice that the province of Uitenhage should henceforward be limited and bounded on the east by the Bushman's River, and consequently that the country to the eastward thereof, with the newly acquired territory between the Fish River and the Kisskamna, and including the field-countries of upper and under Bushman's River, of Bunitje's Hooghte and of Albany proper, should form the province of Albany, whose chief place and seat of magistracy should be the town of Bathurst. Simultaneously with this proclamation it was notified that his Excellency had been pleased to appoint Major James Jones, the commandant on the Frontier, to be Landdrost of the district of Albany (May 25, 1821).

In June following, Sir R. Donkin was able to inform the settlers that the representation he had made on their behalf to Earl Bathurst on the subject of wagon-hire had been attended with success. His Lordship had been pleased to acquaint him that he might dispense with the repayment by the settlers of the sums which had been advanced on their account, adding that this additional boon should enable the settlers to overcome all their real difficulties. This welcome intelligence was communicated to the heads of parties by circular dated 22nd June, 1821, in which the Acting-Governor reiterated that no rations could be issued to them without payment for any period, however limited, and urged that, after the manner in which their brothers had been lightened by taking off the wagon hire, it should be the personal interest of every man, as well as a sense of duty and gratitude, to exert himself so as to place him in the proud independence of living on food of his own earning. A month later the Acting-Governor notified to the heads of parties that arrangements had been made with the Commissariat to continue to them for the settlers present on their respective locations rations till the 30th August, after which date half a ration would be issued up to the 31st December, and thereafter no ration or provision of any sort would be issued.

Meantime, Major Jones had been instructed to have an interview with the Kafir chief, Gaika, for the purpose of cementing the friendly relations which then existed between the Kafir people and the Colony. Lord Charles Somerset had already anticipated this in his instructions to the Rev. Mr. Thompson and Mr. Bronville, missionaries whom he appointed at the request of Gaika among the Kafirs. After expressing his Lordship's anxious desire that inhuman massacres and ruinous plunderings should be put a stop to through the influence of natives and enlightened instructors, his Excellency added, "He was anxious to establish such an intercourse between the Kafir people and the colonists as shall be mutually beneficial ; and for this end he was desirous of obtaining correct statements as to their wants, and also as to the objects which they may be able to bring to Graham's Town for barter." Amongst other things stipulated at this interview was, that an annual fair should be held on the banks of the Keiskama River for the purpose of supplying the Kafirs with such articles as they had been in the habit of obtaining from the Colony through the channel of Government, but which they had not regularly procured since the period at which the disturbances of the year 1818 broke out. The Acting-Governor accordingly issued a proclamation, 20th July, 1821, which specified that the Landdrost of Albany, after having arranged with the Kafir chief Gaika the spot on which a fair should be held, for the object of supplying the Kafirs with such articles as they might require in barter for cattle or the produce of the Kafir country, should give notice within his district and to the Landdrost of Uitenhage and Graaff Reinet of the time fixed and arranged for the intended fair. Regulations were specified as to enforcing strict order ; the appointment of a clerk of the market ; prohibiting any persons from the Colony to attend the fair who had no articles to dispose of so as to prevent crowding ; obtaining as many interpreters as could be collected to facilitate the intercourse of all concerned ; peremptorily forbidding the disposal of spirits, wines, beers, or other liquors, whether by sale, barter, or gift, under penalty of severe punishment ; and in like manner firearms or ammunition were strictly forbidden to be brought to the fair for sale or barter, or to exchange, or give away, with power to the Landdrost to use the most summary means in keeping the peace, and to make such further local regulations as he might find necessary. In his capacity of commandant of troops on the Frontier, the Landdrost was to take such precautions as would be pointed out to him through the military channel to obviate any inconvenience which might arise from unforeseen accidents.

These regulations and arrangements were all for the purpose of establishing law and order in the new Settlement, and by this time the settlers had made progress in the beneficial occupation of their grants of land. They soon found that an area of one hundred acres was much too limited to be of any value. Probably they had by this time discovered that the extent of land grants generally was very much in extent of this acreage, usually not less than six thousand acres, which afforded pasturage for cattle as well as allowed of cultivation. By this time also the number of settlers in the location was materially reduced, many of them having obtained permission to migrate to Graham's Town, Graaff Reinet, Somerset, Cradock, Uitenhage, Port Elizabeth, and even Cape Town, in all which places they found occupation more suitable to their tastes and abilities than agriculture in Albany. Sir Rubane Donkin paid a second visit to the Frontier, inspecting the locations and encouraging the settlers to exertion. He had already proclaimed his intention "to establish a full and permanent seat of magistracy in the Albany district," and now at the request of the settlers fixed on the spot of the future township of Bathurst.[1] With much pomp the first stone was laid on November 9, 1820, inscribed, with that date, " Frances Somerset," in honour of the wife of Colonel Somerset, who conducted the ceremony, "a gratifying sight," as John Goodwin wrote, and the embryo town named Bathurst in honour of the Earl of Bathurst. The second season's harvest was again valueless by the blight of rust, which forced upon his Excellency the consideration of the great distress likely to ensue. Major

---

[1] The situation of Bathurst is extremely unfavourable to defence against such an enemy as the Kafir. It is embosomed in the immense thicket which lines the banks of the Kowie River, thus affording secure cover to the enemy until within a few yards of the dwellings of the inhabitants.—*Moodie*, i. 264.

Jones, the Landdrost of Albany, was therefore instructed to acquaint the settlers that he had come to the determination of affording them such further aid as might be in his power in the unfortunate circumstances in which they were placed. A consignment of a thousand bags of rice was therefore sent to the Commissariat on the Frontier to be issued gratis, subject to inquiry by the Landdrost as to the means and necessities of the inhabitants of the several locations, and upon that information to issue half a pound of rice per day for each individual, whether male or female, or children above five years, and for children under the age of five years a quarter of a pound per diem. Aged persons, sick or infirm women or children, were to be included among those eligible for rations. The issues were to commence on 1st January, 1822, and to be continued for three months. The Landdrost was directed to call the attention of the settlers to the growth of potatoes, which throve well and yielded particularly fine crops, and he was empowered to offer premiums to such as should bring the greatest quantity to Bathurst or Graham's Town markets within a given time, regulating according to his judgment the rate of premium which should be given for a proportion exceeding a fixed quantity of produce.

The number of settlers originally located in Albany consisted of 1,610 men, including 57 directors; of 659 women, and 1,467 children; in all, 3,736, exclusive of detached parties. At the end of 1821 there appeared to be remaining on the location list—

	Men.	Women.	Children.		
Absent, but within the Drostdy	552	403	935	=	1,890
	451	171	365	=	987
	1,003	574	1,300	=	2,877

	Males.	Females.	Children.		
Births on the locations	88	86	—	=	174
Deaths	22	7	48	=	77

There had been twenty-six marriages on the locations. The births, deaths, and marriages of those who were absent are not included. The total number of acres of land ploughed and cultivated amounted to 1,454, and the greatest number of settlers who drew rations at any one time was 931 men, 569 women, and 946 children. The expense of these rations in the year 1820 amounted, after deducting the second and third instalments of their deposits, to 57,000 dollars = £427 10s., and that of 1821 to 195,000 rupees = £14,625.

Mr. George Thompson, an intelligent traveller, visited the Albany Settlement in January, 1821, and again in May, 1823, and gives a pleasing description of the settlers and what they had accomplished.[2]

[2] *Travels*, vol. ii. p. 147.

CHAPTER XVII

THE KOWIE RIVER MOUTH

IT was not unnatural that the settlers should consider a port within easy reach of the Settlement a matter of consequence to their prosperity. They were going to produce wheat in quantities beyond their requirements, and how were they to get their surplus production to other markets? The long and hazardous journey of a hundred miles to reach Port Elizabeth, still in its infancy, with only an occasional small trading vessel calling there, could not be thought of, whilst there appeared within their reach the capabilities of a port within the limits of the Settlement, accessible with little trouble or delay. Among the settlers were several nautical men, besides a party of boatmen under Charles Gurney, from Deal, on the Kentish coast, who had brought a boat with them so that they could engage in the pursuit of fishing at sea. Weeks, formerly a pilot at Ramsgate, and John Burnet Biddulph made a survey of the Kowie River mouth, and reported it practicable for vessels of light draught. In 1821, when Lord Charles Somerset was on the frontier, he was approached by the inhabitants, concurring entirely with them relative to the advantages that must necessarily arise from a port at the mouth of the Kowie River. They asked to have constructed a pier at the Kowie, and allowed direct trade to be carried on between that port and foreign countries, and a custom-house to be erected, and a magistrate appointed there. Lord Charles visited the spot, and named the mouth of the Kowie River, Port Frances, in honour of his son's (Lieutenant-Colonel Somerset) wife, and appointed Mr. Donald Moodie magistrate, one of the most respectable of the settlers, possessing the advantage of a good education, and who, being a half-pay lieutenant R.N., was peculiarly fitted to preside at a seaport. His appointment as magistrate would, it was claimed, be of infinite benefit to the whole of the southern part of the district, by enabling the inhabitants to refer petty cases for adjustment on the spot, exclusive of the frequent necessity of the interference of a police at a seaport. Mr. Moodie's salary was fixed at the moderate sum of 1,200 Rs. (=£90) per annum, and as it was necessary, according to the forms of the Dutch law, that there should be a public prosecutor in all criminal cases brought before the constituted courts, a secretary (clerk) was appointed at 600 Rs. (=£45), and a messenger to the court at 300 Rs. (=£22 10s.) per annum. Three houses for the accommodation of these officials were constructed at an expense of 7,820 Rs. (=£560). As to the request to erect a pier, the Governor cautiously replied that he could not venture to recommend an undertaking of that nature, unless it should be deemed advisable to send out a civil engineer for the purpose of ascertaining the capabilities of that port, as well as of the other ports of the Colony, and of forming an estimate of the expense of any work which might be projected for the permanent improvement thereof,—an object of very great importance, and which his Lordship thought would be well worth the expense attendant upon such an appointment. As to permission to trade with foreign countries, a similar application had been made to him by the inhabitants of Algoa Bay, and to both memorials his Excellency had returned an answer by assenting to grant a license to any particular vessel to trade direct with any specified foreign port, but refused the general permission so to do until the commerce of those ports should increase so as to warrant the establishment of a regular customs department. Lord Charles Somerset had thus so far done all that it was prudent to do in the incipient efforts to establish a shipping port at the mouth of the Kowie River. A trade of some sort had already commenced, and the schooner *Elizabeth*, belonging to Mr. Henry Norman, was the first to enter the river, November 9, 1821, but the unfortunate settlers never realized their ambition to ship wheat from Port Frances.

The Kowie River, like most other African rivers, spreads into several channels at its mouth, not any of them particularly deep or strong in current. For the first ten years of its existence as a port the Custom House stood on the east bank of the river, and the building so used yet exists, and is known by that name, but used as a private dwelling. It was on this side and through the channel flowing into the sea in that direction that the coasters and other light craft entered the Mansfield, and, rounding the Bay of Biscay, as it was then and is still called, were in safe waters. Mr. William Cock, the head of Cock's party, had his residence on the west bank of the river, and was the owner of several farms in the neighbourhood. He conceived the idea of concentrating the channels and causing the ebb and flow to be restrained in one course along the western side, thereby strengthening the volume of water, and in the time of freshets causing a strong scour at the mouth of the river, and assisting to remove the sand-bar which blocked the entrance to the harbour. This bold project was no easy task, not only because Cock had only his own genius to guide him, but also by reason of the labour required to be employed in the work, always difficult to obtain, always uncertain and unreliable. The alteration designed was accomplished by planting stakes in the direction required, so as to block up the one channel and convey the water therefrom into the other, filling up the bed of the disused channel with sand and *débris*. This simple means had the effect desired, and the work remains to this day a monument to the patience and perseverance of this enterprising settler. He had not the means to carry on the work of improving the harbour, which increased in cost, as more substantial work was required as it approached the sea. He, with patriotic zeal, expended his utmost resources in the work of improvement. Under a general ordinance in 1847 for improving the ports and harbours of the Colony, harbour commissioners were appointed, who took what measures they could to improve the harbour; but as their ability to do so depended upon the revenue derived from the imposition of tolls and rates for the use of the quay, landing-place, and moorings, little could be accomplished. In 1852 it was declared that the opening of the Kowie harbour for the reception of vessels drawing from twelve to sixteen feet of water, would be attended with much advantage to a large portion of the eastern Frontier, as well as to the general trade and commerce of the Settlement. Various engineers and other scientific persons had from time to time examined into the nature and causes of the obstruction that existed at the entrance of the harbour, and they were unanimously of opinion that it would be practicable to remove the same in such a way as to allow vessels to pass without danger or difficulty into the harbour. The Legislative Council was approached, through the influence of Mr. Cock, then a member, and supported by the other members from the Eastern Province, to obtain funds to carry on the work, but refused to risk pledging the public revenue to any extent for the purposes of a harbour which the future trade and the revenue to arise therefrom were necessarily more or less conjectural. At the same time it was decided that it would be fit and proper to encourage and assist the proposed work by every means consistent with the principle of not pledging the public revenue for any sum greater than that which there was a reasonable certainty would be repaid by or from the proposed works; and as there was along or adjacent to the left or east bank of the river certain waste crown lands, in extent about 2,200 acres, which land would continue valueless as long as the harbour remained unopened, but which would probably become of very considerable value when the works should be completed, if not sooner, Government finally agreed to contribute on the £ for £ principle to the extent of £25,000, and the responsibility of prosecuting the works devolved upon a Joint Stock Company, of which Messrs. Cock, Cawood, and Wood were prominent directors. The Company was authorized to levy wharfage dues, and, with the proceeds of the sale of the Crown lands mentioned, to preserve the works constructed, Mr. Cock granting a piece of land on the right or west side of the river, in extent 250 square feet, for the purpose of erecting dry stores as buildings which might be needed for the public service. The harbour, when completed, would be taken " to extend from the end next the sea of the piers to be constructed at the entrance thereof up to the spot or place in the Kowie River, at which a line drawn parallel to the line of low water along the sea shore and at a distance from such low water line of one mile would cross the said river." The Company continued to carry on the works till 1868, when it made over the works and property to the Government, and was formally dissolved by Act of Parliament, October, 1869, since which date to the present time the works have been continued by Government, under official superintendence, and largely by convict labour. In 1860, when H.R.H. Prince Alfred paid a visit to the Colony, he laid the foundation of one of the piers on the west side of the river, and in honour of H.R.H., and in commemoration of the event, the port was thenceforward named Port Alfred. A few years after the public offices were removed from Bathurst to Port Alfred, which is thus virtually the chief town of the district, as it is the port of the Settlement; and later still private enterprise has constructed a railway connecting the port with the city of Graham's Town.

CHAPTER XVIII

RELIGION AND EDUCATION AMONG THE SETTLERS

THE religious and educational wants of the British settlers were not overlooked by the local Government. As early as May, 1820, a month after their landing, the Acting-Governor Donkin, reporting on the Settlement, says an allotment of 500 acres of glebe land had been made for the clergyman of Bathurst. At the same time he writes that he neither saw nor heard of any minister who had come out who appeared to be fit to fill the important station of minister of the Church of England in the growing metropolis of a large and increasing population. He urged that Bathurst should be placed on the same footing as Cape Town and Simon's Town; but the actual expense for a clergyman at Bathurst would be lessened, as the fine glebe attached must be taken into account, and a small pecuniary stipend should therefore be granted. "I would," he says, "state the living with all its advantages at something more than £600 per annum." Two clergymen of the Church of England only had come out with the settlers, the Rev. William Boardman with Willson's party, and the Rev. Francis McCleland with the Irish party. Earl Bathurst advised the Governor, 16th December, 1819, that Mr. McCleland "had been accepted as a person properly qualified to officiate as a clergyman to the party in question, and is to be located as such, receiving a moderate stipend for the discharge of his clerical duties." After leaving Clanwilliam, McCleland was sent by Government to Graham's Town, where he arrived in April, 1828, and served the Church at Graham's Town till his appointment to the chaplaincy at Port Elizabeth, which he held till the day of his death in 1853. Of Mr. Boardman there is only the testimony of Mr. Willson, who writes to the Governor 3rd May, 1820: "For the promotion of moral and religious duties, and for the consolation of settlers, I have brought out with me a most worthy and respectable clergyman of the Church of England, the Rev. William Boardman, salary promised him by Earl Bathurst. May I name to him what it is to be?" Boardman officiated at Bathurst and Graham's Town and also was engaged in tuition. He died at Bathurst in 1825. So early as June, 1820, Earl Bathurst writes on the same subject to Governor Donkin: "As it is probable that the system lately adopted by Government for the colonisation of the Cape of Good Hope will carry great numbers of British settlers to that country, it is desirable that permanent means of religious worship and instruction should be secured as well to the original settlers and their descendants as to the natives who will probably

resort to the new Settlement. To attain so desirable an object the S.P.G. have
signified to the Government their readiness to contribute their assistance and
co-operation, as far as the funds of the Society will allow, by providing a regular
supply of ministers and schoolmasters, and have suggested as a means of supporting such an establishment that the newly inhabited districts should be
divided into parishes of moderate size, and that certain proportions of land
should be set apart for the maintenance of the resident clergy. Her Majesty's
Government, fully concurring in the view which the Society has taken of the
subject, I have, conformably to their suggestion, to instruct you to retain in the
neighbourhood of every grant a certain portion of land, not less than one-
seventh of the grants made, for the future support of a Protestant clergy, and
to reserve it in such situations as may afford a probability of its increasing in
value in proportion to the growth and prosperity of the Colony." The settlers
themselves were desirous of an established church, and so soon after arrival as
August, 1820, Mr. J. Ingram wrote to the local Government offering "to build
at his own expense a church 32 feet by 22 feet, tower 30 feet high, with parson-
age, living room 20 feet by 15 feet, two bedrooms 15 feet by 12 feet, and kitchen
14 feet by 14 feet, at Partridge Valley, Clanwilliam, being the most central part
of the British subjects' location, on condition that he and his heirs, being Pro-
testants, have the right of presentation to the living. No clergyman to be
appointed unless of the religion of Great Britain as at present established, and
being regularly ordained." The removal of Ingram and the rest of the Irish
party from Clanwilliam to the Zunsveld prevented the carrying out of this pious
intention. There is also a letter from Mr. J. Sturgis, whose family, he says,
" was well known to Lord Charles Somerset, who left England with Mr. Roberts
(Bailie's party), but without intention of proceeding up country, because he
(Roberts) knew perfectly well that his father, who was curate of St. Margaret's,
Westminster, was in treaty with the Bishop of London and Earl Bathurst for
a mission to the Colony to exercise his functions." On Sunday, June 3, 1821,
Governor Donkin writes, divine service was performed at Bathurst for the first
time in public on the spot intended for the church; and the day following
reports that 2,850 Rs. had been expended for alterations and repairs of the
house purchased at Graham's Town for the residence of the clergyman of the
Established Church settled there. The name of this clergyman is not stated.
In October, 1820, the Rev. W. Wright, LL.D., was selected by S.P.G. as their
missionary to proceed to the Cape of Good Hope. He began his mission at
Wynberg among the coloured population ; Pringle mentions him as the only
clergyman of the Church of England during his residence in the Colony who
was friendly to the freedom, or active in promoting the improvement, of the
coloured classes. Dr. Wright also officiated at Graham's Town when he
visited the Frontier the year following. But he appears to have had the missionary cause more at heart, and penetrated beyond the boundaries of the
Colony, with the view of establishing mission stations among the Kafirs.
On Mr. Boardman's death he was nominated to the chaplaincy of Bathurst,
which appointment, however, he failed to take up. In March, 1821, the Government were advised that the S.P.G. had consented to appropriate, in aid of the

expense attending the erection of a church at Graham's Town, the grant of £500 which they had voted last year towards a similar object at Cape Town.

Nothing, however, was done in the way of procuring a resident clergyman for Graham's Town till 1822, when Lord Charles Somerset wrote to the home authorities as follows, June 22, 1822 : "The increased population of Graham's Town, since it has been permanently fixed upon as the seat of magistracy for the Frontier district, and the prosperity which is likely to reign there under the very judicious and able measures of the present Landdrost, Mr. Rivers, render it imperative that a clergyman should be appointed there without further delay." His Lordship urged that in every respect in point of emolument the chaplain at Graham's Town should be placed on the same footing as the chaplain at Simon's Town. He goes on to describe the qualifications a clergyman should possess in such a community as inhabits Graham's Town and its environs, and adds that he has been at some pains to search out a gentleman of exemplary moral character, and of talent that will command respect. Such an one had been strongly recommended to him by the Duchess of Beaufort—a Rev. Mr. Geary, who was highly esteemed by the Bishop of Gloucester, as well as by the Earl of Liverpool and the Bishop of London. Earl Bathurst was pressed to facilitate his passage, and to urge upon Mr. Geary his embarking as soon as possible, " as his presence at Graham's Town is really of great importance." Beyond this nothing is known of Mr. Geary or his antecedents. He received the appointment and came to Graham's Town, April, 1823. At that time there was considerable opposition to the measures of Lord Charles Somerset, who had reversed the policy adopted by the Acting-Governor, Sir R. S. Donkin. Pringle mentions that Mr. Geary was furnished with a private list in the Governor's own handwriting of obnoxious individuals with whom he was cautioned to have no intercourse.[1] That statement, apparently founded upon Mr. Bishop Burnett's correspondence, has been accepted by subsequent writers, and may be true. If so, it redounds to the credit of the home authorities that the leaders of the opposition to his Lordship's measures should subsequently have been placed in positions of trust, viz., Captain Duncan Campbell, who was the first Civil Commissioner of Albany ; Major Pigott, who was appointed Protector of Slaves ; Mr. Donald Moodie, who was made magistrate at Port Frances ; and Mr. Phillipps, a J.P. Commissioner, who had been sent out to inquire into the causes of complaint against Lord Charles Somerset, and to investigate the affairs of the Settlement. When they arrived at Graham's Town, there was a general illumination and other demonstrations of joy. Mr. Geary's house was one of the first illuminated, and he himself was accused of being out in the street, cheering the mob most loudly, and swinging his hat over his head in a manner

---

[1] Rev. Mr. Geary, Colonial Church, was furnished with a private list in the Governor's own writing of "obnoxious individuals" with whom he was cautioned to have no intercourse whatever ; and among these "marked" persons were Major Piggott, Capt. D. Campbell, and others, as loyal, accomplished, and high-spirited men as could be found in the Colony.—their British spirits of independence, in fact, which refused to truckle abjectly to despotic power, was their real offence. This list afterwards fell by a singular chance into the hands of the very persons stigmatised in it, and, as may be imagined, did not tend to soothe their exasperated feelings.—*Pringle,* 221.

very indecorous (to say no more) in a clergyman.[2] Mr. Geary denied the accusations made against him, except the illumination of his house, and submitted letters to the Governor from certain of the inhabitants testifying that the charges were false, highly injurious and scurrilous. According to Mr. Theal, his letters show Mr. Geary to have been a petty-minded, contentious person, dissatisfied with his position, and Lord Charles Somerset, 29th May, recommended his dismissal from the service, which the home Government confirmed 11th October, 1824. The Rev. Thomas Ireland, military chaplain at Cape Town, was appointed *pro tem.* in Mr. Geary's place, and remained there till 1827, when McCleland was sent up from Clanwilliam, and did duty here till 1830, when the Rev. W. Carlisle was appointed chaplain.

That the Government intended to establish the Church among the British settlers as part of the Established Church of England is clear not only from their creating chaplaincies on the Frontier, but also exercising the right to nominate and appoint thereto; also by incorporating the Church members by the successive ordinances at Bathurst, Graham's Town, Port Elizabeth, Sidbury, and Fort Beaufort, and placing the chaplain thereto on the fixed establishment of the public service. Even in later years, when it was determined to confer the episcopate, Letters Patent were issued to Dr. Robert Gray, D.D., creating the sees of Cape Town; to Dr. John Armstrong, D.D., and again to his successor, Dr. Henry Cotterill, D.D., Graham's Town; and to Dr. J. W. Colenso, D.D., Natal, conferring jurisdiction on the bishops, which were issued by the Crown. And so late as 1865 the right to appoint to the chaplaincies was claimed and exercised by Governor Wodehouse on behalf of the Crown in regard to the chaplaincy at Graham's Town, when the bishop of that see (Dr. Cotterill) nominated Archdeacon Kitton to the vacancy, which nomination Sir P. E. Wodehouse refused to confirm on the ground that Mr. Kitton was a "political person" in having taken part in a meeting at King William's Town, which opposed the annexation of British Kafirland, which that Governor was bent on accomplishing. The bishop urged his claim to exercise this privilege to the Colonial Secretary in London, and carried his point. Lord Cardwell differed from Sir Philip Wodehouse, and it was subsequently intimated to the bishop that the nomination to the chaplaincy was at his disposal.

It was not, however, till 1863 that the English Church in the Colony was freed from the bonds of State patronage and interference by the dictum of the Judicial Committee of the Privy Council in the ecclesiastical *cause célèbre* of Long v. Bishop of Cape Town, when it was declared that "the Church in this country was in no better nor in a worse position than any other religious denomination."[3] Since this emancipation from bondage the English Church has spread throughout the Colony and beyond it in the neighbouring states in a wonderful manner, there being now ten dioceses under bishops, each with a numerous staff of clergy engaged in parochial and mission work, maintaining the stately services of the National Church, conducting educational establishments, and directing attention to the reclamation and Christianization of the

---

[2] Hewitt's *English Church History*, p. 42.
[3] Phillimore, *Ecclesiastical Law*, vol. ii. p. 2245.

native races, remaining also in "full union and communion" with the mother-Church, from whom it continues to receive generous help and support, both by supplying educated men for the work of the ministry, and also by liberal money contributions to Church purposes.

Among the settlers under Mr. Hezekiah Sephton, one of the large parties, was a Rev. William Shaw, a young man twenty-one years of age, married, who may be designated the Apostle of Wesleyan Methodism in this part of the Colony. He was sent out by the Wesleyan Society, and was recognised as a Wesleyan minister to the greater number of Sephton's party, and as such conducted and directed religious services for these settlers. He does not appear to have been placed upon the colonial establishment in regard to salary, nor to have drawn any Government allowance, although he applied for such from the home authorities before embarking, Colonel Birch, the Colonial Secretary, being a Roman Catholic, said he would be "tolerated," but not supported. He was supported by the voluntary contributions of the people amongst whom he ministered. He was instant in season and out of season, visiting, consoling, and cheering the settlers generally by frequent intercourse amongst them. His visits were always welcome. He inaugurated the system of his Society by selecting and appointing local preachers and class leaders, who conducted religious services at stated times and fixed places, such as in Howard's party, about six miles from Graham's Town; in James's party, four miles south-east from Bathurst; in Trappes's Valley, also near Bathurst; and at Salem, on the Assegai River, sixteen miles from Graham's Town, which was the village founded by the Sephton party after they were removed from Reed's Fountain, where they were first located, and the headquarters of the Wesleyan Mission for some time. The Methodists, as they were then called, used a revised version of the Book of Common Prayer, from which were eliminated the form of absolution and the dogma of baptismal regeneration. They were thus as nearly in touch with the Church of England as possible; and in the absence of ministrations from clergymen of that Church, it is not surprising that Mr. Shaw's adherents were numerous, and included many who had been brought up and claimed to be members of the Established Church of England. In November, 1822, the first building intended for Divine worship was, through Mr. Shaw's instrumentality, dedicated for service at Graham's Town. It was situated in Chapel Street, and after the appointment of the Rev. W. Geary, the first colonial chaplain at Graham's Town, was kindly lent to the Episcopalians for Divine service once every Lord's day, and this considerate action was continued till the roof required to be taken off and the building to be considerably enlarged, when the Episcopal congregation was accommodated in the Baptist chapel, which had been completed and opened for public worship about the same time. He remained among the settlers actively engaged in his work of an evangelist till 1823, when he removed into Kaffraria, and founded the mission station called Wesleyville. After the Kafir war that occurred, following in quick succession the occupation of Albany by the British settlers, he returned to Graham's Town, where he conducted the business of the Wesleyan Society, whom he represented, and by whom he had been made superintendent of Wesleyanism in this part of South Africa. He died at the advanced age of 73 in London, December 4, 1872 ; and his adherents erected to his memory a substantial school building, which still exists, known as Shaw College. To his energy and organization is due the spread of Wesleyanism, which is now a powerful factor in the land in promoting the good of its people and the reclamation of the native races.

The London Missionary Society had advanced their stations into the Zunsveld, and placed a missionary in charge of the native congregation at Theopolis, between the Kasonga and the Kowie Rivers. At the time of the arrival of the British settlers it consisted of 17 whites, 186 Hottentots, and 120 other natives of mixed breed. They were considered sufficiently advanced in the knowledge of the Christian religion and the habits of civilization to be constituted a self-governing congregation. The last missionary, the Rev. Mr. Barker, shortly after was withdrawn, and the people were left to themselves. It is sad to add that in 1848, the Hottentots who remained there—the white people having already left and others drifted away—broke out into rebellion without any apparent cause, killed several of the farmers settled thereabouts, who were called out to suppress their revolt, and finally fled the Colony and joined the Kafirs across the Kei River.

In regard to education the majority of the British settlers were educated men and women. The professions to which the heads of the parties and of many others who came with them—officers of the Royal Navy, the army, medical men and other callings necessarily implying a fair education—establish this. Nor can it be said that those who joined the parties, either as dependents under agreement for a term of years or in the hope of improving their condition in the pursuit of their trades, were altogether wanting in rudimentary education at least. A few may have been unable to write or read, men whose callings at home did not require the same extent of useful knowledge. But they were none of them steeped in ignorance. Even among the juvenile immigrants the youth of both sexes had already acquired a fair education. Mr. Thomas Pullen claimed that seven out of the thirteen children he brought out were "fairly educated before leaving England," and there were others who had received similar advantages. Miss Coyle, who came with the Irish party, did so with the intention of devoting herself to the instruction of the female children; and Miss Janet Brown, sister-in-law of Thomas Pringle, obtained a situation as governess in Cape Town ; and Mr. William Elliott, one of Pringle's party, obtained permission to open a classical and commercial school at Cape Town, in conjunction with Mr. A. Duncan, August 28, 1820. So early after arrival as September 30, James Hancock, one of Sephton's party, applied for an eof at Graham's Town to establish a school. The Rev. W. Boardman kept a school at Bathurst and also at Cuylerville, where a substantial school-house was built, which also served for church services. The Rev. Mr. Shaw also had a week-day school at Graham's Town, and Mr. W. H. Matthews opened a school for boys at Salem, which he kept up for many years, and which became the foundation of the educational establishment that now flourishes in that village. Mr. William Howard, from

Chesham, Bucks, came out to introduce the Lancashire system of public instruction, but how far he succeeded or what he attempted does not appear. This was the day of small things, but it is to the credit of the British settlers that they valued education and appreciated the self-denying labours of those who devoted themselves to the wearisome task of instructing youth in the early stages of learning. It is also a sufficient refutation to the calumnious statement circulated in Cape Town a few years later by bigoted zealots, who constituted themselves the protectors of the native races, that the British settlers were for the most part drawn from the workhouses of England, and were altogether illiterate. Government were prompt in sending out schoolmasters to promulgate the English language, which it was determined to introduce into all legal and official proceedings. In July, 1822, Mr. James Rose Innes, M.A. of a Scotch University, arrived at Cape Town with several teachers, who were distributed to the most important districts. One of these, Mr. John Tudhope, was appointed to Graham's Town, where he conducted the public school for a long term of years. Mr. Innes was stationed at Uitenhage, where he resided for several years, until he was appointed May 11, 1839, professor in the South Africa College, Cape Town. He afterwards became Superintendent-General of Education, and removed to Cape Town permanently, where he directed educational matters for the Colony to the time of his death. Since the settlers' day Graham's Town has been known for its intellectual character, the love of its leading inhabitants for literature, and their noble efforts to provide seminaries and colleges for the instruction of the youth of both sexes. It now contains schools for the ordinary curriculum of modern education, and colleges for instruction in the higher departments of classical and technical knowledge, qualifying the students for entry into the learned professions, into the public service, and to take a place in the British universities on admission at Cambridge, Oxford, and Edinburgh. It has not inaptly been termed Modern Athens.

CHAPTER XIX

ADDITIONAL EMIGRANTS

IT is worthy of note how rapidly the arrangements were carried out to expedite those approved as emigrants to the new Settlement in South Africa. All arrangements, as far as the home authorities were concerned, were completed by the end of the year 1819, that is, within six months after the parliamentary vote. Earl Bathurst, in sending to the Governor at the Cape the list of those who had embarked for their destination, appears to have done all that was necessary, and his subsequent correspondence with the local Government had reference to matters of detail in a measure arising out of this extensive emigration from Britain, and the policy to be pursued in reference thereto. Early in January, 1820, however, Earl Bathurst advised the local Government that in addition to those persons who had either proceeded, or were on the point of proceeding, to the Colony as settlers under the conditions and regulations prescribed in the printed circulars, there were many other persons who had made offers of settling in the Colony without any other arrangement than a grant of land proportioned to their means of cultivation and to the number of persons whom they might take out. In all such cases in which the parties had been able to adduce satisfactory proof of their means and qualifications, no difficulty presented itself in assuring them of a grant of land on their arrival in the Colony. In consequence of this assurance, Major-General Charles Campbell engaged to proceed with 100 persons upon condition of receiving land at the rate of 100 acres for every family which might be actually settled on the land allotted to him. In the despatch, 4th January, 1820, advising this undertaking, the local Government were desired to make a suitable grant of land for the erection of the buildings and for the commencement of cultivation by the nine persons [1] named, whom the General proposed sending out to make the necessary preparations for receiving the further number of settlers whom he was to send out. The other persons who engaged to settle at the Cape under similar conditions are specified, viz., Mr. John Leigh with twenty families; Mr. Wm. Currie, Mr. Henry Moore, Messrs. Thomas Peterkin and John Carr, Mr. William Jones, Mr. Walter Meacey, Mr. James Hill, Mr. B. Burnett,[2] Mr.

[1] List Appendix.
[2] A short note of this gentleman is necessary, as his career, like that of Mr. William Parker, was, to say the least of it, extraordinary. Like the head of the Irish party, he became a thorn

Roberts with nineteen families, to all of whom similar indulgence of a corresponding grant of land was to be extended. In all these cases it was pointed out that the parties not having made any deposit in England, they were not entitled to receive any money on their arrival, nor the other advantages which were extended to the settlers sent out at the charge of Government. Henry Lovemore, Mr. Robert Way and Mr. Robert Jackson, were also settlers not connected with any of the parties, who obtained grants of land in the same way as the preceding, and settled in the neighbourhood of Algoa Bay in June, 1820. In addition to the nine pioneers sent out by General Campbell, two further contingents arrived numbering together eighteen, besides his wife and family, six more making a total of thirty-three out of the

in the flesh to the authorities, Parker, formulating grave charges against Sir Rubane Donkin, and Burnett against Lord Charles Somerset. Soon after his arrival in Cape Town, Burnett applied for a grant of land at the Kuyna, but being told in reply to his application that there was no land in that locality to be given out, he came on to Albany. Here he began farming operations at Thorn Valley, about a mile and a half beyond Graham's Town, in the Kowie Valley, which he hired from Robert Hart, a Sergeant in the Cape Corps, who was removed to the Somerset Government Prison. After a time he obtained the grant of the land adjoining that place, in terms of the regulations applicable to those who had brought out the number of persons required. This adjoining piece of land, he alleged, Hart had an eye to, and was in hopes of acquiring, which consequently being lost to him by the grant of it to Burnett, caused the former to be inimical to him. When the rent due to Hart for the hire of Thorn Valley fell due and was not punctually paid, Hart sued for its recovery before the Circuit Court. The proceedings were in Dutch, which Burnett did not understand, and, he alleged, were not explained to him. Judgment went by default, and Burnett was adjudged insolvent. These proceedings irritated him very greatly, and he committed himself to infringing the integrity of the judges, and grossly libelled them and Lord Charles Somerset, to whom he appealed for redress without effect. The end of it was, that Burnett was summoned to Cape Town to take his trial for libel of the officials, and he was sentenced to banishment of the country for five years. Lord Charles Somerset seems to have had a dread of this " dangerous radical," as he termed him, and endeavoured to capture Burnett and transport him to Van Diemen's Land, at that time a penal Settlement of the Crown. But Burnett managed cleverly, not without some extraordinary escapes, with a touch of romance in them, to elude the Governor's vigilance, and got off by a private vessel and returned to England, where he at once began to call to his assistance his friends, some of whom were Members of Parliament and otherwise influentially connected, to expose the tyranny of Lord Charles Somerset and the partiality of the local Government, including the Commissioners, who had him sent out to inquire into affairs generally. His vigorous and strongly expressed memorials and printed publications helped, no doubt, to hasten Lord Charles Somerset's downfall, though it was obvious his statements were exaggerated and that he was suffering from disappointed expectations. Burnett admitted that his statements "abound with violent invective against the Government and some of the public functionaries," but justified the use of his language by the necessity of his case, and by the habit he had of making it plain, beyond possibility of doubt, what he meant ; he could not condescend to use ambiguous terms, or to call a spade "an instrument of husbandry " ! In his printed reply to the report of the Commissioners, Mr. Bigge and Major Colebrooke, on his alleged grievances, he wrote : "I have now before me a detailed history of the cause in appeal, Durr v. Van Reenan, which embraces the fate of the celebrated horse, Kutusoff. I have an elaborate memoir of Mr. Buissine's case, with an authenticated copy of his fatal letter to Lord Charles Somerset. I have *all* the papers connected with the fate of the unfortunate Edwards, and the illicit traffic in prize slaves ; and, above all, I am in possession of a complete development of every particular attending the robbery of the public treasury at the last capture of the Cape " (p. 174).

100 he contemplated bringing out. He obtained a grant of land near the Kasonga, which he called Barville Park (see Appendix). His untimely death, which occurred at his residence, Barville Park, on 9th May, 1822, from the effects of injuries sustained by his fall from horseback, prevented the fulfilment of his engagement to the number originally intended, his two elder sons, with officers in the army, who were about to join their father when the news of the General's death reached them, remaining at home. Another batch of settlers who arrived in June of this year (1820), and came out at their own expense, was Lieut. Richard Daniell, R.N., who numbered thirty-two men, women, and children. He obtained a grant of land on the Bushman's River Heights, which he named Sidbury Park, where he successfully carried on sheep farming by the introduction of the Merino breed. Subsequently he founded a village at this spot, which he called, after his native place in Devonshire, Sidbury, and erected a church for the use of the inhabitants of the village and the surrounding dwellers, to which a chaplain was appointed by Government. These immigrants, who came out at their own expense, made up to a small extent for Captain Grant's party, which at the last moment changed their destination and sailed for North America. The vessel in which they were proceeding, unhappily, was wrecked within sight of their native land, and most of the party drowned. To five persons who were attached to a party consisting of above thirty families who had embarked for the Clyde in September, 1820, and who were unfortunately lost in the transport *Alcoma*, Earl Bathurst consented to waive the regulation in their favour that grants should not be made to any party consisting of less than ten families. These five persons were to enjoy the same advantages as had been granted to the rest of the settlers. They were: John McLaren, 36, joiner; John McLean, 34, turner; James Clark, 30, merchant; Robert Thomson, 30, bricklayer; Thomas Reid, 26, lawyer; and Agnes Reid, 22.

CHAPTER XX

REVERSAL OF LORD CHARLES SOMERSET'S POLICY

WHILST on the Frontier, Sir R. S. Donkin, in company with an officer of the Royal Engineers, inspected the line of demarcation agreed upon with the Kafirs and the spots at which Lord Charles Somerset had commanded forts to be erected for the protection of the border. In reporting to the home authorities what he had done on his own judgment and responsibility, he conveyed the idea that Lord Charles Somerset's plans were unsuitable and unnecessarily expensive. "Instead," he said, "of allowing a ponderous fortress, cannon-proof, to be erected under the name of Fort Willshire, at an immense expense, and which would not have been near finished at this date (June, 1821), I caused a fortified barrack, perfectly adequate to every defence against Kafirs, to be constructed in its stead, which has long been completed and occupied by 250 men, the number originally intended for Fort Willshire." Here was a substitution of his own views for the direct command of his superior officer,—a breach of discipline among military men of the most serious character. Again, with regard to the second fort, which had been planned and directed to be erected at a given spot by General Lord Somerset, Sir Rubane wrote that it had not been begun "because the chief engineer and himself both concurred in thinking that instead of placing it where first proposed, it might be placed more advantageously nearer the sea." And a further reason for delaying the order for the construction of this fort was added, viz., "that he had it in contemplation to locate a body of the disbanded Royal African Corps in that direction, which, if accomplished, would afford a fortified village as a right flank to the colonial frontier line of defence." And then, if the projected location of part of this disbanded corps proved impracticable, disregarding the orders of his superior officer already given, he would place a fortified barrack, similar to the one he had already placed on the Keiskama, on the best military point he could select. It is difficult to understand how a military officer of Sir R. S. Donkin's standing could have so completely overlooked his duty, which was to obey,[1] not to set up

---

[1] It is remarkable that so judicious a writer as Mr. Theal should speak of Lord Charles Somerset entertaining a "dislike" (p. 183) to Sir Rubane Donkin; and Mr. Noble terming it "umbrage" (p. 55) which he had taken owing to a reprimand that Sir R. Donkin had given to Colonel Somerset, the Governor's son, for some breach of military discipline. Neither expression points to the true cause of offence, which was undoubtedly this neglect of duty and respect for authority displayed by the extraordinary acts of Sir R. Donkin. Chase, himself a

his own judgment and carry out his own views. Fredericksburg, as the location was termed, was given out in grants of 2,000 morgen to each of the officers of the Royal African Corps, on condition that they should engage among them at least sixty men of the corps, and occupy the ground personally. Their names were Captains M. J. Sparks, and R. Birch, Lieutenants A. Heddle, W. Cartwright, C. McCombie, and J. P. Sparks, Ensigns A. Matthewson, A. Chisholm, and C. Mackenzie. It was within the ceded territory, on the Beka River, between the Keiskama and Fish Rivers, the territory that had been mutually agreed upon by the Kafirs, and the Colony should be considered neutral. It might have formed a fortified village, as Sir R. Donkin terms it, and been a *point d'appui* for the right of the line of demarcation between the Colony and the Kafirs; but it was a flagrant breach of a settled treaty. The disbanded corps was composed of Hottentots, who had acted as guides, dispatch riders, and sharpshooters, officered by colonists. The Hottentots would not be likely to have any regard for the Kafirs, whom they had encountered as foes, and would be a thorn in the flesh to them; and the officers, no longer entitled to command the Hottentots, might not be able to control their desire to measure assegais with their now proximate neighbours. Moreover, the grants of land which the Acting-Governor Donkin promised to the officers who elected to settle at Fredericksburg, were more extensive than those made to the settlers at Bathurst. It was submitted the cases were not analogous. The officers of the Royal African Corps had served their country, were on the spot, and did not put the Government to any expense for their transport thither, and they took with them a considerable number of men also free of expense to Government. It is further added, with a candour not exactly of a diplomatic character, "that if the extent of land asked for had not been granted, the officers would not have gone to the Beka, and the Settlement could not have been effected." Before occupation the land was worth nothing; it could be occupied only by such numbers, and by such a class, of men as were sent there. When the Settlement took root, all the adjacent lands would, under the protection of their fortified village, acquire the same value as the lands in the rest of Albany, and could then be measured out accordingly. In commenting upon this scheme of Sir R. Donkin's, which Lord Charles Somerset did immediately after his return to the Colony, it was pointed out that a population of the best disposed persons in this tract of country would defeat the only system his experience had taught him could tend to check the Kafir depredations. Moreover, the population placed there was composed of such a description of persons that a military force of thirty-three men was required to keep them within the limits of good order. The Kafirs, as could have been foretold, recommenced their old

settler, does not see the cause of discord. He says: "Unfortunately for the peace and progress of the Settlement, differences having arisen, out of some infraction of military routine, between Sir Rubane and the son of the absent Governor, an officer on the Frontier, occasioned such a breach, that it began to be rumoured that Lord Charles Somerset, whose return was daily expected, being moved by his son, had expressed entire displeasure at all the acts of Sir Rubane, and was disposed vindictively to reverse them,—a rumour too quickly realized" (*Annals*, p. 281).

depredations on the colonial side of the Fish River, and cattle belonging to a settler had been stolen, and an English lad who was herding them was murdered. With regard to the fort which he had directed to be erected, and which Sir Rubane Donkin had characterized as "cannon-proof" and needlessly expensive, considering the means and weapons of the Kafirs,—which also implied that Major Holloway, of the Royal Engineers, who had charge of the work, had been wanting in skill or judgment,—Lord Charles Somerset felt it due to himself and to that officer to refer General Donkin's dispatch to Major Holloway for report. From this report it appeared that the work which Lord Charles Somerset had directed to be erected was not built with greater solidity than was absolutely necessary, the walls being only two feet thick; that they were built of stone because it was not only more durable, but cheaper than brick. That being termed "cannon-proof," it would be a waste of time to refute; that the stopping that work on account of its expense and erecting another did not stand upon more correct grounds, as it would have taken only £450 to have finished the work in the most complete and efficient manner in addition to the £279 already expended, whereas the new building had cost £281, so that the intended saving had caused an additional expenditure of £37, exclusive of taking all the materials which had been prepared for the work which was stopped, the expense of which materials was included in the £279. In point of situation, it was pointed out that the present work has every fault, being so low and near the river as to be under it, scarcely habitable on account of the health of the troops, and, in a military point of view, it is equally objectionable, being commanded entirely within 100 yards from the abrupt rising of the ground on the opposite bank of the river, whereas the abandoned work possessed every local advantage [Dispatch No. 12]. This extraordinary action of Acting-Governor Sir R. Donkin was the blot on his escutcheon, disastrous to the settlers, and the beginning of a policy of change in the Government of the Kafirs, continued by subsequent Governors, who, like General Donkin, saw fit to alter the plans and reverse the action of their predecessors. On the return of the Governor to the Colony, Sir R. Donkin embarked for England, and his name no longer figures in the history of the Settlement.

Immediately after his return to England, General Donkin published a pamphlet entitled, *Letter to Earl Bathurst*, in which he exposed the misdoings of the Governor, Lord Charles Somerset, in connection with the Settlement of the British settlers, which drew forth a scathing Reply, in which he was mercilessly dealt with by an anonymous writer, generally supposed to be Mr. Wilberforce Bird, who had been in the colonial service. Sir R. S. Donkin also made several attempts to get into Parliament, with the view of bringing Lord Charles Somerset, Governor at the Cape, before the House of Commons, but only succeeded in getting returned for Berwick in 1832, when Lord Charles was already dead. He thus, with Messrs. Bishop Burnett, Edwards, and others, became a source of much annoyance to the Governor for whom he had acted. He was a man of superior education, and published several interesting works relating to military service. It is sad to think that he terminated his life by committing suicide by hanging, at Southampton, 1st May, 1841.

CHAPTER XXI

LORD CHARLES SOMERSET'S GOVERNMENT

LORD CHARLES SOMERSET returned to Cape Town in H.M.S. *Hyperion*, bound to South America, and resumed his government 1st December, 1821. His landing was ominous to Sir Rubane Donkin. Lord Charles disdained to avail himself of the carriage and escort sent by him to conduct the Governor to Government House, and his re-entry therein is described as "coming in at one door as Sir Rubane Donkin went out at the other." The cause of offence became apparent soon after. The settlers had now been in occupation of the territory assigned to them twenty months or so; but to have expected the settlers to thrive who were located six hundred miles from the market of the capital of the Colony, from which they were shut out by mountains and distance involving a journey of over a month by ox-wagon to reach it,—to expect men to become wealthy who were placed on a coast one hundred miles distant from the sea, presenting no harbours, and having bays as tempestuous as the ocean itself, rivers unfit for navigation, a frequent drought of five or six months, and an insufficiency of water for the greater part of the year, was too much to look for. He became aware, very soon after entering on office, of the deplorable state, verging on starvation, to which the immigrants were reduced by the failure of their crops, notwithstanding their exertions to maintain themselves, and the generous assistance that had been rendered them by the local Government. In January, 1822, his Lordship advised the new Landdrost of Albany, Mr. Rivers, that 500 mirds of the best Cape seed wheat of the beardless sort had been consigned to the commissariat department for distribution to the heads of parties in such proportions as they should require for the supply by produce of what would be necessary for the consumption of the persons located under each head of party for one season, provided it was made clear that the head of the party had sufficient land prepared for the reception of the seed intended to be given to him. Three hundred and sixty bags of Bengal wheat had previously been sent to Mr. Hart, at the Somerset farm, to be disposed of to such settlers as should require it at prime cost— of 20 Rs. per bag of 150 lbs. The exigency of circumstances required this; but very soon after his arrival Lord Charles Somerset, in a dispatch dated 13th December, 1821, reported to the home Government that Sir Rubane Donkin had abandoned the principle of defence which he had laid down in October, 1819, namely, the forts along the Keiskama, and leaving vacant the ceded territory between the Fish River and the Keiskama by locating two hundred discharged men of the Royal African Corps on the Beza River, near the outward limits of that country, with some officers to whom grants of land had unfortunately been made. He delayed his visit to the Frontier till February, 1823. Meanwhile he reversed Sir Rubane Donkin's acts and appointments in all directions. Naturally of a haughty and imperious disposition, he could not endure that his plans and arrangements should have been thwarted and his entire policy disregarded. Whether it might have been better, seeing these were done, need not be discussed. It certainly seems unfortunate that the fair at Fredericksburg, which by this time was successful as a trading place with the Kafirs, should all at once have been prohibited. Open and legitimate barter had been carried on here in elephants' tusks, corn, gum, mats, baskets, skins of wild animals, etc., in exchange for beads, buttons, blankets, pots, brass and tin ware, the value of which had begun to be appreciated by the Kafirs. However, the fiat went forth, Fredericksburg was abandoned, the grants of land to officers and men settled there were cancelled, and the civil appointments that Sir Rubane Donkin had made were severally annulled. Major Jones, who had been provisionally appointed Landdrost, and also Commandant of Albany, an appointment which had been kept in suspense for Colonel Graham should his health allow him to return to the Frontier, and who had retired to Simon's Town as Commandant of that post, was considered too recently arrived in the country to be confirmed in that position by Earl Bathurst. Major Jones was highly popular among the settlers[1] as Landdrost, but the appointment of Commandant of Albany was a grievous blunder on the part of Sir Rubane Donkin, if he was aware that it had been reserved for Colonel Graham, and was a further instance of his acting on his own judgment regardless of consequences and without first ascertaining whether the late gallant holder of that appointment would or could then take it up. In place of Major Jones, Lord Charles Somerset appointed Harry Rivers, Esq., to the Landdrostship of Albany, in whose integrity and ability in the discharge of the difficult and laborious duties of that office the Governor pledged himself to Earl Bathurst, adding that the public would be advantageously served. It is oftentimes difficult to take the place of a popular official, especially when his removal is thought to be due to caprice or personal dislike. The successor in such cases is viewed with disfavour at once, and not received with cordiality. Such was Mr. Rivers's fate; he became unpopular, and his removal to Swellendam was the only way of getting rid of the prejudice created against him as Lord Charles's nominee.[2] Sir Rubane Donkin's intention to make Bathurst "a full

---

[1] "He was gentle, brave, open and kind-hearted; well acquainted with human nature, pushing the point of honour and right-thinking, as well as right-doing, to a chivalrous extreme. He was of noble descent, and first cousin to the Duke of Norfolk" (Donkin's *Letter*, p. 40).

[2] Sir R. Donkin says of Mr. Rivers: "A man who had never been above twenty miles beyond Cape Town, where but little is to be learnt of the real state of the interior, a man who had never held any Colonial office but that of Wharf-master, which was created for him by Lord Charles Somerset, and who originally held a small office in the East India Company's service; a man, in short, who, from the moment of his arrival in Albany, threw everything

and permanent seat of magistracy" for the convenience and advantage of the settlers,³ was nipped in the bud by the removal of headquarters, civil and military, to Graham's Town, an act of strategy necessary in consequence of the abolition of the forts erected by Lord Charles Somerset. Not any of Sir Rubane Donkin's appointments were allowed to remain. The unfortunate settlers suffered for this sudden display of power and temper. It was the beginning of that wavering system which characterized the subsequent Government on the Frontier, each commander preferring his own views rather than carrying on the policy adopted by his predecessor. As may be supposed, the settlers were not disposed to sit down tamely and endure the confusion and mischief which these acts of Lord Charles Somerset caused. They were hurtful to themselves, and incomprehensible to the Kafirs, who hoped to see their way to re-occupy the Zunsveld, and had already begun to penetrate amongst the scattered settlers, and despoil them of their cattle. Public meetings were held to discuss the situation, and to approach the Governor on the baneful effects of his arbitrary acts. The Kafir chief Macomo had been allowed to take possession of the fertile valleys of the Kat River in 1821, and thereby became a source of apprehension to the colonists. The Boers who had vacated the Zuurveld on the incoming of the British settlers, and taken up their abodes in the Tarka and other parts near to the Kat Mountain, became alarmed and adopted the course they had invariably pursued of moving further off from the scene of danger, of which they had premonitory indications. The settlers passed resolutions at public meetings, remonstrating with the Governor, and, apprehensive that their complaints would not be attended to, they took the manly course of appealing to the home Government against the arbitrary and unjust acts to which they were subject. Lord Charles Somerset did not improve his position, or allay the irritation he had created, by the issue of a proclamation, May 24, 1822, that public meetings convened without the sanction or authority of the Government for the time being, or, when such sanction or authority cannot be conveniently obtained, without the sanction and authority of the chief local magistrate, for the discussion of public measures and political subjects, were and should be deemed contrary to law. This proclamation seems to have been founded on one by Governor Sir George Yonge, Bart., dated February 19, 1800, relating to clubs, which were required to render an exact account of their origin and the nature of their institution; and was relied upon by Lord Charles

into confusion: with whom Lord Charles Somerset subsequently quarrelled, and whom he removed after he had completed the destruction of Bathurst and the subversion of all my institutions" (*Letter*, p. 39).

³ "The establishing of Bathurst was no hobby-horse, or favourite fancy, of mine. The idea of it not even my own. The necessity of some central point of re-union for the settlers, and for the civil magistracy away from Graham's Town, which was distant from the majority of the locations, and was the military station, and on that account not desirable as the point on which all the infant civil institutions of a rising Colony were to be appended, was first suggested to me by some of the settlers themselves, who generally were the best judges of their own wants. But I am indebted for the selection of the site to the local knowledge of Colonel Cuyler, who had been thirteen years Landdrost of the adjacent district of Uitenhage, and to the discriminating judgment of Mr. Henry Ellis, Deputy Colonial Secretary" (*Letter*, p. 43).

Somerset in his prosecution of Fairbairn, Dr. Philip, and Pillans for holding meetings to form a Literary Society.[4] This shameful and invidious restraint upon the liberty of speech and freedom of discipline, which is regarded as the birthright of British subjects, fell into disuse, but was not formally repealed until December 12, 1848, by Ordinance No. 15, during the Government of General Sir Harry Smith. Not to be browbeaten by this check upon their independence of speech and action, the leaders in the agitation made known their position to His Majesty's Government by memorial addressed to the Secretary of State. The manly, dignified tone in which this memorial was written is a proof of the intelligence and education of the settlers, which, from the moderation in which it was couched, was bound to command respectful attention. It was as follows, dated March 10, 1823 :—

Memorial dated March 10, 1823.

"The subscribing colonists in South Africa, who emigrated in the year 1819, under the patronage of their native Government, are compelled, by a sense of justice to themselves and of duty to the Government under whose auspices they embarked, to lay before your Lordship a statement of the real circumstances which have prevented their advancement.

"Whatever may have been the individual disappointments and failures incidental to so numerous an emigration, they do not present themselves to Her Majesty's Government with any complaint of the natural disadvantages of the country to which they have been sent; and they have ever been actuated by one undivided feeling of respect and gratitude for the liberal assistance of the British Government,—a feeling which future reverses can never efface.

*　　*　　*　　*　　*　　*　　*

"Although the settlers must lament that in its earlier stages the prosperity of their Settlement has been checked in several important instances through the misapprehension of the general or local authorities, yet they gratefully acknowledge the prompt and generous exertions of Government in providing the means of subsistence on the commencement of the Settlement, and in alleviating, as far as possible, the severe visitations of repeated and total failure of their wheat crops; and they cannot omit their expression of particular gratitude to the Acting-Governor Sir Rubane Donkin, who devoted to their prosperity a great share of his personal attention, to whom they owed the establishment of a town in the centre of the new Settlement, as the seat of its magistracy; and a system of military defence, during which they were free from Kafir depredations. By these measures, as well as by making arrangements for a friendly intercourse with the Kafirs, and by his solicitous attentions to the interests and wishes of the settlers, he inspired them with a degree of energy and hope of which they have now left only the recollection."

The settlers go on to say in their paper, that having been prevented by authority from holding a meeting of a small number of the principal settlers, for the purpose of submitting certain points to the Governor: "Being thus pre-

---

[4] Pringle's *Narrative*, p. 207

vented from communicating with the Colonial Government, they have for twelve months continued to labour under the effects of a series of measures calculated only to extinguish the small remains of enterprise and confidence that had survived the numerous disappointments they had previously encountered; and when at length their situation, from the increasing and unpunished incursions of the Kafirs, had become really insupportable, they were reduced to the necessity of requesting permission to meet in the manner pointed out to them as legal, for the purpose of making their situation known to His Majesty's Government; but, as this also has been virtually denied to them, they are obliged to content themselves with offering to your Lordship this imperfect, but faithful, sketch of their situation in general, but more particularly of the uniform reversal of every measure previously resorted to for their advantage. As it does not appear that many natural obstacles are opposed to their advancement, they are induced to submit a candid statement of the artificial disadvantages by which they are surrounded, in the confident hope that this Settlement will not be allowed to fall a sacrifice to them. The establishment of the town of Bathurst as its seat of magistracy was of the most material service to the Settlement, as, from its situation in the centre of the smaller parties, it served to sustain in its vicinity a denser population than the circumstances of the country could otherwise admit of. Its superior advantages of soil, its vicinity to the only part of the coast found capable of communicating with the sea, and the erection of the residence of the chief magistrate at the public expense, had induced many individuals to expend their means in establishing themselves there; and the removal of the seat of magistracy and the withdrawing of the troops and Government support from a town upon which they had fixed their first hopes, and upon which depended all their future prospects of a market, has been productive of the worst effects upon the interests and welfare of the Settlement in general, as, besides its directly ruinous consequences to individuals, it has drawn away the population from the nucleus of the Settlement, and created a general distrust in the stability of the measures of Government. But the most pressing and insupportable of their grievances arise from the constant depredations of the Kafirs, who have within a few months committed several murders, and deprived the Settlement of the greater part of its cattle. These depredations are in a great measure produced by relinquishing that line of policy which held out to these tribes a hope of procuring by friendly barter such commodities as their newly-acquired wants have rendered necessary, and which they are now obliged to procure by force or theft, by withdrawing the military force from, and discountenancing, the new Settlement at Fredericksburg, and permitting thereby the Kafirs to plunder and force the settlers to retire, and ultimately to burn it to the ground. By withdrawing from the Fish River a line of posts which had previously effectually protected the settlers, by refusing aid to the more advanced farmers, plundering parties have been encouraged to drive therein, and afterwards to extend their incursions to all parts of the Settlement, and even beyond it. By exasperating that tribe which had hitherto preserved the appearance of friendship, in attempting to seize their chief Gaika in his own village, and by withholding from the local military authorities that discretionary power with which they were formerly vested,—which, by enabling them to enforce summary restitution, showed the Kafirs that the offence would be instantly followed by the punishment, whereas, by waiting the decision of the Commander-in-chief, 600 miles distant, in every emergency, offences are allowed to accumulate to an alarming amount, and the slender means of defence the Settlement possesses, deprived of the power of acting with promptitude, is forced to present to the Kafirs at once the appearance of enmity and weakness.

"It thus appears to the colonists, that instead of the new settlers ever deriving any advantages from the civilization of the savages, the existing measures can lead only to a war of mutual extermination."

The paper concludes with a hope that better days await the memorialists, and is thus signed :—

GEO. PIGOT.
D. CAMPBELL.
THOS. PHILLIPS.
and 200 others.

The heads of parties and many others among the general body of settlers were of the middle class of English society. Mr. John Bailie may be mentioned by way of illustration.[5] Another was Major Pigot, once a cavalry officer. He took out with him £5,000 to lay out in improvements amongst the settlers, besides having several hundred pounds a year of income. He built a good house on his grant of land, which he called Pigot Park, cultivated a large tract of land, and sunk £3,000. In the circle of the acquaintances of the settlers were men of position and influence, which included noblemen and landed gentry who had assisted them with pecuniary means and in other ways to emigrate. This was notably the case with the Nottingham party, who had been provided with funds for their undertaking by the contributions of several noblemen and gentlemen of the county of Nottingham. These patrons addressed Earl Bathurst on the subject of the grant of land that Mr. Thomas Calton, of North Collingham, Notts, who proceeded in charge of a party of sixty able-bodied settlers, would be entitled to under the regulations. These benefactors conceived that it would be more expedient that the grant of land that would accrue to Mr. Calton should be made to the Rev. J. Thomas Becher and Edward Smith Godfrey, Esq., of that county, as trustees for the subscribers at large, the object of the subscribers being to ensure the welfare of these settlers, which they hoped to promote by maintaining the exercise of their superintendence over them and their proceedings.[6] It is natural to suppose that in the enforced position the settlers found themselves by the harsh and despotic conduct of Lord Charles Somerset, these friends and patrons should support the memorial addressed to the home Government to obtain redress of

---

[5] See *ante*, chap. xiii.

[6] The grant was so made out, December 20, 1823. The deed was cancelled by Proclamation of 6th March, 1845, and the area subdivided and granted in sections to individual members of the party.—*Letter from Surveyor-General, Cape Town, to author.*

their grievances. There can be no doubt that this representation of their despised condition in private quarters that were likely to be successful in bringing them to light was responded to, and through this channel pressure was brought to bear upon the Government, resulting in the appointment of a Royal Commission. The enlarged scope of inquiry which the gentlemen appointed were to make, shows the force and effect of the memorial and the support it must have had from men of influence. The Commissioners appointed were Messrs. Bigge, Colebrooke, and Blair, and they received full authority to inquire into all laws, regulations, and usages prevailing in the Colony, and into every other matter in any way connected with the administration of the Civil Government, the state of the judicial, civil, military, and ecclesiastical establishments, the revenue, trade, and internal resources. These plenary powers indicate the necessity of a sweeping reform of what was complained of; and the inquiry not being undertaken in a perfunctory manner, but carried to the fullest extent, and extending over a period of four years, resulted in the recommendation of changes in the laws, customs, and usages, which were part of the heritage of the conquest of the Colony, but now, under British occupation, had to give way to those which belonged to a more enlightened period and a more liberal Government.

There was an apprehension in England soon after the arrival of the settlers that the new Settlement at the Cape of Good Hope would become tainted with slavery. The want of labour among the settlers themselves, the fact that their fellow colonists of Dutch extraction were slave-holders, and the knowledge that slaves were bought and sold openly without restriction, were not unlikely to create this apprehension among the anti-slavery party in England that was now exerting its influence to extinguish the slave trade all over the world, especially throughout the British Colonies. On July 27, 1822, Mr. Wilberforce, in the House of Commons, moved an address on the subject of slavery at the Cape of Good Hope, " in consequence of his having received information which induced him to believe that unless proper measures were adopted, there was great danger of a slave colony being formed in that quarter. The emigrants who were now settling, or had lately settled, at the Cape, finding a few old colonists in that very extensive territory who were in possession of slaves, would be very apt to follow a similar course. It was therefore requisite to give a sort of general warning to the new settlers, that they must abandon all idea of employing their capital in the purchase of slaves, or of cultivating their possessions by such labour. From the nature of the country, however, in question, from the example afforded by the existence already of slavery in a slight degree; and from the facility there was for introducing slaves both by land and by sea, very vigorous measures of prevention would be necessary. Already in the grants of land a condition was inserted that the soil should not be worked by slaves; but it too frequently happened that the conditions of such grants were very quickly forgotten; and besides, the condition, if observed, would only prevent the employment of field slaves; and it was universally admitted that domestic slavery, if it were the cause of less physical suffering to the slave, produced the greater degree of moral degradation in the master. If the condition attached to the grant of land was insufficient to prevent the extension of slavery, no less difficulty would be found in applying the system of registry which was adopted in our West Indian Settlements. He therefore moved, "That this House has learned with great satisfaction that H.M. Government, with a just abhorrence of slavery and a provident dread of the evils which would result from its extension, has made it a condition in the grants of land which it has recently allotted within the new Settlements of the Colony of the Cape of Good Hope, that no slave labour should be employed in their cultivation, also that His Majesty has established a registry of the slave population,—that nevertheless from the great extent of the Colony, from its contiguity to countries whence slaves may at no distant period be easily procured, from the remoteness of many of the farms that are scattered over its surface, and from the thinness of the population, the due execution of all laws enacted for the government of those countries, particularly those for preventing the illicit extension of slavery, must be rendered extremely difficult, more especially where self-interest shall tempt powerfully to the violation of them, that the regulations so justly introduced into the colonial grants applies only to predial slavery, whereas domestic slavery, while it is in itself at least as great an evil, would prove a strong temptation to the needy and indolent to procure drudges for their own use, and would operate with a still more pernicious influence on the feelings and habits of the new settlers,—that as to the expediency of a registry, the House cannot but fear that a slave registration for so extensive a Colony, comprising thousands of square miles, where the places are very thinly scattered and divided from each other by wide tracts of a desert and unpeopled country, cannot be so constituted and regulated as materially to check, much less effectually to prevent, the fraudulent introduction of slaves, where facilities exist for such introduction,—that under such circumstances no effectual means can be devised for preventing abuses injurious to the best interests of the settlers themselves, pernicious to the natives of Africa, derogatory to the honour of this country, but the extending as far as possible by a fundamental law to the new African Settlements the same just and liberal principles of colonization, with such exceptions only as the slaves actually in the Colony may render necessary and beneficially established as at Sierra Leone." This motion was agreed to. It was well that attention was at this early date directed to the possibility of slavery being adopted by the settlers, for slaves had already been sold publicly on the Graham's Town market, and Sheffield mentions that Kidwell, one of the settlers, bought a female slave at a public sale for £7 10s. for the purpose of giving her her liberty;[7] and there is a mortgage bond dated so late as November 13, 1827, in which John Mandy, of Graham's Town, acknowledged himself to be indebted to John Daniel Kownspek, of Cape Town, in the sum of 3000 Rs. (£22 10s.), the price of a slave, named Picton, he had that day bought and taken possession of.

The settlers were reduced to a very miserable condition in 1823. For three years in succession their crops of wheat had been famished by drought or destroyed by a species of blight called rust. The soil and climate were discovered to be unfit for purposes of tillage husbandry. The resources of the settlers were wholly exhausted. Depredations by Kafirs became common, their cattle carried

[7] p. 228.

off in droves, the colonists—Dutch as well as English—attacked by the plunderers in open day and some of them savagely murdered. Wretchedness was at its height. Without food, without clothing, without suitable abodes, without the commonest necessaries of life, all their privations and misfortunes were attributed to the reversal of Sir Rubane Donkin's plans. The unwearied exertions of benevolent individuals at Cape Town, turned into a "society for the relief of the settlers in South Africa," aroused the world to a sense of their dreadful and almost hopeless situation. Funds were collected at Cape Town, in England, and in India; 120,000 Rs. (=£9,000) were subscribed, and by the wise administration of these funds, blessed in their appropriation, an impetus was given, which materially, as if by magic, improved the face of Albany. The spiritless were cheered, the naked clothed, the hungry fed, and, through the aid of loans of money, a plan suggested by the wisdom of the sub-committee on the spot, the renewed capital stimulated and invigorated the palsied state of the settlers. Heaven blessed the deed. A decrease of blights, more favourable harvests, together with the augmentation of the allotments of land, enlivened the hopes of the settlers, and enabled them to recover themselves.

CHAPTER XXII

LORD CHARLES SOMERSET'S REPORT ON THE SETTLERS

IN March, 1825, the Governor made a report to the home Government upon the location of the British settlers and the Frontier generally. Lord Charles arrived at Graham's Town on February 6, and was, he says, received by the community there with every mark of attention and respect. After having visited the chief part of the locations, and taken into consideration the several reports of Mr. Commissioner Hayward[1] on the petitions for land, he made such extensions of grants to the British settlers as he conceived most equitable, and as the industry evinced by the grantees entitled them to. Some individuals who had petitioned for lands which were reserved for public purposes were excepted from this general extension, but afterwards applied for other places, and their memorials were to have due attention.

The principal drawback to the prosperity of the settlers was the want of labourers. With the view of supplying this want, Mr. Currie, one of the settlers, and Lord Charles himself, submitted a scheme to attain this desirable object, but it does not appear that either proposal was found practicable. The rate of wages at this time for a very indifferent labourer is quoted at 3s. per diem, with food and a bottle of wine; for a mechanic, 7s. 6d. to 9s. per diem, with the same allowance of food. It was pointed out that nothing which the earth can be made to produce would repay such an expense in cultivation, exclusive of which it placed the labouring class out of its proper sphere and demoralized it, almost all the artificers and many of the labourers devoting two or three days each week to drinking, and working only the remaining ones. Whilst among the settlers, and listening to their cry for labour, the utmost solicitude was expressed to his Excellency that he would submit their earnest request that Government would take upon itself to send out, free of expense, their wives and families, a list of whom, with the number thereof, and their respective places of residence in Great Britain and Ireland, would be forwarded. With a view of meeting the urgent demand for labour, of which the settlers stood so much in need, Lord Charles reported that about a year since an immense tribe, called Mantatus, were impelled by famine into the territories of the inhabitants north and north-east of the Colony—the Guquas. Being

---

[1] An officer of the Commissariat appointed by the Colonial Government to proceed to Albany in order to inquire into and report upon all claims or disputes relative to lands, either in the occupation or expectancy of the British settlers.

defeated by the latter, they retreated, but left numbers of their women and children in a state bordering on starvation behind them. Many of these fugitives had wandered into the Graaff Reinet district, and it had become a question how to dispose of them. The Governor directed that they should be apprenticed to the settlers in Albany for terms not exceeding seven years, according to their ages, under very strict conditions as to treatment, etc. This appeared the best way of disposing of these unfortunate beings, because the settlers were prohibited from employing slaves, which rendered it impossible that any of these vagrants could emerge into that state or be substituted for them. A register of these persons was to be kept, and no transfer could be allowed without the authority of the magistrate and a previous enregisterment thereof. Lord Charles Somerset reported specially that as regards the settlers all the communications he had with them during his stay in Albany led to the gratifying conclusion that they entertained the best feeling towards His Majesty's Government and towards himself, adding that should they shortly be supplied with that indispensable requisite—labour—they would ultimately succeed beyond the expectations even of the projectors of the measure of emigration.

A Court similar to that at Port Frances was also constituted at this time at Algoa Bay, where an English population was rapidly increasing,—the Government Resident and Commandant, Captain Evett, being appointed to preside therein, with a secretary and messenger, at the same rate of salary to the Commandant as was fixed in the year 1820, viz., 1,200 Rs. per annum.

The establishment of a magistrate at Bathurst was also desirable, but nothing was done on that head, as there were not more than four or five families resident there. However, to give encouragement to extend that place, his Excellency established a Grammar School there, and notified his intention to grant lots of ground gratis, upon an obligation to build to a specified extent and with staple materials.

The Governor further reported that a town of considerable importance might be formed where the Government farm, called the Somerset Farm, had hitherto been established. It is a beautiful spot, and the land of the most fertile description, and so situated that the whole can be irrigated. The plan of a town had therefore been made out, and nearly 300 erven, or building lots, consisting of 150 feet in front and 450 feet in depth, had already been measured. Ninety-four of these lots were to be offered for sale on the 13th and 14th of the month following [April], and it was expected they would fetch on an average 500 Rs. each. They were to be sold under an obligation to erect dwellings of certain dimensions within a given time, and composed of burnt brick or stone. The other erven would be put up for sale from time to time in such proportions as the demand for them might dictate. In order to give encouragement to this river town, the establishment of the Deputy Drostdy of Cradock, "a miserable place," which, Lord Charles said, "never could advance," was removed thither, and a portion of the northern side of the Albany district, which was inconveniently extensive, was added to the limits of the new district of Somerset, which was established as a Drostdy. It was not intended at that time to go to any but a very inconsiderable expense in converting the buildings of the farm to the purposes of a seat of magistracy. With a very slight alteration a large store could be converted into a very commodious temporary church, a farm-house, into a very good school, and a strong-built wagon-house into a prison,—other dwellings would accommodate the officers attached to a Drostdy.

A statement of comparative expense of the arrangements lately made in the Albany and Somerset districts with those that previously existed, was enclosed, by which a saving of 8,804 Rs. per annum was made, exclusive of the annual interest that would arise from the sale of the erven, which would increase as the place flourished and as fresh demands for erven were made. In this estimate it was pointed out that credit had been given for the expenses of the Albany levy, which had been abolished, considering that the happy state of security in which Lieutenant-Colonel Somerset's able system of defence of the Frontier had placed the settlers with regard to the Kafirs had rendered it no longer necessary.

The unprecedented success of the weekly fairs with the Kafirs, which Lord Charles re-established under strict regulations at Fort Willshire, was announced with great pleasure. The articles received in barter from them consisted of 40,000 lbs. of ivory, a like quantity of gum, etc., within five months, amounting in value to 96,000 Rs. (£720). For originating as well as carrying into execution this most advantageous measure, his Excellency stated that he was entirely indebted to Lieutenant-Colonel Somerset, whose intimate acquaintance with the disposition of the Kafirs and their respective chiefs had enabled him to induce them to enter warmly into the measure, and his Excellency considered it as the greatest boon that His Majesty's Government could have bestowed on the Kafir nation. In proof of this there never had existed anything but the most complete good order, regularity, and strict observance of the conditions on the part of the Kafirs since its first establishment in June last. It was projected to establish another fair more to the southward, as Fort Willshire was rather too distant from the best-affected Kafir tribes.

Having received many pressing applications from Mr. Rivers to be employed in any other department under Government, Lord Charles Somerset removed him from Albany to the Landdrostship of Swellendam, and appointed W. B. Dundas, Esq., Captain of the Royal Artillery and Brevet-Major in the army, an officer who had been highly recommended to him, and who, he learnt with pleasure, was much respected and had been cordially received by the English population in the district.

Concluding his report on the district of Albany, Lord Charles Somerset pointed out that the expense of all the establishments within that district must for a long time be a dead burthen upon the revenue of the Colony, as the district chest would be unable for many years to come to provide for the necessary disbursements. No tax on the lands granted to the settlers would be payable until the year 1830, nor had they been called upon for payment of the usual taxes on their families, cattle, etc. They were in debt to the Government for the amount of the rations issued to them by the Commissariat department; and should it not be the intention of His Majesty's Government to enforce the payment of that debt, which, without a single exception, his Lordship asserted, they possessed not the means to discharge, he would take the opportunity of making known to them, if so authorised, the beneficent intentions of Government on that head, to direct that at the commencement of the year 1826 they be called upon to pay their quota of the established taxes received annually at the Opgnaff.

CHAPTER XXIII

ALTERATIONS IN THE LAWS AND ESTABLISHMENT OF A FREE PRESS.

ONE of the earliest benefits of a substantial character which accrued to the settlers as a result of their representations to the local Government upon the laws of the Colony, which they did not understand or like, was that relating to the law of inheritance by the Roman-Dutch law, which was the law introduced by the Dutch settlers, and which was guaranteed to the burghers and inhabitants of the Colony by the Articles of Capitulation in 1806. Marriage lawfully contracted and not preceded by any ante-nuptial contract, created a partnership between husband and wife, under the sole administration of the husband, in all property, movable or immovable, belonging to either of them before the marriage or coming to either during the marriage, until the date of its dissolution. The idea of separate property is entirely excluded, and a perfect community exists. On the dissolution of the marriage by the death of either of the spouses, after the payment of the liabilities of the common estate, the partnership being dissolved, the survivor, whether husband or wife, has a right to one-half of the clear property of the community, the other half being the portion of which the pre-deceased could by will dispose, or devolving on his or her heirs *ab intestato*. This law relating to testamentary disposition of property was calculated to defeat the expectations of those who had emigrated from the United Kingdom and become settlers within the jurisdiction of the local Government; and Lord Charles Somerset was directed and authorized to make provision by proclamation that it should be thereafter considered lawful, regular, and of full force for all residents and settlers in the Colony, being natural-born subjects of the United Kingdom of Great Britain and Ireland, to enjoy the same rights of devising their property, both real and personal, as they would be entitled to exercise under the laws and customs of England; provided, however, that in case any such natural-born subject should enter into the marriage state without making a previous marriage settlement (called, in the colonial law-term, ante-nuptial contract), the property in such case, both real and personal, would be administered and divided according to colonial law, notwithstanding any subsequent testamentary devise, unless such subsequent testamentary devise were made in conjunction with the wife of the party, according to colonial law on that head. This important Proclamation dated 12th July, 1822, was successfully relied upon in the case of Shaw *v.* Shaw before the Supreme Court (Menzie's Reports, vol. ii., part v., p. 443), and is still in force as law. Whatever may have operated upon Lord Charles Somerset to meet the requirements of the settlers, whether the knowledge that representations had been made to the home authorities on some subjects that he could have prevented, this was the last of his Proclamations of any general importance. On February 9, 1825, a Council was established to "advise and assist in the administration of the Government." The Council consisted of seven members, all appointed by the Crown; three of these were settlers, viz., Messrs. Cock, Godlonton, and Wood, and subject to removal at any time. After this date the laws of the Colony were no longer issued as Proclamations of the Governor, but as "Ordinances of the Governor in Council." These Ordinances numbered sixteen up to the end of 1825, after which period Lord Charles Somerset no longer figures. The first of these Ordinances, dated 28th May, 1825, was for "introducing the use of the English language in the judicial transactions of the Court of Magistracy at Algoa Bay, (Port Elizabeth) and assigning proper limits to the territory within which the said Court is authorised to exercise its jurisdiction," which Ordinance remained in force till 14th May, 1829, when it was disallowed or superseded by the Charter of Justice. No. 2, dated 6th June, 1825, was for making British silver money a legal tender in discharge of all debts due to individuals and to Government, at the rate of one shilling and sixpence for each paper six-dollar; and No. 6 promulgated an Order in Council for giving currency to, and fixing the value of, British silver and copper money throughout the Colony. No. 11, dated 10th October, 1825, related to the office of Fiscal, assigning certain duties specially to his charge, and separating therefrom the administration of the police; and No. 12, of same date, appointing an officer to be entrusted with the administration of the police and the prosecution of police cases arising within the jurisdiction of Cape Town,—both which Ordinances only lasted till 1829, when they were disallowed and superseded by the Charter of Justice. No. 14, dated 17th October, 1825, was for abolishing the duty of 2½ per cent. levied on movable property bought in at public auction, and for reducing from 2½ per cent. to 1 per cent. the duty levied on immovable property bought in at public auction, if disposed of by private contract within six weeks after such attempt at public sale, which was disallowed 14th May, 1829. The last Ordinance, No. 16, dated 17th November, 1825, was for opening the trade in cattle with the Kafir tribes at the fair established by Government at Fort Willshire, and at such other fairs as may hereafter be established by Government for that purpose, which was repealed by Ordinance No. 23, in September, 1826.

The right of free discussion which the British settlers claimed and exercised, together with the bold defiance they gave to the suspicions entertained of their disloyalty and disaffection to the Government, had the effect of exciting in the Dutch and native population a spirit of vigilance and attention that never existed before to the acts of the Government, and which rendered all future exercise of authority virtually impossible that was not founded on law.

These were some of the changes in the laws which the settlers, by their firm attitude of independence, had wrung from a despotic Governor before their appeal to the home Government for redress of their grievances. More important results followed from that appeal upon the recommendation of the Commissioners who had been sent out to enquire into and report upon them. The most valuable of these was the Charter of Justice, whereby, under Letters Patent, dated 24th August, 1827, the Supreme Court was established. The Charter provided that all judicial proceedings should be in the English language exclusively. From 1st January, 1823, all documents issued from the Colonial Office were in the English language, and from 1st January, 1825, all official notices were promulgated in that language; but the order for its exclusive use in all judicial acts and proceedings took effect after 1827. The Supreme Court established under the Charter consisted of a Chief Justice and two puisne judges. A Circuit Court was to be held in every district once in every six months; Magistrates superseded Landdrosts to hold an open court twice a week, or as often as necessary, and with these changes the English language was ordered to be used in all official proceedings and business. An Executive Council was appointed to assist the Governor with advice in matters of importance or difficulty. The Royal Commissioners had also recommended that a separate and distinct Government should be created for the Eastern Districts, owing to the embarrassment to which all measures, both of executive and judicial authority, were liable, from the great extent of territory that the Colony included, and which had received His Majesty's approbation. A measure of this kind had become necessary from the increased progress of business and correspondence with the remote districts on the Frontier occasioned by the settlement of the British immigrants, the importance of applying some uniform and consistent principles to the intercourse of the Colonies with the Kafirs and other tribes by preventing their collision and checking the desultory warfare that had prevailed along a considerable portion of the Frontier. Unfortunately this wise suggestion was not adopted, and subsequently the Frontier inhabitants suffered from the vacillating and temporizing policy of succeeding Governors, and experienced the disadvantage of a Government at a remote distance, not easily and quickly reached and not in sympathy with Frontier residents.

Up to the time of the arrival of the British immigrants there was no publication of any kind of the character of a general newspaper. In Sir George Yonge's time, July 15, 1800, Messrs. Walker and Robinson had permission to set up a printing press and publish a weekly newspaper at Cape Town. But the production was nothing more than a Gazette in which Government notices, proclamations and advertisements appeared. Mr. Thomas Pringle, who came out as head of Pringle's party to locate his relatives and friends at the Baboons River, conceived the idea of publishing a newspaper at Cape Town to treat of political, social, and general topics, and with that object in view induced his friend and countryman Mr. James Fairbairn to come to the Colony, join him in the enterprise, and assist him in editing the paper. Such a publication as Pringle contemplated would have been an advantage to the Colony, and to Cape Town in particular, helping to diffuse liberal ideas and keep colonists aware of what was going on in the Colony and abroad. A feature of the proposed newspaper was the verbatim reporting of cases in the Courts and speeches at public meetings. The project was discountenanced by Lord

Charles Somerset, who was afraid his despotic acts would be published to the world. Permission was refused to the publication; then it was allowed subject to approval of the editorials and other matter before being published; finally the printing plant was seized and put under seal by the Governor's orders. Pringle and Fairbairn were not men to submit to arbitrary proceedings of this character, and they used the influence they had in England to get the barriers to free publication completely removed. Their history of this strange attempt to gag the Press is related at length in Meurant's *Sixty Years Ago*, and is a disgrace to the Governor who used the Fiscal (Attorney-General) and others to do his bidding in a despotic manner. Meurant had come out as a lad about the time of the British immigrants, served his time in the Gazette printing office at Cape Town, and was personally cognisant of the repeated attempts to stifle and ruin Pringle and Fairbairn and their newspaper. The moderation and persistence with which these enlightened men appealed to the authorities in London succeeded at length, in defeating Lord Charles Somerset, and securing to the Colony the advantage of freedom from censorship and the liberty to set up a newspaper as they had projected. Godlonton, who was a printer by trade and had come out with Bailie's party, followed in the wake of Pringle and Fairbairn, and took over from Meurant the Press he had set up in Graham's Town, and published with marked ability the *Graham's Town Journal* for a long term of years.

The quiet of the Colony was disturbed by these arbitrary acts of Lord Charles Somerset which made him extremely unpopular. Many of the reports that were circulated in England against his Excellency carried falsehood or misrepresentation on the face of them. But still there remained enough to show that he had neither the patience, nor the candour, nor the liberality of spirit, without which the discretion necessarily entrusted to a colonial Governor will for the most part degenerate into capricious tyranny. The proceedings against Pringle, Fairbairn, and Greig, to smother their newspaper enterprise, were bad enough. An enlightened British public would sympathize with their brethren across the ocean in their efforts to establish a free Press; and the persistent efforts of this autocrat to stifle it out of existence would create contempt and disgust. But what damaged Lord Charles Somerset in the eyes of all lovers of independence was his absurd conduct in regard to a Literary Society which upwards of sixty of the most respectable individuals in Cape Town wished to establish. It reads like a satire upon education to learn that Lord Charles would have no concern with the scheme, condemned it as illegal, and induced the Chief Justice and some others of the members to withdraw their names. A memorial was then presented to him, signed by about forty of the principal inhabitants, requesting merely his permission to establish the proposed society, and pointing out the identity of its constitution and objects with those of the Royal Society patronized by the King of England, etc. To the application of this memorial Lord Charles Somerset gave a positive refusal: 1st, Because they had promised to form themselves into a society "without any previous reference to his Excellency," which he designated as a' "wilful" disregard of the existing authority at the Cape; 2nd, Because it was improper to permit the establishment of an association which might have a tendency to "produce" political discussion ! In these affairs there may have been circumstances in the background which might have tended to exasperate the Governor ; but could there be a greater fault than to carry into the affairs of administration private feelings of resentment or partiality, however well-founded those feelings may have been? The Royal Commissioners could not be unaware of vagaries such as these, which, with the other acts of official tyranny, clearly disqualified his Lordship for the Government entrusted to him. His friends in office had an inkling of the reflections and grave charges against him that would be contained in the report the Commissioners would present to Parliament as the result of their labours. Lord Charles obtained leave of absence to come to England to meet and answer those charges, but in reality it was to retire from office altogether, which he did, leaving the damaging statements in the report by the Commissioners where they were. It is with the retirement of Lord Charles Somerset from the Government of the Colony of the Cape of Good Hope that this narrative ends. The limits of the work proposed have been reached. It is for another pen to take up the history from this point and continue it for a further period. The materials abound with the advantage of reference to the records of the time carefully preserved, and in the English language, and with the running commentary upon current events of an active, enterprising, Free Press, one of the results of the British Settlement of 1820.

Lits Van Riebeck's name will remain associated with the first Settlement of Europeans at the Cape, so will Lord Charles Somerset's name be identified with the introduction of the first body of British settlers after its conquest by British arms, whereby the Colony of the Cape of Good Hope became *de facto* a British Colony, and thereafter became an integral part of the British Empire Lord Charles Somerset will also be remembered as the first Governor to introduce superior blood stock to improve the breed of horses and cattle in the Colony. His stud farm at Worcester, his cattle-breeding and agricultural farm at the Kleine Post nearer to Cape Town, and his experimental farm on the Frontier where Somerset East now stands, intended to produce food supplies for the Commissariat for the use of the troops stationed on the Frontier line of defence, were substantial advantages to the colonists, but were turned to his prejudice by his adversaries, who identified the Governor personally with instances of jobbery in horses and cattle which could not be concealed or denied. His Lordship died 20th February, 1831.

BRITISH SETTLERS WHO ROSE TO DISTINCTION

A SHORT notice of the more prominent immigrants who did useful work in their day and generation in the country they had come to occupy, whose memory will remain green and long associated with the early history of Graham's Town, will be a fitting close to this work.

DUNCAN CAMPBELL.

1. The first of these, in virtue of his official position, is Captain Duncan Campbell, a half-pay officer of the Royal Marines, who came out in the *Weymouth* at the head of a party consisting of thirteen men, eight women, and eight children from Hampshire. After an unsuccessful attempt at farming on the Endless River (Zonder End) with Southdown sheep that he brought with him, he was removed to Albany. He was not long in coming into prominence, being appointed Heemsraad, with Mr. Miles Bowker, another settler, under Major Jones, whom the Acting-Governor, Sir Rufane Shaw Donkin, had made Provisional Landdrost of Albany. This appointment he held for a short time only, neither he nor his colleague being able to concur in the arbitrary acts of the Governor, Lord Charles Somerset. When, however, changes were made in the condition and style of the appointments previously prevailing under the Dutch system of Government, Captain Campbell was appointed Civil Commissioner and Resident Magistrate of Albany in 1828. During the administration of Sir Benjamin D'Urban, then Governor of the Colony, he was in 1833 appointed Commissioner-General of the Eastern province, a more important office, in succession to Captain Andries Stockenstrom, who was retired on pension. When that, however, was abolished, he resumed his duties as Civil Commissioner, and in 1836 was required to perform the duties of Resident Magistrate of Albany as well. There was a good deal of feeling, even at this early date, in the history of the Eastern Frontier, on the benevolent policy of Sir Benjamin D'Urban, the causes of the war of '34-'35, and the treatment of the Kafirs by the colonists, which was greatly accentuated by the Rev Dr. Philip and his party in Cape Town, who did all they could to calumniate the settlers, charging them with perpetrating atrocities on the Kafirs. This strongly-marked party feeling led to the appointment of Captain Andries Stockenstrom as Lieutenant-Governor of the Eastern Province, with whom Captain Campbell came into unpleasant collision, and figured as defendant in an action at law instituted against him by Stockenstrom for "maliciously and unlawfully causing and procuring him to be falsely charged with having deliberately fired at and killed a

Kafir child" during the operations of a Commando under Captain Fraser in 1813, which was carefully inquired into by the Supreme Court before Wylde, C. J., and Menzies and Burton, J. J., in 1838, with the result that the shooting of the Kafir was held proved, but that the deed was a lawful military act, which established Captain Campbell's plea of justification fully and satisfactorily. Stockenstrom pursued his hostility against Captain Campbell in a further accusation of neglect of duty in allowing the land books of Somerset to fall into arrear, which was the immediate cause of his retirement, his health giving way. Whether Captain Campbell was entitled to a retiring allowance rested on the accuracy of Stockenstrom's charges. Campbell retorted by taking up a newspaper scandal and accusing Stockenstrom of corruption in having received a free grant of the farm Maastrom, consisting of 5,000 morgen of the best land in the old ceded territory. The charge and counter-charge came before the Secretary of State, and was referred to the Governor of the Colony, Sir George Napier, who completely exonerated Captain Campbell, and he was allowed a pension of £200 a year. Stockenstrom was able to show that he had obtained the farm from Sir Rubane Shaw Donkin in a perfectly honourable manner, at a time when land was being given away by the Government to any official who applied for it. Captain Campbell is described by Sir Rubane Donkin as "a man full of energy and expectation, a gentleman of considerable acquirements, with a strong tincture of the military character." He was a married man thirty-nine years of age when he arrived in the country, but left no issue to inherit his honourable name. He resided on his farm on the race-course flat above Graham's Town, which he called Thorn Park. A valued correspondent writes: " Captain Campbell always lived on his farm, three miles from Graham's Town, on the Fish River side of the town. In my girlhood I used to stay with Mrs. Campbell, frequently for months together. She was a bright and cheerful woman; the old Captain was quiet and thoughtful, and a great politician. Major White, of Table Farm, would frequently ride over and dine with the Captain, talk politics for hours, often till one o'clock in the morning. Then Major White would jump on his horse and ride home in the dark. Captain Campbell was one of the first sheep farmers in the Eastern Province, and perhaps the first man who ever made it pay. He had a good overseer, and took great interest in sheep farming."

HOUGHAM HUDSON.

2. Captain Campbell's successor in office as Civil Commissioner and Resident Magistrate of Albany was Mr. Hougham Hudson, "a man of Kent," from Canterbury, who came with Mr. Dyason's party in the *Zoroaster*, as a young man twenty-six years of age, with a wife and one child. He found farming in the Zuurveld unsuited to his tastes and habits, and obtained permission to leave the location, and removed to Graaff Reinet in 1821. A clerkship in the Landdrost's office happening to be vacant, he availed himself of the opening, and was appointed thereto. By dint of industry, zeal and integrity he was successively promoted to the office of District Clerk and Magistrate at Port Elizabeth. He was much esteemed by Sir Benjamin D'Urban, Governor of the Colony,

and at the close of the war of '34-'35, when the settlers were permitted to return to their homes for the purpose of getting in crops of grain, an arrangement was made whereby a little assistance was given to those who were utterly ruined. Of the money lent by Lord Charles Somerset to the sufferers by the flood of 1822, a portion had been repaid. Sir Benjamin D'Urban appointed Mr. Hudson a Commissioner to lend this fund again, which amounted to £6,792, in small sums to the most distressed of the settlers. This fund was augmented by £9,019, received for captured cattle sold by auction, and these amounts were distributed in proportion to losses sustained. After this Mr. Hudson was appointed Agent-General of the New Province of Queen Adelaide, stationed at Graham's Town, where he was also to perform the duties of Resident Magistrate, which office he ceased to hold in 1836, when he was appointed Secretary to the Lieutenant-Governor (Stockenstrom) of the Eastern Districts; and finally, on the retirement of Captain Campbell, became Civil Commissioner and Resident Magistrate of Albany, which office he held till his death in 185-. In all these positions of trust and importance Mr. Hudson proved himself an active, faithful public servant, discharging his duty effectively, and to the entire satisfaction of his superiors.

WALTER CURRIE.

3. Sir Walter Currie may next be mentioned. His father, Lieutenant Walter Currie, a purser in the Royal Navy on half pay, came with Mr. Willson's party in the *Belle Alliance*, and lived on the location assigned to Mr. Willson's party, south of Manley's Flat, otherwise called Beaufort Vale, near Bathurst. Subsequently he acquired a farm near that, which he called Langholm. Here young Currie was brought up from infancy, being only one year old when his parents arrived in Albany. In the war of '34-'35 he took the field as a volunteer in the corps of Guides, under the command of Captains W. Bowker and R. Southey. After the war Walter Currie returned to his farm, declining a commission in the Army offered him by Sir Benjamin D'Urban, and on his father's death removed to the little Fish River, near Somerset, where he had a sheep farm. During the war of '46 he did good service, scouring the country and driving the Kafirs from their strongholds. In 1850 he disarmed the disaffected Hottentots at Theopolis, and made prisoners of the ringleaders and took command of several wagon trains between Graham's Town and Cradock. In 1852, when Governor Sir George Cathcart arrived and found the Eastern Districts in a still insecure state, he was appointed Commandant of the Albany District in the new corps, which was styled the Frontier Armed Mounted Police, in which corps he distinguished himself by his valour and daring, to which Sir George Cathcart gave expression in garrison orders, 12th January, 1853. On Sir George Grey's arrival, realizing the importance of a constant patrolling police force on the Frontier, arrangements were made to organize the force permanently, and Currie was appointed to continue at its head and superintend its management as General Commandant. Under this new force Currie distinguished himself in the expedition against Queesha and Vadanna in the Queen's Town district, and the after expulsion of the paramount chief

Kreli from beyond the Bashee. These services were brought to the notice of Her Majesty the Queen by special despatches from Governor Sir George Grey, and Currie received the honour of knighthood, and also to mark His Royal Highness Prince Alfred's appreciation of his services during the long and interesting tour which that member of the Royal Family made in 1860. Sir Walter Currie's routing and dislodging of rebellious Hottentots and Korannas, who had established themselves on the islands of the Orange River near its mouth, and were a source of annoyance and damage to the colonists in that part by their predatory and lawless habits, was a service in which daring and hardship were equally combined, but which brought his active career to a termination. The fatigues of that campaign and the successive drenchings in reaching the islands and getting back to land, brought on an attack of acute rheumatism which rendered him a cripple till his death, which occurred at his residence, Oatlands, near Graham's Town, July 7, 1872. He left no descendant to bear his honoured name.

WILLIAM COCK.

4. Mr. William Cock, the head of Cock's party, who, with several other small parties, came out by the *Weymouth* transport, was located on the banks of the Kowie, near its mouth. He was a young man, twenty-six years of age, married, and had three children when he landed. His first impressions were inseparably associated with an inlet which engaged his attention to his dying day, and for which he never faltered in predicting for it full importance. Blighted harvests, flooded rivers, and Kafir depredations were only the more prominent difficulties the pioneers were called upon to contend with, and which, to a large extent, caused a break up of the locations and the dispersion of the settlers. Among the latter was Mr. Cock. Intuitively a man of business, a printer by trade, and constitutionally active and pushing, he was soon found at Graham's Town, then in its infancy, elbowing his way and joining others in laying those commercial foundations upon which subsequent generations have securely built. At one time he was a contractor to Government for supplying the Mauritius with salted beef and other provisions, compelling him to go over to that Island and to St. Helena; anon in partnership with the wealthy Cape Town firm of Heideman, Hodgson & Co.; and again establishing a successful wholesale business in Graham's Town in connection with the same firm. Amid all this bustle of life and clash of commercial competition, while his energy was conspicuous, his integrity was equally so. After a few years of successful enterprise the partnership with which he stood connected was dissolved by mutual consent, Mr. Cock retiring from it with a moderate competency. Here again, it is remarked in the obituary notice of him published at the time of his death, that the attraction which drew him to the Kowie was remarkable. In the course of the firm's previous business transactions a good deal of land had been either taken over or purchased; and among these were several farms at the mouth of the Kowie. These assets were, at his own desire, allotted to him, and he then gave practical effect to the idea he had always cherished of forming the Kowie estuary into a commercial harbour. A brief visit to his beautiful native country of Cornwall

I

did not dissipate these sanguine hopes. He shortly returned to the Cape, and in conjunction with Messrs. Hayton succeeded in establishing another mercantile business in Graham's Town. After a few years he retired from this, and then concentrated his whole attention on the improvement of the harbour. This was only done at the expense of immense personal labour and an almost ruinous outlay of capital. It may be said that for a time he stood alone in this project, and it is impossible to overestimate the pluck which enabled him to sustain the weight of responsibility resting upon him, and that too coupled with discouragement of the most depressing character. It was during this period of his career that he was nominated by the Governor of the Colony, Sir Henry Pottinger, a member of the Legislative Council, thus opening up to him a new phase of colonial life. As a member of the Legislature no one ever displayed more sturdy independence or approved himself a more ardent lover of his country. It was impossible to be associated with him without feeling assured of the firmness of his political principles or of his readiness to stand up and do battle for the rights and welfare of his fellow colonists. It was at this time, during his membership in the old Legislative Council, that he succeeded, in conjuction with his only colleague from the Eastern Province, Mr. Godlonton, in getting the Bill for the improvement of the Kowie passed into law. This was conceded grudgingly, and then only on condition that half the £50,000 required for the work should be raised by the people themselves, impoverished as they were by the innumerable difficulties which at the time surrounded them. This Act was a great step in advance, which however only excited him to more incessant exertions and more vigilant oversight. The issue may be anticipated. He wore himself out in the service of his country and in a most laudable attempt to carry to perfect completion a grand idea ; and though he eventually broke down, he was permitted to see, to a large extent, the fruition of his most sanguine hopes. He died at Graham's Town, February 9, 1876, aged eighty-three years.

ROBERT GODLONTON.

5. A settler whose name will remain familiar even to a succeeding generation, and whose fame will not die out, was Mr. Robert Godlonton, one of Mr. Bailie's party in the ship *Chapman*. He was born in London in 1794, and having to fight his way in the world, was, at an early age, apprenticed to the trade of a printer in one of the largest London offices. Thomas Stringfellow, who became Civil Commissioner and Resident Magistrate of Fort Beaufort, was employed in the same establishment, and the two friends, then married, attached themselves to Mr. Bailie's party and came to Albany with the settlers of 1820. On his first arrival he shared the hardships of the pioneer settler's life on a location. That they were not trivial, may be gathered from the fact, often mentioned by Mr. Godlonton, of the walks with a companion or two from the Fish River mouth, over the roughest hills and bush paths into Graham's Town, to get a few loaves of contractor's bread, then considered an epicurean luxury, with which they would walk back again to share it with their families and friends. The hardships and uncertainty of location life, as soon as Government rations were no

longer forthcoming, caused him to remove to Graham's Town. After a short time he accepted employment in the Landdrost's office at Graham's Town and the revenue department of the Eastern Province, under Captain Duncan Campbell, whose confidence he fully obtained. One of the chief responsibilities of his office was the collection of taxes, the "Opgaaf" as it was then called, a duty attended both with difficulty and serious responsibility, involving as it did the collection of taxes based upon the pastoral wealth of the farmers, collected from the rural population by visitation from farm to farm. On these expeditions his only safe was his wagon-box, and his honesty the only security the Government could obtain. Whilst in office, he had offers of promotion in the service, but declined these offers, preferring to embrace one far more congenial to a man of literary tastes. He was a man of intelligence, with a strong determination, and resolute in maintaining the rights and liberties of the people, strongly opposed to the tyranny and oppression of Lord Charles Somerset's rule. This made him a chosen leader, and he was amongst the foremost to oppose that Governor in his attempts to suppress the popular voice. In the same ship with himself, and of the same party, was Dr. Edward Roberts, who brought a printing press to be used by Godlonton under his control, in conjunction with Stringfellow and Mollett, who were also fellow emigrants in the same vessel, of the same party, and of the same trade. It was contemplated producing a newspaper as a means of communication between the settlers and other inhabitants and friends at home. The project, however, came to nothing, as on arrival of the vessel and the discovery of this "infectious machine," Sir Rubane Shaw Donkin, the Acting-Governor, confiscated it, paying its cost to Dr. Roberts. Mr. Noble, in his *Past and Present* (p. 44), says Godlonton and Stringfellow had been engaged in the King's printing office, Schackelwell, and that Mr. Rutt, the manager, anxious to give them a fair start, had given them a complete plant for a printing establishment, upon the understanding that if they were successful, he should be paid for it; if not, no demand would be made for it. Stringfellow was allowed to go ashore, and by negotiation with the Government printer the amount of the invoice was paid and remitted by Dr. Roberts to Mr. Rutt in England. This press and material were, some years after, sent to Graaff Reinet to be used for printing Government notices and similar innocuous matter. By a strange irony of fate, this identical press was, after a considerable interval, purchased by Mr. Godlonton, by whom it was preserved in "cotton and lavender" as one of the curiosities of the past. It is impossible to do justice to the character of this remarkable man in a short memoir, or to refer in detail to all the political movements which he directed and successfully accomplished. There was no more strenuous and unflinching champion of the rights and liberties of the subject, no more valiant defender of the character of the immigrants against the unjust and uncharitable aspersions that were levelled at them, and the calumnies that were circulated against the settlers at the seat of Government and in England. It was not till December, 1831, that the *Graham's Town Journal* was launched by Mr. L. H. Meurant, to which Mr. Godlonton was one of the principal contributors. It was in order to share an interest in the venture, of which he subsequently became the sole proprietor, that he relinquished his position in the Civil Service. He conducted the Journal with marked ability for a long period of years, and which was popularly termed the "Settlers' Bible." He published several pamphlets of great service at the time, notably his *Narrative of the Irruption of the Kafirs in* 1834-5, and his *Case of the Colonists in reference to the Invasions of the Kafirs in* 1835 and 1846. The influence thus gained led to his being chosen as one of the two elective members, Mr. Cock being the other, to represent the Eastern Province under the first form of constitutional government that was granted to the country. Upon the Colony having its constitution developed by an increase of elective representatives, he was at once returned. He lived to see the fruits of his incessant labours in the cause of political freedom and progress, the eventual concession of responsible government, though he and his colleagues did all they could to delay the introduction of that step, holding that the Colony was not sufficiently advanced to take upon itself self-government, and that the Eastern Province would be ruled by the Cape Town party, who were hostile to the settlers and to Frontier development. In 1858 he, with his family, re-visited his native land after an absence of thirty-eight years, spending three years renewing old associations and friendships. On his return to the Colony he retired from the prominent position he had so long occupied in public life and from editorial duties, but in his retirement enjoyed a vigorous old age and the unaffected respect and attachment of his fellow citizens and of colonists at large. He died at his residence, Beaufort House, Graham's Town, May 30, 1884, at the advanced age of ninety-one years. A marble monument was subsequently erected over his grave in the Wesleyan Cemetery bearing the inscription :

ROBERT GODLONTON,
Born in London, 24th September, 1794,
Died at Graham's Town, 30th May, 1884.

A British Settler of 1820. The recognised Father of the Press in the Eastern Province of the Colony, and for many years a valued member of the Legislative Council of the Cape of Good Hope.

" Mark the perfect man, and behold the upright, for the end of that man is peace."—*Psalm* xxxvii. 37.

GEORGE WOOD.

6. A colleague of Mr. Godlonton's throughout his parliamentary career, and a co-operator with him in every undertaking for the good of the Settlement, was George Wood, who came with the Sephton or Salem party in the *Aurora*, as an apprentice to Mr. Richard Smith, being then fourteen years of age, and subsequently to Mr. William Thackwray. He was early thrown on his own resources, and his industry, energy, and aptitude for business soon obtained for him a good position. As his large family of sons and daughters grew up around him, assisting him in the shop and store, he prospered as no other settler did, and died reputed a millionaire. As a business man he was shrewd and far seeing, cautious to a degree, but never above hard work. He was no counter-jumper of the modern style, and never feared soiling his fingers. He

donned the shopman's apron and swept his own shop long after the prosperity of his business would have justified the employment of others to do manual work, and withal was as courteous to his customers and as good a hand at driving a bargain as the best of modern salesmen. He recognised the nobility of work, he practised it himself, and brought up his sons in the practice of it. As prosperity rewarded his efforts he increased the sphere of his business operations, built "larger barns" and storehouses, and speculated so judiciously that wealth flowed in upon him almost without a check. His business instincts were early taken advantage of by the promoters of trading, insurance, and trust companies, and none of these prospered so well as when he was the practical managing director. The Eastern Province recognised in him a man of wide experience and sound judgment, and for many years returned him in at the head of the poll, or among the first five at each general election. He was most punctual and diligent in attendance on his duties in the Legislative Council, even when advancing age and infirmity deprived him of the use of his legs, and when he had to be carried and wheeled from place to place, hauled on board ships and lifted to upper rooms in hoists. His spirit was an indomitable one. Such pain and paralysis of the limbs as he suffered would have curbed the spirit and deprived many more robust than he of all energy and interest in public affairs. He was most punctual in attendance at his office, at the Divisional Council meetings, at Board Meetings, and, when in session, at Parliament, retaining up to the last, even when sight and hearing had failed him, a memory of the most retentive and tenacious description. His public benefactions were considerable. His assistance was never asked in vain for any worthy object, whether in the promotion of institutions connected with religious or secular bodies. He gave liberally whether for the erection of the Cathedral Tower, for the erection or founding of the Wesleyan High School, or for the Baptist Sunday School. The one exception to the local institutions with which his name might have been naturally associated was the Jubilee Memorial Tower. He was deemed to young to be ranked among the Settlers, only those of eighteen years of age and upwards being so regarded. This slight he resented very much, and in consequence the tower was built without any money assistance from himself or any of his sons. He died at his residence, Woodville, Beaufort Street, Graham's Town, 1st November, 1884, aged seventy-nine years and six months.

SAMUEL CAWOOD.

7. Another colleague of Mr. Godlonton's in political strife, and a co-operator with him in various local undertakings, was Samuel Cawood, who came with his parents with Mr. Hazelhurst's party in the transport, John being then thirteen years of age. Godlonton, Wood and Cawood have always been bracketed together as Fathers of the Settlement. At one time the firm of Cawood Brothers, of which Samuel was a member, were contractors to the Imperial forces, and in a large way of business. Samuel Cawood owned landed property in Lower Albany, and was unceasing in his efforts to induce farm owners and others to cultivate cotton on their lands, the seeds for which he

procured with some difficulty and expense, and distributed gratuitously. He was in consequence familiarly called "King Cotton." He was one of the most active promoters of the meeting at Graham's Town of such of the settlers as survived with their direct descendants to celebrate the Jubilee of their arrival and landing in Algoa Bay in 1820. And as the result of that gathering of the settlers and the interest that the proceedings evoked in the history of the Settlement, he was mainly instrumental in raising a permanent monument in the shape of the "Settlers' Memorial Tower," Mr. Godlonton laying the foundation stone amidst much enthusiasm. Six or seven years later the Town Council of Graham's Town determined to build a Town Hall, when it was suggested that this Memorial Tower should form part of it. When the tower was up to its first floor, it was determined to convert the upper bell-turret into a clock chamber. The corner foundation stone of this Town Hall was laid with much ceremony by his Excellency Sir Bartle Frere, then Governor of the Colony, during the mayoralty of Mr. T. M. Parker. The old memorial foundation stone was subsequently removed and relaid by Mr. Godlonton as the foundation stone of one of the buttresses of the present tower, which is 120 feet high. A clock with illuminated dials has been put into the Settlers' Memorial Tower. The Town Hall was publicly opened by Samuel Cawood, Acting-Mayor, 7th May, 1882, when the tower was completed, which is as much a memento of himself as of those whose advent it is intended to honour and commemorate. In 1855 he was returned to Parliament and continued to represent his constituency for seven consecutive years. Then came a break of nine years in his useful Parliamentary career, until, in 1869, at the General Election, he was returned to a seat in the Legislative Council, which he occupied until 1873. In 1872 he entertained at a banquet at Graham's Town the then Governor, Sir Henry Barkly, and 200 of the leading citizens whom he had invited to meet his Excellency. In 1880 he was elected Mayor of Graham's Town. He died at his residence Waybank House, Graham's Town, 15th June, 1887, aged 79 years. The descendants of the Cawood family are of the most numerous of the British Settlers, and are to be found in almost every part of the Frontier districts as well as in the neighbouring States.

RICHARD SOUTHEY.

8. Another of the settlers who rose to distinction, and whose career has been one of exceptional brilliance and usefulness, is Sir Richard Southey, who came with his parents as a lad, eleven years of age. Southey's party, of which his father, Mr. George Southey, was the head, came from Somersetshire. They were located between Manley's Flat and Bathurst, with Holder's and Greathead's parties for immediate neighbours. Like other of the sons of the settlers growing up in the district, he acquired the language and became familiar with the habits and customs of the Kafirs, and acquainted with the numerous by-paths through which those marauders penetrated into the Settlement and robbed the settlers of their cattle. During the war of 1835 he, with his brother George and other young sons of the settlers, formed a Corps of Guides to direct the military forces under Colonel, afterwards Sir Harry, Smith, to reach

the Kafirs and fight them in their stronghold, the Fish River Bush. In this capacity he did good service, which led to his employment under Sir Benjamin D'Urban's Government as Magistrate in the New Province of Adelaide, subsequently abandoned. He then returned to Graaff Reinet, where he resided for ten years. On the return to the Colony of Sir Harry Smith as Governor in 1847, he was appointed Secretary to the High Commissioner and accompanied him through the Colony, the Orange Free State, and Natal, and was present at the battle of Boomplaatz in August, 1848. Mr. Southey was left as President of the War Tribute Commission, formed for the purpose of levying fines upon persons who had been engaged against the Colony, both as a punishment and to pay expenses. Within six months he collected and paid into the treasury £9,000. In 1849 he was appointed Civil Commissioner and Resident Magistrate of the large district of Swellendam, which, even in those days, contained many disaffected persons, whom, however, he managed to conciliate and reduce to obedience to law and order. In 1852 he acted as Colonial Secretary during the absence on leave of Mr. Montagu, till his return in 1854, when he returned to Swellendam. In 1855 Mr. Southey was appointed Secretary to the Lieutenant-Governor General Jackson, who was also Commander of the Forces on the Frontier, and resided at Graham's Town. In 1859 he was appointed Auditor-General, but had to give up that appointment to Mr. E. M. Cole who had been nominated by the Home Government. But soon after he again acted as Colonial Secretary during the absence on leave of Mr. (now Sir) Rawson W. Rawson. Finally, in July, 1873, Letters Patent were issued appointing him first Lieutenant-Governor, of the Province of Griqualand West, which difficult and responsible position he held till 1875, when the Imperial Government decided to withdraw local Government, and eventually annexed the province to the Cape Colony. In 1891 his long and meritorious services were acknowledged by the distinction of knighthood. Sir Richard Southey is still alive and well, living at Wynberg, near Cape Town.

APPENDICES

APPENDIX I
CAPE PARLIAMENT

British Settlers of 1820 who were elected to represent the Eastern Districts in the Legislative Council.

1854	Robert Godlonton, resigned.		George Wood.
	George Wood, resigned.		Robert Godlonton.
1856	William Cock, resigned.		Samuel Cawood.
1858	William Southey.	1866	James Cotterell Hoole.
1859	I. Cawood, deceased.		John Centlivres Chase.
	Charles Pote.		Richard John Painter.
	William Southey, disqualified.	1868	Charles Henry Caldecott.
	James Henry Greathead, resigned.	1869	George Wood.
			Samuel Cawood.
1860	Samuel Cawood.	1870	James Cotterell Hoole.
1862	Robert Godlonton.	1872	Responsible Government Bill passed.
	George Wood.		
1864	Charles Pote.		

British settlers of 1820 who were elected to represent Eastern Districts in the House of Assembly.

		Constituency.
1854	James Mortimer Maynard	Cape Town.
	Thomas Holden Bowker	} Albany.
	William Cock, resigned	
	James Collett, forfeited his seat.	} Cradock.
	William Thornhill Gilfillan	
	Richard John Painter	Fort Beaufort.
	Charles Pote, resigned	} Graham's Town.
	James Thackwray, deceased	
	Robert Mitford Bowker	Somerset East.

		Constituency.
1855	William Wright, resigned	} *Cradock.*
	Charles Scanlan	
	Joseph Cawood	*Graham's Town.*
	William Wright, elected and resigned	*Victoria East.*
1856	Charles Slater	*Graham's Town.*
1857	Charles Henry Caldecott	*Cradock.*
1859	Samuel Cawood	} *Albany.*
	Charles Slater	
	Charles Scanlan	} *Cradock.*
	Charles Henry Caldecott, resigned	
	Robert John Painter	} *Fort Beaufort.*
	William Stanton, incapacitated	
	Robert Mitford Bowker	*Somerset East.*
	Thomas Holden Bowker	*Victoria East.*
1860	Joshua Cawood	*Port Elizabeth.*
1864	John Edwin Wood, resigned	} *Albany.*
	William Miles Bowker	
	Charles Scanlan	*Cradock.*
	George Samuel Wood	*Graham's Town.*
	John Centlivres Chase	*Port Elizabeth.*
	Richard John Painter, resigned	} *Somerset East.*
	Robert Mitford Bowker	
	Jonathan Ayliff, resigned	*Victoria East.*
1865	Reuben Ayliff	*Uitenhage.*
1866	George Slater	*Albany.*
1867	Joseph Gush	*Victoria East.*
1869	George Slater	} *Albany.*
	Joseph Gush	
	William Ayliff	*Fort Beaufort.*
	Reuben Ayliff	*Uitenhage.*
	William Stanton	*Victoria East.*
1870	Thomas Charles Scanlan	*Cradock.*
	Robert Mitford Bowker	*Somerset East.*
	Reuben Ayliff	*Uitenhage.*
1872	Responsible Government Bill passed.	

APPENDIX II
EARL BATHURST'S DESPATCH, No. 280

Names of the persons under whose direction the Settlers proceed.	Number of families composing party.	Their present residence.	General Remarks.
England.			
Bailie, John	101	London	Is accompanied by a physician and two surgeons.
Biggar, Alexander . . .	12	Hampshire	
Bowker, Miles	10	Wiltshire	
Bradshaw, Samuel . . .	12	Gloucestershire	
Campbell, Captain Duncan	13	Hampshire	
Carlisle, John	11	Staffordshire	
Clarke, William	31	London	Mr. Clarke is a surgeon.
Colling, Thomas	101	London	
Colston, John	12	Somerset	
Crause, Lieutenant R.M. .	12	Kent	
Dalgairns, C.	11	London	
Damant, Edward	25	Norfolk	Is accompanied by a surgeon.
Dixon, John Henry . . .	11	London	
Dyason, George	20	London	
Erith	10	Surrey	
Ford, Edward	10	Wiltshire	
Gardiner, Edward . . .	16	Warwickshire	
Greathead, James Henry .	11	Worcestershire	
Gurney, Charles	13	Kent	
Hawkins, John	40	Oxfordshire	
Hayhurst, Richard Whitby and Michael	32	Lancashire	
Holder, William	11	Gloucestershire	
Howard, William	15	Buckinghamshire	
Hyman, Charles	11	Wiltshire	
James, Samuel	20	Wiltshire	
Liversage, Samuel . . .	17	Staffordshire	
Mahoney, Thomas . . .	16	London	
Mandy, John	11	Surrey	
Menezes, William	12	Kent	

Names of the persons under whose direction the Settlers proceed.	Number of persons composing party.	Their present residence.	General Remarks.
England (*continued*).			
Mills, Daniel	10	London	
Morgan, Nathanael . . .	12	London	Mr. Morgan is a surgeon.
Mouncey, Charles. . . .	12	Yorkshire	
Neave, J.	12	Lancashire	
Osler, Benjamin	11	Cornwall	
Owen	11	London	
Parkin, John	11	Devonshire	
Pigot, George	20	Berkshire	
Richardson, James . . .	11	Yorkshire	
Rowles, Thomas	10	London	
Scott, George	14	Surrey	Is accompanied by a surgeon.
Smith, George	21	Lancashire	
Smith, William	11	London	
Southey, George	27	Somersetshire	
Stanley, John	11	Lancashire	
Turvey, Edward	14	London	
Wainright, J.	11	Yorkshire	
Wait, William	54	Middlesex	
White, T..	12	Nottinghamshire	
Willson, Thomas	102	London	Is accompanied by two surgeons.
Wales.			
Griffith, Valentine	22	Montgomeryshire	Is accompanied by a surgeon.
Philipps, Thomas	20	Pembrokeshire	Is accompanied by a surgeon.
Scotland.			
Grant, Captain	400	Highlands	Is accompanied by a Minister of the Church of Scotland and by an adequate number of surgeons
Pringle, Thomas	12		
Ireland.			
Butler	12	Wicklow	
Ingram	27	Cork	
Parker.	124	Cork	Is accompanied by a clergyman of Church of England, by a physician, and by an apothecary.
Synnot	11	Wicklow	

APPENDIX III
LIST OF THE SETTLERS OF 1820

WITH the Ships by which they came out, the Heads of each "Party" into which they were divided, and the names of each Settler and their Wives, and the Children who Landed with them, with the ages of each in 1820. Copied from the original in the Archives of the Colonial Government. This List does not correspond with the Alphabetical List also in the Archives, many names being omitted on both.

PER SHIP "NAUTILUS"

Left Gravesend December 3, 1819, arrived in Table Bay March 17, Algoa Bay April 9, 1820.

SETTLER.		WIFE.		CHILDREN.	
G. Scott's Party, Surrey.					
Scott, George, Director					
Ubsdell, George	23	Betsy	23	William	7
				Mary	6
				Eliza	2
Younger, John, Dr.	26			Thomas	16
				Charles	14
Hughes, Charles	28				
Bolus, Thomas	26				
Martin, William	29	Esther	28	Mary	½
Ranson, William	28	Isabella	25	William	5
				Mary	4
Shone, Thomas	31	Sarah	25	George	7
				Thomas	4
				Sarah	1
Webster, William	21	Elizabeth	20	William C.	10
Griffin, Edward	21	Ann	23	Ellen	1½
Clarke, William	30	Mary	25		
Biles, John	32	Charlotte	30	Charlotte	1
Davis, Thomas	28	Mary	24		
Gregory, Joseph	19				

SETTLER.		WIFE.		CHILDREN.	
(No name) . . .	35	Emily . . .	26	Major . .	9
				Edward . .	7
				Charles . .	6
				Emily . .	3
				Henry . .	1
Crause, John . . .	26	Amelia . .	25		
Attwell, Richard . .	48	Ann . . .	47	Edwin . .	16
				Sarah . .	13
				James . .	11
				Brooke . .	9
Phillips, Thomas . .	35	Alice . . .	35	Robert . .	10
				Alice Ann . .	8
				Thomas . .	6
				Maria . .	4
				George . .	1
Mellett, Samuel . .	40	Margaret . .	38	Rebecca . .	13
				John . . .	9
				Samuel . .	6
Attwell, William . .	22				
Martinson, George . .	37	Sarah . . .	38	Louisa . .	13
				Charles . .	11
Dredge, William . .	29	Elizabeth . .	25	Samuel . .	
				Susanna . .	3
				Mary . .	2
Attwell, Richard L. . .	19				
Spiller, Charles James .	28	Catherine . .	27	Mary . .	5
Morecroft, James . .	26	Sarah . .	28	George . .	6
				James . .	1
Owen's Party, London.					
Owen, Thomas, Director .	38	Elizabeth . .	35	Thomas . .	5
Owen, Samuel William .	40	Judy Ann . .	35	Margaret . .	13
				Mary . . .	12
				Elizabeth . .	6
				Ellen . .	4
				Frederick John .	2
				Infant 19 days	
Brown, James . . .	22				
Pullen, Thomas . .	43	Dorothy . .	36	Dorothy . .	20
				Adelaide . .	18
Mr. William Metilerkamp, of		Zumburg, ob.	Cuton	Augusta, ob. Oct., 1894	16
Park in 1876				Thomas . .	15
				Edward . .	14
				Tindall . .	12

SETTLER.		WIFE.		CHILDREN.	
				Julia .	10
				William .	8
				Ellen .	7
				Harriet .	5
				Charles .	2
				Lavinia .	1
Ann Dyke, 36, in family of		Thomas Pullen.			
Stanley, William . .	20				
Stanley, Francis . .	42	Mary Ann . .	41	Mary Ann . .	15
				Francis . .	13
				Joseph . .	11
				Nathanael . .	9
				John . .	2
Whiley, William . .	31	Deborah . .	31	Mary Ann . .	11
				Caroline . .	10
				Emma . .	8
				William . .	6
				George . .	4
				Edwin . .	2
				James . .	1
Cole, William . . .	22				
Kolbe, George A. . .	20	Margaret . .	19		
Wall, Allen William	47	Mary . . .	36	John . . .	13
Church, Henry . .	25	Elizabeth . .	21		
Knowles' Party.					
Knowles, Thomas . .	32	Elizabeth . .	30	Augusta . .	10
				Edward . .	8
				Frederick Pegler	6
				Stephen . .	4
				Eben. Phil. .	2
				Solo. E. . .	1
Blackbeard, Francis .	27	Elizabeth .	27	G. Francis .	3
				Robert . .	1
Whiting, Thomas . .	27				
Surmon, William Henry .	23	Louisa H. . .	23	William Henry .	1
Crane, John . . .	23				
Hawkes, Frederick . .	21				
Chipperfield, J. . .	20				
Cooper, J. H. . . .	28				
Wilson, John . . .	33	Hannah . .	30	Joseph . .	6
Smith, John . . .	40	Mary Ann . .	33	Alfred . .	3
				Eliza . . .	$1\frac{1}{2}$

SETTLER.		WIFE.		CHILDREN.	
Mandy's Party, Surrey.					
Fagan, Peter	39	Mary	38	Richard	13
				Thomas	12
				Mary	11
				Elizabeth	9
				Frances	7
				Jane	6
				Peter	5
				William	3
				Ann	3
Mandy, John, Director	31	Mary Ann	29	John	6
				Stephen	5
Gower, Richard	30	Mary	28	Edwin	7
				Frederick	2
				Mary	1
Mandy, Joseph, Coachmaker	23				
Fitzgerald, Michael	30	Sarah	29		
Fitzgerald, James	35	Margaret	22		
Williamson, Thomas	28	Sarah	30		
Smith, Portius	29	Mary	27	Sarah	7
				Thomas	4
				Sophia	2
Hunt, Richard	26	Ann	24	George	6
				Mary	1
White, Edward	24	Jane	25	Edward	4
				Richard	1
Miller, William	29	Sophia	26	Emma	2
				Mary	22
Miller, Thomas	29	Mary Ann	25	Sarah	7
				Thomas	4
				Sophia	2
				Mary Ann	1

APPENDIX III

PER "CHAPMAN"

Landed April 20; arrived at Table Bay 17th March, 1820; 18th April, 1820, the first to go from P. E.; in 96 wagons, arrived at Cuylerville on 28th, 7 miles from Kafir's Drift, 40 miles from Graham's Town.

SETTLER.		WIFE.		CHILDREN.	
Carlisle's Party, Staffordshire.					
Carlisle, John, Director	22				
Chadwick, Samuel	20				
Chadwick, William	18				
Chadwick, James	18				
Hayes, Samuel	—			Samson	13
				Samuel	8
Bassett, Benjamin	39				
Bellfield, George	18				
Wheeldon, Samuel	18				
Rowe, William	22				
Carlisle, George		Hannah		Mary	—
Carlisle, Frederick	—			Rupert C.	13
Bailie's Party, London.					
Goodes, John	25	Anna	24	Sarah	3
				Charlotte	1
Goodes, Joseph	29	Ann	28	Mary Ann	3
				Elizabeth	2
Flanegan, Tim	38	Mary	40	James Frederick	10
				Arthur S.	7
Burnett, Bishop				Mary Ann	15
				Elizabeth	3
King, Richard	27				
Plewman, Thomas	23				
Plewman, Michael	40	Isabella	37		
Biddulph, Simon	50	Ann	48	Louisa	24
				William	14
				Francis	12
Biddulph, James Henry	20				
Biddulph, John Burnet	22				
Gunning, Barthol.	42	Mary	32		
Adams, Thomas P.	39	Mary	30	Mary	4
				Frances	1
Leeder, James	28	Ann	30	Ann	3
				James	1

K

130 BRITISH SOUTH AFRICA

SETTLER.		WIFE.		CHILDREN.	
Hoole, James	31	Jane	32	James	8
				Abel	4
				Jane	1
Godlonton, Robert	25	Mary Ann	—	Mary Ann	—
Forbes, William	27	Mary Ann	27	Alexander Wm.	17
				Mary Ann	4
Stringfellow, Thomas	30	Ann	30	Ann	5
				Mary	3
				Sarah	1
Vokins, Henry	38	Lucy	36	Mary Ann	17
Ball, William	31				
Lawler, John	32	Anne	30	Mary Ann	—
McNamara, Mary	28				
Matthew, Augustus Thomas	19				
Bellmore, Henry	29	Ann	28		
Duffy, John	42	Ann	44	Charles	10
				George	4
Cox, John Edward	25				
Barton, George	21				
Rose, John	27				
Hockley, Daniel	32	Elizabeth	29	Daniel	6
				Elizabeth	4
				Harriet	3
				Frances	—
Griffin, Thomas	34	Sarah	31	Thomas	8
				Joseph	3
				James	2
				Sarah	9
				Elizabeth	6
				Harriet	4
				Margaret	—
Gray, William	19				
Cowper, William D.	21				James	10
Low, James	20				
Low, William	19				
Franz, Christopher	29	Ann	25	Helen	—
				Ann	1
Bowles, John	29	Sarah	27	John	1
				Amelia	2
Garland, Joseph	44				
Hobbs, William	31				
Mills, Thomas	21				
Blair, William	47	Jane	50		

APPENDIX III

SETTLER.		WIFE.		CHILDREN.	
Reed, William . . .	45	Elizabeth . .	37	Charles . .	11
				Louisa . .	9
				James . .	7
				George . .	1
Reed, William, jun. . .	22	Eliza . . .	20		
Reed, Henry . . .	18				
Mead, Thomas .	20				
Adams, Matthew . .	20				
Walker, John, Dr. .	21				
Thompson, John . .	26	Mary . .	29	John . . .	6
				James . .	—
Oldham, Thomas . .	27				
Oldham, Edwin . .	21				
Taylor, Richard . .	30				
Oldham, Joseph . .	33	Dorcas .	30	Harriet . .	12
				Mary Ann . .	7
				Lucretia . .	3
				Joseph . .	1
Heath, John Hy., Solicitor	26	Maria . .	23	John Henry .	2
Bayne, Alexander . .	36	Elizabeth . .	33	Rhoda . .	11
				Jane . . .	5
				Robert . .	4
				Alexander . .	2
Roberts, Dr. Edw. . .	27				
Anderson, George . .	48	Isabella . .	45	Benjamin . .	14
				Isabella . .	8
Anderson, Robert . .	26				
Anderson, George, jun. .	24				
Anderson, William . .	21				
Harrison, William . .	30	Ann . . .	30	George . .	2
				Mary . .	—
Harden, William . .	25	Maria . .	25	Jane . . .	4
				Maria . .	2
Seymour, William . .	32	Sarah . .	29		
Saunders, John . .	22				
King, George . .	31				
Hewson, Thomas William	42	Elizabeth . .	38	Isabella . .	14
				Eliza . . .	11
				Frederick Wm. .	8
				Emma . .	3
Wade, William . .	20				
Heyell, Thomas . .	19				
Hewson, Ed. Benjamin .	19				

SETTLER.		WIFE.		CHILDREN.	
Wakeford, Thomas .	34	Mary . .	36	Thomas . .	13
				William . .	12
Futter, George .	38	Sarah .	35	George . .	9
				John . . .	7
				Sarah . .	5
				Elizabeth . .	2
Tucker, Henry .	31				
Lloyd, Henry J. .	28	Rebecca .	26	Henry T. . .	6
				William R. .	4
				Charles . .	1
Somerville, James .	29				
Whittall, Francis .	22				
Lecet, John . .	39				
Crause, Captain C., Director	29	Mary Emma .	27	Charles . .	6
		Helen (sister) .	25		
		Arabella „ .	21		
Chase, John Centlivres .	24	Arabella .	30	Louisa. Died Bay Biscay .	1
Marillier, Philip Richard .	27				
Ford, James Ed. .	50	Frances .	40	Frances Jane .	14
				James Samuel .	13
				George Henry .	11
				Edward Samuel	9
				John H. . .	3
Shortman, James .	19				
Bailie, John . .	31	Amelia .	28	Charles T. .	10
				Arch. H. . .	8
				Thomas C. .	6
				John A. . .	4
Bovey, Robert .	27				
Divine, Tim .	33	Eleanor .	30	John . . .	11
				Bridget . .	6
				Jeremiah . .	4
				Catherine . .	2
Leonard, John. .	29	Elizabeth .	25	Mary Ann . .	3
				Elizabeth . .	2
Hart, William . .	46			Eliza . .	19
				Henry G. . .	10
O'Flynn, Dr. Daniel .	27	Margaret. Died Dec. 23, 1854 .	28		

APPENDIX III

PER "NORTHAMPTON"
Arrived at Table Bay, 26th March, 1820

SETTLER.		WIFE.		CHILDREN.	
Pigot's Party, Berkshire.					
Pigot, George	45			Catherine	17
Grabb, C.	22			Sophia	15
Webb, William	19				
Tombs, John	20				
Gunter, Thomas	19				
Innis, William	20				
Povey, John	40	Mary	30	John	16
Quince, John	25	Jane	20		
Comley, William	26	Ann	24	Mary	2
Heath, Thomas	34			William	17
Marshall, Charles	23	Charlotte	23	Charles	6
				John	3
				Thomas	2
Alder, William	26	Mary	24		
Goddard, James	39	Fanny	35	Benjamin	15
				Ann	10
				Mary	6
				Betsy	4
				John	1
Hiscock, James	23	Sarah	22		
Boucher, John	20			Philip	14
Brooks, Henry	30	Mary	25	Caroline	4
				William	3
				Ellen	1
Pratt, George	35	Hannah	20	John	15
Saltmarsh, Charles	20				
Hutton, T.	22				
Gibbs, William	31	Rachel	29	Charles	14
				William	12
				Henry	10
				Thomas	7
				Mary	2
Mahoney's Party, London.					
Mahoney, Thos., Director	35	Ann	36	Eliza	14
				Daniel	13
Hambley, George	36	Sarah	36	Sarah	16
				Eliza	14
				Jemima	11
				George	9
				Frederick	5

SETTLER.		WIFE.		CHILDREN.	
Bateman, Jeremiah	32				
Jusan, William	25				
Tomlin, George	29	Harriott	25		
Jeffries, Samuel	35	Mary	30		
Sheanan, Edward	23	Ellen	24		
Holland, Dennis	40	Mary	35	Mary	17
				John	16
				Daniel	13
				Allen	7
Lamb, Cornelius	30	Margaret	23	Thomas	1
Carty, Florence	27				
Freemantle, Richard	38	Sarah	31	John	13
				Eliza	4
				George	1
Cornday, Andrew	35	Ann	30	Eliza	9
				Michael	6
Holland, D., jun.	18				
McFarlane, James	40				
McFarlane, J., jun.	18				
Patten, Alexander	37	Jane	34		
Clarke's Party, London.					
Clarke, Dr. William	25	Catherine Eliza	27	C. Holliday	14
Marshall, Henry	28	Mary	24	Henry	3
				Mary Ann	1½
Taylor, John	38	Mary	40	John Watson	8
Fell, John	37	Jane	39	Jane J.	11
				John W.	9
Hough, John	39	Elizabeth	40		
Wentworth, William	35	Frances M.	24	William	13
Harvey, Richard	40	Sarah	36	Sarah	13
				Elizabeth	11
				Mary Ann	9
				Job	4
				Ruth	2⅔
				John	.7 months
Stubbs, John	35	Ann	34	Elizabeth	13
				John	12
				Thomas	10
				William	6
				Ellen	3
				Richard	1

SETTLER.		WIFE.		CHILDREN.	
Brown, John	28	Ann	25	Elizabeth	4
		Charlotte	23	Ann	2
Blackmore, George	33	Sarah	34	Mary Ann	9
				Elizabeth	5
				Harriet	1
Durham, William	31	Sarah	32	George	3
				Lydia	2
Davis, David	40			Eliza	13
				David	8
Box, John	29				
Marshall, John	40	Mary	24	Mary Ann	1½
White, Richard	40				
White, John	18				
Saunders, John	36	Ann	33	John Thomas	4
Fancutt, Thomas	28	Ann	32	Louisa	11
				Thomas	9
Warner, Ebenezer	28	Louisa	28	Thomas	10
				William	4
Mainman, Thomas	25				
Harrison, William	34				
Honey, Jeremiah	36	Ann	30	Sarah	10
				Elizabeth	8
				Ann Webb	5
				*Cordelia	3
				Harriet	2
				†Frances	
Desert, James	30				
Evans, James	32	Mary	30		
Thom, George	28				
Charsley, Edward	18				
Pannymore, Thomas	18				
Fulton, Thomas	18				
Goulden, John	18				
Williams, Isaac	18				
Dawson, James	18				
Robertshaw, William	18				

Wm. Smith's Party, London.

Smith, William, Director	26	Anna	24	John	13
Cornfield, John	21	‡Eliza Cornfield	27	Richard Bland	13

* Died at sea Feb. 20.   † Born at sea, March 16.
‡ Born at sea, Feb. 24.

SETTLER.		WIFE.		CHILDREN.	
Hobson, David	22				
Hobson, Carey	12				
Warmington, A.	19				
Edkins, John	28	Ann	29	John	7
				Thomas	—
				Joseph, 1 month	
				Eliza } twins,	
				Sarah } 7 months	
Bagot, Captain Robt. Wood	35	Letitia	35	Harriott	17
				R. O'Conner	16
				Edward	.8 months
Rooke, James	25	Sarah	28	Henry	3½
				Rhoda	2
Picket, William	27	Maria	27	William	7
				Ann	5
				Phillip	1
				Rebecca	1
Scott, John	20				
Thackwray, William	40	Dorothy	43	Dorothy	15
				Ann	13
				William	11
				Joseph	9
				James	4
Thackwray, John	18				
Dalgairn's Party, London.					
Dalgairn, Charles, Director	42			Agnes	14
				Eliza	11
				Magdalene	8
Blackmore, John	28	Mary	26	Elizabeth	2
Williams, William	40	Mary	36	Mary	4
				*James	1
Eatwell, William	33	Emma	30		
Hill, Richard	32	Sophia	30		
Bailey, William	21				
Tharratt, Thomas	39	Ann	34	John	6
				Tobias	5
Denham, Stephen	26	Martha	26	Mary	2
				Martha	.6 months
Stephenson, Frederick	20				
Haw, Simon	37	Margaret	27	Charles	1

* Died at sea, Jan. 6.

PER "OCEAN"
Arrived at Table Bay, 29th March, 1820

SETTLER.		WIFE.		CHILDREN.	
Adcock, Christopher	35	Elizabeth	29	William	7
				George	4
				Edward	2
Damant's Party, Norfolk.					
Damant, Edward, Director	33	Mary	27	Ann	13
				Eliza	2
Atherstone, Dr. John	29	Elizabeth	37	Guybon	5
				Catherine	4
				Elizabeth	3
				Emily	2
Damant, John	34				
Frost, Philip	32	Elizabeth	30	Philip	11
				James	10
				William	7
				Edward	6
				John	4
				Mary	1½
Smith, Stephen	27	Ann	27	Henry	5
				*Harriet	1
Tee, Richard	34	Mary	30	Richard	8
				Mary	7
				Charlotte	5
				Elizabeth	2
Hames, Joseph	20				
Durell, Henry	27				
Atherstone, Thomas	26				
Thompson, William	21				
White, William	28				
Lawson, Philip	22				
Jeley, William	26				
Cooper, John	27				
Stirley, Thomas	54	Ann	44	Thomas	17
				John	15
				Mary	12
				Lydia	8
				Maria	6
				William	3
				James	1
Wells, John	20				

* Died at sea, 5th Feb., 1820.

SETTLER.		WIFE.		CHILDREN.	
Purvis, Henry . .	32				
Stirley, Thomas .	19				
Gibbon, Edward .	21				
Francis, John . .	24				
Jacobs, John . .	21	Catherine .	20		
Matthew, Jno. . .	22				
Luke, John . .	19				
*Price, John . .	25				
Males, Thomas .	18				
Dixon's Party, London.					
Dixon, Jno. Hy., Director	32	Margaret .	36	Mary .	9
				Emma .	6
				Eliza .	4
				Sarah .	2
Webb, Richard .	29	Elizabeth .	22	Edward .	2
				Richard .	3
Henman, Robert .	34	Mary Ann .	36	Mary Ann .	7
				Elizabeth .	2
Fuller, Henry .	25	Susannah .	23	George .	4
				Charles .	1½
Vice, John . .	30	Elizabeth .	28	Elizabeth .	2
				Ann .	3
Carney, James . .	28	Elizabeth .	29	Elizabeth .	3
Vice, James . .	24	Sophia .	30	John .	8
				James .	3
				†Sarah Eliza (Henman)	
				‡ Samuel (Vyce) .	
Daniel, Joseph .	36	Elizabeth .	35	Richard .	7
Paxton, Jesse . .	39	Sarah .	39	William .	13
				Charles .	11
				George .	7
				Henry .	5
				Elizabeth .	4
				David .	2
Marsden, George .	40	Elizabeth .	34	Elizabeth .	8
Wyatt, John . .	31	Jane .	34	§ Jane .	7
				Amelia .	4
				Ann Mary .	3
				‖ John .	2

* Died at sea, 14th Feb., 1820.   † Born at sea, 17th March, 1820.
‡ Born at sea, 19th Feb., 1820.   § Died at sea, 3rd Feb., 1820.
‖ Died at sea, 5th Feb., 1820.

APPENDIX III

SETTLER.		WIFE.		CHILDREN.	
Morgan's Party, London.					
Morgan, Dr. N., Director	27	Mary	22		
Halse, Thomas Henry	27	Susan	20	Henry	2½
				William	6 months
Philips, George	29	Ann	26	George	3
				James	1
Thomas, James	26	Martha	21	Harriet	8 months
Thomas, William	29	Elizabeth	30	Elizabeth	6
				Rebecca	5
				William	3
				Jane	1
Gadsden, Robert	24	Sophia M.	19	James V.	6 months
Poultney, James	28	Ann	21	Ann	4 months
Kestall, Charles	32	Grace	28	John	10
				Eliza	8
				Susannah	5
				Charles	1
Allen, Robert	30	Susan	28		
Telke, Joel	28	Sarah	31	Elizabeth	7 months
Floodgate, Edward	28	Mary	28		
Jinks, Joseph	37	Sarah	21	Mary Smith	13
Howard's Party, Bucks.					
Howard, William, Director	42	Elizabeth	39	John Henry	17
				William	15
				Mary Ann	14
				Thomas	10
				Emily	1
Bainbridge, Thomas	39	Elizabeth	38	Elizabeth	13
				Jane	12
Tarr, William	32	Susannah	35	John	9
				Maria	3
				Sarah	2
Harper, Henry	30	Mary	37	James	14
				James B.	12
				George B.	8
				Elizabeth	6
Wellan, Giles	38	Rachel	29	Alice	6
				Elizabeth	1
				* Sarah	
Felton, George Henry	19				

* Born at sea, 28th Feb., 1820.

SETTLER.		WIFE.		CHILDREN.	
Vaughan, John	19				
Niland, John	29	Catherine	25		
Poulton, John	42	Ann	35	Ann	13
				John	11
				Mary	10
				Samuel	9
				Eliza	8
				Sarah	6
				Charles	5
				Charlotte	3
				Ruth	1
Heath, George	23				
Cadle, John	24	Sarah	28	Mary	8
				Elizabeth	3
				William	1
				John	3 months
Mehrtens, Sicba	25	Ann	24		
Hanger, Edward	30	Harriet Sophia	26	Caroline	6
Healey, Edward	34	Mary	28		
Watts, James	32			Edward George	12
				George	10

PER "HENNERSLEY CASTLE"

Arrived at Table Bay, 29th March, 1820

SETTLER.		WIFE.		CHILDREN.	
Phillips' Party, Pembrokeshire.					
Phillips, Thos., Director	44	Charlotte	41	Edward	16
				Catherine	14
				Charlotte	13
				Sophia	12
				Frederick	10
				Emma	6
				John	4
		Ann John	25	} Servants	
		Mary Owen	20		
		M. Thomas	18		

APPENDIX III

SETTLER.		WIFE.		CHILDREN.	
Currie, Dr. Robert, Surgeon	25				
Rhenish, John	30	Catherine	30	William	11
Davis, John	38			William	13
Jones, John	21				
Gittins, John	23				
Butler, Richard	19				
Phillip, William	21				
James, Benjamin	21				
Davis, John	23				
James, John	21				
Davis, William	21	Mary	25		
Matthias, Thomas	22				
Pugh, David	23				
James, David	18				
Mack, John	19				
Owen, Robert	23				
Whareham, Samuel	18				
Esmond, William	18				
Southey's Party, Somersetshire.					
Southey, George, Director	39	Jane	38	Sophia	16
Skinner, Elizabeth (servant)				William	13
				Richard	11
				George	9
				Elizabeth	7
				Henry	4
				Cannon	1
Parsons, James	26				
Glass, Thomas	35	Ann	33	Elizabeth	15
				John	13
				Daniel	9
				Thomas	6
				James	4
				Ann	1
Berry, Thomas	21				
Style, Thomas	40	Mary	36	Ann	13
				Hannah	10
				Sarah	8
				James	6
				Elizabeth	4
				William	2
Hutchings, James	19				

SETTLER.		WIFE.		CHILDREN.	
Berry, William. . .	27	Mary . . .	30	Elizabeth . .	4
Thomas, James . .	38	Mary . . .	34	Jane . . .	10
				Humphrey .	6
				Ann . . .	4
				Thomas . .	2
				Isaiah . .	2
Thomas, E. (spinster) .	18			Arabella . .	1¼
Ingram, Thomas . .	27				
Stack, William . . .	26				
Biggs, John . . .	42			William . .	13
Biggs, John, jun. . .	19				
Bradshaw's Party, Gloucestershire.					
Bradshaw, Sam., Director	34				
Brent, Thomas. . .	36	Grace . . .	27	Thomas . .	6
				Sarah . .	3
				John . . .	2
				James . .	1
Baker, Thomas. . .	38	Esther . .	25	Elizabeth . .	13
				Hannah . .	12
				Thomas . .	11
				Sarah . .	10
				Ann . . .	8
				Rachel . .	2
				Enoch . .	1
King, Joseph . . .	37	Ann . . .	25	Joseph . .	11
				Philip . .	8
				Charles . .	6
				Anna . . .	3
King, Henry . . .	32	Sarah . . .	26	Samuel . .	5
				Anna . . .	3
				Rhoda . .	1½
				George . .	1
King, Philip . . .	30	Maria . . .	30	Richard . .	8
				Andrew . .	5
				Elizabeth . .	3
				John . . .	1
King, Edward . . .	18	Sarah (spinster) .	17		
King, Henry . . .	28				
Alfred (bro.) .	10				
Wiggell, Isaac . . .	30	Elizabeth . .	31	Eli . . .	9
				George . .	7

APPENDIX III

SETTLER.		WIFE.		CHILDREN.	
				Joseph	3
				Elizabeth	1
Willcocks, John	25	Sarah	20		
Bennett, Samuel	36	Ann	40	Ann	5
				Elizabeth	3
Cook, John	22				
Newth, William	40	Sarah	30	William	13
				Benjamin	3
				Thomas	2
				Elizabeth	1
Carter, Robert	36	Elizabeth	36	Thomas	13
				John	12
Greathead's Party, Worcestershire.					
Greathead, Jas., Director	24	Martha	20	John H.	1 month
Greathead, William	20				
Laco, John	24				
Bate, William	20				
Davies, Josiah	33	Sophia	24	Daniel	3
				Sarah (born on board)	
Brown, William	22				
Collins, William	25				
Wilks, Samuel	25				
Simmons, W.	37				
Hartell, John	44	Mary	38	John	13
				Emma	8
Holder's Party, Gloucester.					
Holder, William, Director	30	Sophia	25	Sophia	3
				Eliza	2
Webb, John	34	Sarah	30	Eliza	7
				Frederick Jas.	5
				Henry, James	3
				Sarah	1½
Powell, James	32	Sarah	32	Priscilla	9
				Sarah	5
				Philip	3
				F. James	1¾
Hancock, John	23				
Hiles, Fred.	38	Mary	35	William	11
				George	9
				Ann	6

SETTLER.		WIFE.		CHILDREN.	
Roberts, William . . 25		Maria. . . 24		John . . . 3 William . 4	
Guest, John . . . 34		Ann . . . 40		John . . . 9 William . 7	
Kidwell, Alexander . . 38		Sarah . . . 32			
Woods, Samuel . . 17					
Shepstone, John . . 24		Elizabeth . . 25		Theophilus . 3	
Tainton, Richard . . 24		Ann . . . 22			
Currier, William . . 24					

PER "AMPHITRITE"
Arrived at Table Bay, 29th March, 1820

SETTLER.	WIFE.	CHILDREN.
Nightingale's Party.		
Nightingale, Dr.T., Director 37		
Matthews, Francis . . 38	Elinore . . 26	
Lettersted, Jacob . . 22		
Sedgwick, John . . 21		
Haynes, Robert . . 31		
Black, William . . . 32	Elizabeth . . 22	Elizabeth . . 1
Greenleaf, James . . 29		
Wood, Joseph . . . 20		
Thomas, David . . 27		
Leach, Charles . . . 59	(drowned)	
Bowyer, Thomas . . 40	(absent)	
Bishop, William Kant . 20		
Eagar, Edw. . . . 20		
Thornelow, William . . 20		
Anson, John . . . 45	Elizabeth . . 45	Henry . . 13
		Elizabeth . . 13
		Ambrose . . 12
		Hannah . . 10
		Sarah . . 8
Anson, John, jun. . . 21		
Bridge, John . . . 36	Ann . . . 43	Mary Ann . . 16
		Henry . . 13
		Eliza . . . 12
		Ann . . . 8
Gammon, Charles . . 19		
Barnard, David . . 20		
Brest, Henry . . . 54	J. M. . . 46	

APPENDIX III

SETTLER.		WIFE.		CHILDREN.	
Wilkinson's Party.					
Wilkinson, J. M., Director	28				
Wilkinson, George	20				
Gaugain, Philip	31				
Satchwell, Richard	21				
Smith, James	37	Mary Ann	26	Sophia	8
				James	3
				Sarah	2
Humphreys, Robert	18				
Cleaver, John	28				
Cleaver, Joseph	24				
Harris, James	26				
Placey, Charles	29				
Neale, James	25				
Oakes, John	21				
Welsh, Michael	25				
Fletcher, Edward	29				
Donnelly, John	14				
French, John	14				
Jenkins, James	28				
Jenkins, Charles	24				
Jenkins, Joseph	20				
Cannon, Philip	26				
Tucker, George	25				

PER "JOHN"

Arrived at Table Bay, 19th April, 1820

SETTLER.		WIFE.		CHILDREN.	
Hazelhurst's Party, Lancashire.					
Hazelhurst, Richard, Dir.	51	Ellen	—	Sarah	17
				Maria	15
				Jane	12
				John	9
Stirzaker, Henry	40				
Counsel, Andrew	40				
Walker, John	31				
Murray, James	40	Mary	39		
Tudor, Charles	29	Bridget	28	Annie	12
				Mary	7

L

SETTLER.		WIFE.		CHILDREN.	
Watson, George	33	Jane	31	Margaret	5
				Edward	1½
				Deborah	6
				William	¾
Bold, John	46	Hannah	46	Mary	23
				Grace	21
				Joshua	16
				Martha	11
				Caleb	9
Bold, Peter	18	M. Hudson	27	James	7
				Sarah	6
				Richard	1½
				Elizabeth	1½
Sharples, Henry	21				
Derbyshire, Thomas	24				
Bisset, John	40	Ann	35		
Kelbrick, Robert	21				
Foxcroft, Robert	38	Ann	40	Margaret	20
				Thomas	13
				James	11
				Robert	9
				William	7
				John	3
Peel, Thomas	24	Mary	21		
Kidd, Thomas Jenkins	32				
Gradwell, William	21				
Gradwell, Stephen	20				
Cawood, David	43	Mary	33	Joshua	16
				Elizabeth	13
				Mary	12
				Samuel	10
				Sarah	5
				Joseph	9
Cawood, James	21				
Cawood, William	19				
Cawood, John	18				
Bradley, John	46	Mary	47	Mary	18
				Ann	7
Robinson, James	21				
Oxley, John	25				
Hartley, Benjamin	36	Elizabeth	31	Helen H.	13
				Margaret	12

APPENDIX III 147

SETTLER.		WIFE.		CHILDREN.	
Griffiths, William	. 33	Ellen . .	. 33	Jane G. .	. 7
				Maria .	. 5
				Mary . .	. 2
				(an infant born)	
Halsthead, Richard .	. 36	Ellen . .	. 31	Thomas	9
				James .	. 4
				Nancy .	. 2
Clark, George . .	. 28	Elizabeth Mary .	22	George 10 months	
Buffry, Samuel .	. 38	Lucy . .	. 40		
Eccles, Robert	. 43				
Eccles, Thomas	. 31				
Kent, James . .	. 27	Ellen . .	. 22	Richard John .	½
Mouncey's Party, Yorks.					
Mouncey, Chas., Director.	40	Sarah . .	. 39	William	13
				James	10
Taylor, William .	. 39			Ann .	6
South, William . .	. 39	Lydia . .	40	Mary .	8
Hewson, Joseph .	21	Elizabeth .	. 20		
Guest, William . .	. 26			William .	8
Carlisle, George .	. 22	Hannah .	. 22	Mary . .	1½
Shillito, Samuel .	. 39	Isabella .	. 40	Samuel .	13
				Isabella .	10
				Henrietta .	8
				Mary . .	. 2
Carr, Thomas . .	. 35	Mary . .	. 34		
Carr, George . .	. 28				
Shillito, Thomas .	. 18				
Ogle, Henry . .	20				
Fox, William . .	. 34				
Stanley's Party, Lancashire.					
Stanley, John, Director .	37	Sarah . .	. 27		
Ashbrook, George .	. 27	Catherine .	. 24	Mary . .	. 6
				Eliza . .	. 4
				George .	. 2
Howard, Thomas .	. 24				
Calverley, William .	. 35	Jane . .	. 28	William .	14
				James .	5
				Eliza . .	2
Currie, James . .	. 28	Mary . .	. 28	Ann . .	. 3
				Margaret . 3 weeks	

SETTLER.		WIFE.		CHILDREN.	
Bowyer, Thomas . .	25				
Milton, Hugh . . .	21				
Brogden, John . . .	22				
Shepherd, Solomon . .	30	Elizabeth . .	24	Elizabeth . .	1
Wainwright's Party, Yorks.					
Wainwright, Jonathan, Dir.	48	Elizabeth . .	50	Ann . . .	20
				Ellen . . .	17
				Edward . .	14
Wainwright, Daniel . .	23				
Cockcroft, Charles . .	35	Harriet . .	36	Thomas . .	13
				William . .	9
				Mark . . .	7
Bentley, Francis P. . .	37	Elizabeth . .	31	William . .	9
				Susannah . .	8
				John . . .	4
				George . .	3
Stirk, William . . .	30				
Stirk, Joseph . . .	18				
Duffield, George . .	20				
Young, Thomas . .	36				
Braithwaite, William .	38				
Hartley, William . .	40				
Whitehead, George . .	25				
Liversage's Party, Staffordshire.					
Liversage, Sam., Director	30	Ann . . .	35	Elizabeth .	8
				Ann . .	6
				Catherine .	3
Hunt, William . . .	22				
Forrester, Richard . .	31	Mary . . .	30	Sarah . .	10
				John . . .	5
				Joseph . .	3
Mountford, William . .	33	Ann . . .	31	Thomas . .	8
				Mary . . .	7
				William . .	2
Venables, Daniel . .	40	Jane . . .	37	John . . .	15
				Sarah . .	13
				Elizabeth .	10
				Thomas . .	8
				Eliza . . .	5
Breeze, Charles . .	33				

APPENDIX III 149

SETTLER.		WIFE.		CHILDREN.	
Payne, Thomas . .	32	Sarah . .	33	Thomas .	10
				William . .	8
				James . .	6
				John . . .	2
Manley, Thomas . .	35	Margaret . .	30	Ralph . .	12
				John . . .	10
				William . .	2
Ford, William . . .	30	Harriet . .	27	George . .	5
				John . . .	3
				William . .	1
Robinson, Abraham .	25			Joseph . .	5
				Ann . . .	3
Scott, Joseph . . .	35			Mary . . .	7
				Thomas . .	6

PER "STENTOR"
Arrived at Table Bay, 19th April, 1820

SETTLER.		WIFE.		CHILDREN.	
Smith's Party, Lancashire.					
Smith, George, Director .	34	Mary . .	27		
(late of 95th Rifle Brigade).					
Walker, Richard . .	29	Martha . .	28	Joseph . .	2
				Elizabeth	3 months
Walker, Joseph . .	22				
Long, Jeremiah . .	40	Ann . .	33	James . .	13
				Jeremiah . .	11
Milton, John . . .	33	Ellen . .	39	Elizabeth . .	17
Warner, Henry . .	37	Elizabeth . .	34	Mary . . .	13
				Joseph . .	12
				Rosina . .	7
				Caroline . .	2
Hayes, Thomas . .	47				
Buckley, John . . .	27	Sarah . .	33	Hannah . .	8
				Jane . . .	6
				John . . .	4
				Alfred . .	2
				Edward	3 months
Bonsall, George . .	24	Sarah . .	21	Henry . .	2
				Ann . . .	1
Flinn, Daniel . . .	42	Catherine . .	42	Ann . . .	13
				John . . .	9

SETTLER.		WIFE.		CHILDREN.	
Elliott, William . .	23	Ellen .	22	Jane . . .	5
Wedderburn, Christopher	48	Ann .	.	William . .	20
				Ann . . .	
				George . .	
				Elizabeth .	
				Esther . .	5
Duxbury, Samuel . .	40	Margaret . .	39	William . .	15
				Hannah . .	5
				John . . .	3
Kirkman, John . . .	33	Mary . . .	31	Hannah .	11
				Albert . .	7
				Mary . . .	4
				Margaret . .	2
				Martha . .	1
Capper, Thomas . .	24	Mary . . .	30		
Forrest, Ralph . . .	26				
James, John . . .	26	Mary . . .	27		
Beardman, Thomas . .	47	Ann . . .	42	Maria .	13
				Ann . .	5
Holt, John .. .	38				
Manchester, John .	22				
Richardson's Party, Yorks.					
Richardson, James, Direc.	25	Sarah . . .	29	Elizabeth . .	12
				Martha . .	8
				James . .	8
				John . . .	4
				Emma . .	3
Hulley, Richard . .	34	Ann . . .	33	Richard . .	9
				Ann . . .	6
				Sarah . .	4
				Francis . .	1
Clayton, William . .	32	Judith . .	30	John . . .	7
				Ann . . .	5
				Elizabeth .	3
Clayton, George . .	29				
Denton, William . .	26	Mary . . .	26	William .	1
Denton, Charles . .	38	Hannah . .	39	Ann . .	13
Welch, Luke . . .	25	Mary . . .	30		
Kennedy, Jonathan .	24				
Mosley, Sophia . .	20				
Bradshaw, John . .	24				
Noon, Richard .	21				

APPENDIX III

SETTLER.		WIFE.		CHILDREN.	
Griffith's Party, Cardiganshire.					
Griffith, Val. } Directors	29	Mary } Sisters	25		
Griffith, Charles }	31	Cornelia }	22		
Griffith, Dr. John	24				
Griffith, Eliza (sister)	19				
Powell, Benjamin	25	Elizabeth	26	Eliza	5
				John	3
Hairbottle, Richard	32	Jane	28	Richard	8
				Ann	1
				William	3 months
Morris, William	30	Catherine	31	Ann	3
				William	2 months
Brown, David	32				
Williams, John	33	Sarah	26	Thomas	14
Jones, John	19				
Jones, Jenkins	20				
Jones, John	19				
Thompson, David	26				
Powell, William	22				
Forrest Eliu	22				
Lloyd, John	18				
Wright, Daniel	26				
Doe, Richard	28	Mary	19	Ann	
Noble, Mark	28				
Gardiner, J.	22				
Morton, William	24	Mary	19	Henry	2 months.
Diggery, Richard	28				
Williams, John	32			John	5
Neave's Party Lancashire.					
Neave, John, Director	30				
Huddleston, Richard	25	Sarah	26	Betsy	5
				John	2
Keegan, Jno.	32	Jane	23		
Knowles, Richard	35				
Downing, Thomas	21				
Fleetwood, John	20				
Geary, Richard	21				
Ramn, F. G.	22				
Simmons, James	20				
Tyler, James	32				
Quilham, Richard	35	Ann	30	Ann	12
Gregory, Thomas	24				

SETTLER.	WIFE.	CHILDREN.
White's Party, Notts.		
White, Lieut. Thos., Direc. 27		
Bespun, William . . 25		
Parr, John . . . 30	Ellen . . . 30	
Singleton, William . . 33	Mary . . . 40	Elizabeth . . 14
		John . . . 9
		Charlotte . . 6
Streets, William . . 21		
Smith, James . . . 18		
Oswell, John . . . 33	Mary . . . 35	Sarah . . 16
		John . . . 6
Whalton, Edward . . 30	Jane . . . 38	Joseph . . 15
		Mary . . . 13
		Elizabeth . . 10
		Rebecca . . 8
		Edward . . 3
Peach, George . . 20		
Noon, Richard . . 18		
Germaine, Richard . . 50		
Pearson, Jos. . . . 19		

PER "WEYMOUTH"

Arrived at Table Bay, 26th April, 1820

SETTLER.	WIFE.	CHILDREN.
Gurney's Party, Kent.		
Gurney, Charles, Director 42		Charles . . 7
Hubbard, Joseph . . 22		
Woodland, John . . 20		
Claringbould, Richard . 22		
Basden, James . . . 20		
Darby, John . . . 23		
Carter, John . . . 44		
Webster, George . . 27	Jane . . . 21	Thomas . . 12
		Robert . . 9
		George . . 3
Qeough, Patrick . . 25	Rebecca . . 25	Henry . 6 weeks
Cronk, John . . . 37	Ann . . . 37	Mary Ann . . 14
		John . . . 8
		Frances . 6

APPENDIX III

SETTLER.		WIFE.		CHILDREN.	
Bubb, George	21				
Terry, Mal.	18				
Watson, Richard	18				
Menezes' Party, Kent.					
Menezes, Wm., Director	29	Mary	25		
Green, John	39	Ann	30	Hannah	9
				Mary	7
				John	6
				James	5
				Thomas	3
				William	2
Oliver, John	27	Mary	24	Alexander	2
Cummings, Alexander	24	Elizabeth	26		
Hayward, George	21	Mary	17		
Hayward, William	22				
Bowles, Richard	35	Elizabeth	36	H. Amos	16
				E. Amos	13
				C. Amos	12
				E. Bowles	10
				R. Amos	9
				T. Amos	7
				S. Amos	6
				E. Amos	4
				J. Bowles	1
Eastland, Thomas	39	Sarah	—	George	13
				Thomas	11
				James	9
				Celia	6
				Elizabeth	3
				Jane	1
Sweetnam, Thomas	36	Jane	35	James	7
				Hannah	5
Hayward, James	25	Mary	24	Ruth	3
				William	1
Dickson, Richard	39				
Reed, James	29	Sarah	31	Joseph	8
				Emily	4
				Mary	1
Biggar's Party, Hants.					
Biggar, Alex. Henry, Dir.	39	Mary	39	Margaret	19
				Ann	18
				Mary	16
				Jane	14
				Georgina	12

SETTLER.			WIFE.			CHILDREN.		
						Agnes	.	10
						Charlotte	.	8
						Robert	.	7
						Alixiana	.	3
						Helen	.	1
Knowles, Richard	.	32	Mary	.	40	Sarah	.	19
Pollard, George	.	36	Ann	.	35	Mary Ann	.	7
						Thomas	.	6
						Jane	.	3
						George	.	1
Pedlar, Henry	.	30	Elizabeth	.	35	Mary Ann	.	7
						Henry	.	5
						Elizabeth	.	2
Bingle, Thomas	.	39	Sophia	.	27	Elizabeth	.	19
						Thomas	.	10
						Eleanor	.	8
Faircloth, George	.	33	Mary	.	32	James	.	9
						Elizabeth	.	4
Ellicott, James	.	27						
Godfrey, Robert	.	27	Martha	.	28	Henry	.	5
						Martha	.	1
Page, Thomas	.	25	Ann	.	33			
McDonald, James	.	31	Mary	.	23	Alexander	.	1
Cole, Robert	.	22	Jane	.	21	Robert	.	(infant)
Epsey, George	.	29	Mary	.	25			
Sanderson, George	.	31	Ann	.	28	Ann	.	9
						Margaret	.	7
						Caroline	.	5
Parkin's Party, Devon.								
Parkin, John, Director	.	32	Elizabeth	.	30	William	.	9
						John	.	6
						Robert	.	2
Cross, Richard	.	25	Charlotte	.	27	Charlotte	.	1
Maysh, James	.	28	Jane	.	24			
Clogg, William	.	29	Maria	.	27	William	.	3
						Maria	.	1
Parkin, George	.	24	Jane	.	26			
Heresgood, William	.	42						
Sprague, John	.	26	Sermiford	.	27			
Newcombe, Robert	.	31				W. Lexthorn	.	16
Canterbury, Charles	.	25						
Leach, Benjamin	.	30	Ann	.	30	Ann	.	4
Dobson, James	.	27	Ann	.	27	John	.	5
						Mary	.	4

APPENDIX III

SETTLER.		WIFE.		CHILDREN.	
Ford's Party, Wilts.					
Ford, Edward, Director	38	Jane	39	James	17
				John	16
				Patience	13
				Elizabeth	11
Dicks, James	23	Dinah	22	John	(infant)
Ralph, Richard	29	Elizabeth	28	Harriet	4
				Samuel	1
Ralph, Joseph	27	Elizabeth	28	Joseph	3
				Mary	¾
Miles, Robert	27	Ann	20	William	2
Dicks, James	38	Jane	39	Robert	17
				Uriah	14
				James	12
				Joseph	10
				Jonah	8
				Eliza	6
Jennings, James	28	Mary	30	James	3
Dicks, Ephraim	38			Ephraim	16
				Joseph	15
Crouch, Richard	29	Sarah	30	John	1
Payne, Elijah	25	Mary	22	Mary	1½
Campbell's Party, Hants.					
Campbell, Captain Duncan, Director (half-pay Marines)	39	Susan	—		
Stroud, John	30	Elizabeth	30		
Horton, Robert	40	Elizabeth	26	Elizabeth	1
Wills, John	29	Mary	30	Margaret	7
Penny, George	32	Nancy	30		
Shepherd, George	23	Elizabeth	30		
Gladstone, William	20				
Goff, George	18				
Jordan, Charles	26	Martha	25	Charles	3
				Parish Boys:	
				Edgecombe J.	16
				Lichfield, C.	13
				Chance, R.	13
				Hawkins, J.	13½
Littlefield, John	40	Mary	38		
Lovelook, William	40				
Kiminish, J.	19				
Littlefield, John	18				

SETTLER.		WIFE.		CHILDREN.	
Hyman's Party, Wilts.					
Hyman, Charles, Director	21	Elizabeth	26	John Wheeler	14
Trollip, Stephen	19	Mary	20		
Farley, Daniel	28	Elizabeth	26	William	5
				Joseph	2
				Sarah	2
Trollip, John	22	Elizabeth	20		
Trollip, Joseph	38	Sarah	39	Hester	18
				Benjamin	16
				Rhoda	13
				Jacob	11
				Joseph	9
				Mary Ann	7
Debman, Isaac	38	Mary	39	Eliza	17
				John	16
				Ann	13
				Isaac	11
Trollip, William	24	Patience	22	Alfred	1
Weakly, Joseph	27	Emma	36	Mary	5
				Joseph	3
				John	1
King, John	23	Eleanor	24	John	2
				Sarah	1
Neat, William	22	Susan	23	Jane	1
Adams, Edward	21				
Cock's Party.					
Cock, William, Director	26	Elizabeth	27	William Fred.	4
				John Anderson	—
				Loveday Ann	1¾
Collier, Abraham	38	Mary	30		
Forward, William	33	Elizabeth	28	William	2
Lyon, George	26				
Coleman, John	28				
Whitehead, John	37	Sarah	36	Thomas	15
				George	6
				Hebe	4
				Sarah	2
Thomas, Joseph	28	Elizabeth	24	John	¼
Warden, Benjamin	23	Elizabeth	24	Elizabeth	¼
Woodman, William	29				
Jarman, Joseph	26				
Jones, William	26				
Hopler, John	22				

APPENDIX III

SETTLER.		WIFE.		CHILDREN.	
James, George . . .	20				
Dean, Charles . . .	30				
Emleslie, Robert . .	48	Sarah . .	34	Elizabeth .	7
				Sarah .	5
				William .	3
Doyleley, Samuel . .	32	Mary . . .	27	Fanny .	6
				Samuel .	2
Palin, Roe John . .	22				
Joats, John . . .	36				
Leppan, James . .	30	Ann . . .	35	Ann . .	5
				Christopher	2
				Mary . .	1½
Bayley, Simon . .	27	Ann . . .	29	Thomas .	3
Simpson, Thomas . .	48	Ann . . .	43	Dorothy .	10
				Clara .	6
Ingram, Charles . .	48				
Sanders, John . . .	30	Martha . .	27		
Rhodes, John . . .	46	Henrietta . .	38	George . .	8
				Charles . .	6
				Edward . .	3
Booth, Henry . . .	22				
Evans, Charles . . .	43	Mary . . .	26		
Brown, Stephen . .	48	Sarah . . .	36	William . .	4
Nicety, William . .	40	Elizabeth . .	33	John . . .	19
				Elizabeth .	12
				James . .	5
				Thomas .	3¼
Martin, Edward . .	40	Ann . . .	38		
Martin, Edward, jun.	21				
Beale, William . . .	42	Mary . . .	35	William . .	13
				George . .	11
				Henry . .	8
				Mary Ann .	6
Williams, Thomas . .	30				
Overe, Thomas . .	48				
Overe, John, jun. . .	24				
Bradley, John . . .	25				
Bassett, William . .	35				
Field, Thomas . . .	25				
James, John . . .	38				
Rogers, Philip . . .	48				

Bowker's Party, Wilts.

Asten, John . .	25				

SETTLER.		WIFE.		CHILDREN.	
Bowker, Miles, Director (From Newton, Salisbury).	55	Ann Maria.	35	Wm. Monkhouse	17
				Miles.	14
				John Henry	12
				Mary Ely.	11
				Bertram.	10
				Robert M.	8
				Septimus.	6
				Octavius.	4
Stanford, John.	35	Maria.	28	John.	7
				Letitia	5
				Jane.	2
				Sophia.	infant
Hayter, John.	20				
Down, George Hooks	25				
Lines, Richard.	20				
Ingram, William	24				
Adams, Henry.	36				
Bezant, Charles	34				

James' Party, Wilts.

SETTLER.		WIFE.		CHILDREN.	
James, Samuel, Director.	31	Elizabeth.	33	Edward.	8
				Eliza.	5
				Stephen.	2
				Samuel W. } infants	
				Thomas	
Hobbs, Philip.	26	Charity.	25	Daniel.	3
				Sarah.	1
Rogers, Robert	25	Sarah.	26	Rebecca.	4
				Emma.	1
Rendall, James	44	Rebecca.	33	Mary.	14
				Jane.	9
				Elizabeth.	7
				James.	3
				Sarah.	1
Henton, Richard	33	Sarah.	36	Rebecca.	10
				George.	7
				Leonard.	4
				Jane	6 months
Usher, James.	36	Sarah.	36	Elizabeth.	16
				Joseph.	14
				Sophia.	9
				James.	5
				John.	4
				Ann.	4

SETTLER.		WIFE.		CHILDREN.	
Pinnock, Philip	32	Betsy	26	Harriet	3
				Joseph	1
Banks, William	25	Sarah	22	James	2
				William	½
Barter, William	22				
Warren, Thomas	44	Mary	42	James	14
Lanham, Thomas	30	Elizabeth	27	Mary A.	10 months
Oslers' Party, Cornwall.					
Osler, Benjamin, Director	44	Jane	45	Stephen	13
				Mary Ann	12
				Amelia	10
				Elizabeth	6
Bridgeman, John	19				
Dale, John	24	Mary	17		
Pearse, Charles B.	35	Ann	32	Eldred	11
				Charles	8
				Horatio	6
Eva, Richard	24	Elizabeth	22		
Richards, Joseph	25	Sally	21	Sally	3
				Phillis	1
Blee, Richard	22	Penelope	19		
Goodman, Henry	23	Elizabeth	20		
Weeks, James	29	Grace	25	Elizabeth	2
Mallett, William	45	Elizabeth	46		
Ball, James	44	Ann	45	James	6

PER "EAST INDIAN"
Arrived Simon's Bay, 30th April, 1820

SETTLER.		WIFE.		CHILDREN.	
Parker's Party, Irish Party, Cork.					
Parker, William, Director (Ex-mayor of Cork.)	42	Eleanor Alice	39	Mary	16
				Ann D'Estre	13
				Thomas S.	9
				Lucia	6
				Wm. D'Estere	4
				Nercet D'Estere	1
Eliza Coyle (governess)					
		Bridget Murphy	20		
		Mary Robinson	24		

SETTLER.		WIFE.		CHILDREN.	
McClelland, Rev. Francis	24	Eliza	20		
Johnson, John	28	Margaret	27		
Bryne, Patrick	30				
Archer, John	21	Jane	21	John	1 month
Shaw, Samuel Edw.	32	Ann	23	Edward	1
		Ann Daniell	49		
Roberts, William	29	Sarah	24	John	1
Coughlan, Cornelius	20				
Murray, James	48	Sarah	40	Richard	16
				George	13
				Mary	10
				Margaret	8
				Martha	6
				Sarah	4
				James	2
Armstrong, John	30	Catherine	27		
Armstrong, Lawrence	28	Ann	25		
Armstrong, James	28				
Armstrong, Moses	26	Jane	25	Samuel	6
				William	2
Franne, Percival	23				
Forbes, Alexander	27				
Forbes, Edw.	27	Harriet	27	Alexander	2
Foster, James	21				
Barber, William	23	Ann	25		
Folliott, John	24	Eleanor	23		
Scanlen's Party.					
Scanlen, William	40	Hannah	34	William	16
				John	13
				Charles	8
				Thomas Ross	5
				Hannah (*m.* Sam. Roberts	4
Hunt, Thomas	35	Sophia	25		
Norman, William	36	Jane	33		
Allison, James	44	Ann	39	Sarah	15
				John	12
				Margaret	10
				Mary	8
				Joseph	3
				Ann	1
Allison, James, jun.	18				
Walter, Alexander Alyne	31	Jane	30	Abel	2
				George	1 month

APPENDIX III

SETTLER.		WIFE.		CHILDREN.	
*Holditch, Dr. R. . . 30		Mary . . 22			
(Prov. Surgeon, Clanwilliam.)					
Woodcock, Robert . . 37		Susannah . . 36		Samuel . . 7	
				Charlotte . . 4	
Fryer, Richard . . . 25		Eliza . . . 20			
(Shipbuilder.)					
Blythe, Nathaniel . . 25					
Wolmsley, Anthony . . 27		Sarah . . . 25			
Boucher, Charles . . 22		Mary . . . 22			
(Fisherman.)					
Dickinson, Robert . . 45				Emily . . 13	
(Cabinetmaker.)				Frederick . . 11	
				Alfred . . 9	
				Henry . . 6	
Greenwell, Thomas . . 30		Ann . . . 30		Edward . . 6	
(Labourer.)				Thomas . . 5	
Latham, Joseph . 30				William . . 16	
(Gentleman.)					
Latham, Henry . . 20					
(Carpenter.)					
Baker, George . . . 34		Ann . . . 47		George . . 13	
(Machinist.)				Richard . . 6	
Eddy, John . . . 28					
Wolgrove, John . . 34					
Pote, Robert . . . 34		Margaret . . 34		Charles . . 10	
				Agnes . . 7	
				Harriet . . 5	
				Ann . . . 2	
Kavanough, James . . 24					
Stone, James . . . 22		Charlotte . . 22			
Stone, Charles . . . 23					
Francis, David P. . . 36		Hannah . . 28			
Tilbrook, George . . 27		Ann . . . 22			
Sheldon, John . . . 36					
Ella, Peter . . . 33		Effy . . . 30		Elizabeth . . 6	
				David . . 3	
Moss, John P. . . 42					
Barish, Ralph . . . 25					
Douglass, William . . 39					
Seton, T., late Captain					
Madras Establishment . 44		Sarah . . . 22		William Page 16	
Hare, John . . . 34		Esther A. . . 28		William 7	
				Martha 4	
				John . 2	
Walsh, William . . 22					

* Drowned as per letter of Landdrost of Stellenbosch, dated Dec. 25, 1822.

M

SETTLER.		WIFE.		CHILDREN.	
Leary, Timothy	24				
Foley, John	40	Barbara	—		
Matthews, Thomas	21				
Hayse, John	40	Mary	34	Robert	16
				Richard	13
				Ann	12
				Mary	10
				Jeremiah	5
				Catherine	3
Barry, John	42	Margaret	36	John	16
				Michael	13
				Eleanor	9
				Johanna	8
				William	7
				John	5
				Mary	1
Clarke, George	24				
Quinn, John	40	Mary	27	Michael	8
				John	6
				Catherine	1
Cooney, Samuel	22	Margaret	18		
Whelan, William	42	Mary	—		
Clarke, Thomas	38	Ann	38	Joseph	15
				Ann	13
				Elizabeth	12
				Susannah	5
				Harriet	4
Jobson, John	21	Sarah	21		
Nelson, William	32	Elizabeth	31	Harriet	12
				William	6
				Elizabeth	2
Smith, John	41	Mary	31	John	13
				Jane	11
Quinn, John	30	Mary	26	Anne	10
				John	8
				Jane	6
				Elizabeth	3
Hawks, George	21				
Newlan, James	21				
Taylor, John	20				
Ross, Richard	24	Elizabeth	24	Mary	17
				Colin	2
Moore, William	21				
Moore, John	20				
Conn, William	26				
Parker, William S.	20				

PER "FANNY"
Arrived at Simon's Bay, 1st May, 1820

SETTLER.		WIFE.		CHILDREN.	
Butler's Party, Irish, Wicklow.					
Butler, Capt. Thomas, Dir. (Dublin Militia.)	43	Elizabeth	33	Joseph	11
				James	6
				Matilda	1
Fowler, Thomas	36			John	13
Murray, Edw.	21	Jane	19	(Child born on board)	
Harrington, Thomas	22	Frances	20		
Devine, James	36	Margaret	26	William	12
				Ellen	4
Whelan, John	21				
Byrn, Murtagh	33	Jane	30	Patrick	13
				William	7
Magier, William	36			Thomas	8
Toole, Michael	21	Honora	20		
Healey, John	21				
Goss, Michael	21				
Walsh, Lawrance	40				
Synnot's Party, Irish, Wicklow.					
Sinnott, Capt.Wm., Director	45	Elizabeth	20	F. Houston	15
				Walter	12
				Robert	2
				George	$1\frac{1}{2}$
				Ann	—
Scannel, John	21	Johanna	21	George	10
Spires, William	30	Sarah		James	8
				Mary	6
				Margaret	4
				Sarah	2
				Elizabeth	$1\frac{1}{2}$
Cowser, Robert	20				
Caliston, William	28				
Tuimie, Joseph	21	Mary	19		
Kennedy, James	25				
Thompson, Robert	26				
Short, Robert	18				
Young, Robert	28	Margaret	28	Samuel	8
McDonald, Patrick	25				

BRITISH SOUTH AFRICA

SETTLER.		WIFE.		CHILDREN.	
Ingram's Party, Irish, Cork.					
*Ingram, John, Director	35				
Pierce, Patrick	21				
Agnew, William	25	Honora	22		
Forster, John	40	Mary	34	Mary	9
				James	7
				Harriet	3
				George	2
				John	2 months
Barry, John	23				
Hanley, William	32				
Begley, Gerald	42	Margaret	36	Gerald	12
				Terence	10
Begley, Joseph	44	Mary	40	Joseph	13
				John	8
				Ellen	4
Begley, David	22	Mary	17		
Begley, Timothy	24	Catherine	19		
Gresnock, John	30	Mary	34	Mary	13
				Ann	11
Griffin, Patrick	34	Mary	28	Mary	5
				Michael	2
Hearn, Thomas H.	24				
Quinn, Thomas	30				
Mukin, Thomas	32				
Woodley, Simon	26	Jane	24		
Barry, Michael	22				
Bennett, Thomas	28	Margaret	27	George	9
				William	5
				Julia	4
				Thomas	2
Coffie, John	22				
Crawley, John	28	Mary	22	Humphrey	3
Hannan, John	25				
Rearden, Daniel	34	Margaret	28	Michael	9
				John	2
Callaghan, Cady	30	Johanna	25	Johanna	11
				Bridget	7
				Helen	5
				Morgan	4
				Daniel	2
Rowley, Richard	19				
Lehane, John	24				
Lehane, David	22				
Keilley, Dennis	28				

* Returned to England, and in February, 1823, entered into an arrangement with Earl Bathurst and took out 183 men, 59 women and 105 children ; arrived at Cape Town in winter of 1823.—Theal, p. 239.

APPENDIX III

PER "ALBURY"

Arrived at Simon's Bay, 1st June, 1820

SETTLER.		WIFE.		CHILDREN.	
Calton's Party, Nottingham.					
Calton, Dr. Thomas, Dir.	40	Martha	. . 39	Charles	12
				Henry .	10
				Sarah .	7
				Mary .	3
				Frederick .	1
Calton, Thomas, jun.	. 18				
Dennison, George .	36	Hannah	. . 29	Ann . .	7
				George .	5
				Henry .	2
				Charlotte .	½
Palmer, George . .	. 36			Jervase .	. 14
				Matilda .	. 2
		Atkin, Elizabeth .		Benjamin .	. 12
				George .	. 3
		Atkin, Sarah .			
Pulgm, George . .	. 36				
Webster, Thomas .	. 21				
Sykes, William .	. 44				
Goulding, George .	. 21				
Draper, Thomas .	. 33			Thomas .	. 8
Harris, James . .	. 19				
Wright, William .	33				
Palmer, Thomas .	. 22				
Bradfield, Edmund .	. 22				
Bradfield, John .	. 25				
Bradfield, Joseph .	. 19				
Bradfield, John, sen.	. 46	Mary .	. . 45	Ellen . .	. 20
				Mary . .	. 16
				Richard .	. 12
				James .	. —
Cross, John .	. 36	Mary .	. . 31	Matilda .	. 9
				William .	. 7
				Charles .	6
				Mary Ann .	. 3
Morris, John . .	. 28	Esther E. .	. 25	William .	. 9
				Jane . .	. 7
Pike, William .	. 41	Mary .	. . 44	Sarah .	. 17
				Eliza . .	. 16
				William .	16
				Mary .	4

SETTLER.		WIFE.		CHILDREN.	
Pike, Thomas	. 19				
Poole, Matthew	. 34				
Radford, Joshua	. 19				
Hunt, William	. 44	Mary	. 50	Sarah	. 20
				Ann	. —
Sheppard, Henry	. 28	Hannah	. 26	William	. 6
				Eliza	3
				Ann	1½
Timms, Thomas	. 40	Elizabeth	. 40	Charles	13
				Edward	. 12
				Thomas	9
				Eliza	. 7
				Louisa	. 5
Torr, Thomas	. 29	Ann	. 20	Selina	. 7
				James	. 4
				Eliza	. 3
				George	. 1
Elliott, William	. 25	Elizabeth	. 22	Nathanael	. 3
				William	1
Goulding, Thomas	. 30	Elizabeth	. 27	George	6
				William	4
Nelson, Thomas	28	Mary	. 24	William	3
				Matilda	1
Hodgkinson, George	. 21				
Holland, Henry	. 22				
Radford, Richard	. 25				
Crooks, William	. 23				
Foulds, Henry	. 22				
Valentine, Peter	. 24				
Brooks, Thomas	. 24				
Brown, George	. 22				
Keeton, Benjamin	. 19				
Meats, William	. 27				
Bradford, Edward	. 23				
Driver, Edward	. 23				
Elliott, Mark	. 21	Sarah	. 20	Alfred	. 1
Muggleton, George	. 36	Sarah	. 46		
Allison, Francis	. 40	Elizabeth	. 30	William	. 17
				Mary	. 9
				Eliza	. 6
				Samuel	. 4
				Ann	. 2
Sansom, George	. 24	Dorothy	. 23		
Hartley, William	. 24	Sarah	. 25		
Hartley, Thomas, jun.	. 18				

SETTLER.		WIFE.		CHILDREN.	
Hartley, Thos, sen. . . 48		Sarah . . . 39		Mary . . . 22	
				Ann . . . 20	
				Hannah . . 16	
				Eliza . . . 13	
				Sarah . . 10	
				Jeremiah . . 7	
				Henry . . 4	
Jackson, Samuel . . 33		Dorothy . . 33		Samuel . 4	
				William 2	
				Eliza . 1	
Wright, Joshua . . 22		Elizabeth . . 21			
Belson, Thomas . . 26		Mary . . . 27		{ Eliza . . 5 Thomas . . 4 John . . ½	
Jarman, Thomas . . 26					
Thiele, William . . 19					
Edlestone, Thomas . . 45					
Smith, John . . . 20					

PER "BRILLIANT"
Arrived at Simon's Bay, 30th April, 1820

SETTLER.	WIFE.	CHILDREN
Pringle's Party, Scotland.		
Pringle, Thomas, Director 30	Mrs. Pringle . 32	
	Eliza Syker . 30	} Servants.
	*Janet Brown . 35	
Pringle, Robert, Director . 61	Mrs. Pringle . 45	Robert, Dods . 10
		Catherine . . 9
		Beatrice . . 4
Pringle, John . . 29		
†Sydserf, Charles . . 21		
Rennie, George . . 23	Mrs. Rennie (his moth er)	
Rennie, John . . 22	Elizabeth (his sister) 15	
Rennie, Peter . . . 20		
Mortimer, Alexander . 23		
Somress, James . 19		
Eckurn, James . . . 20		

* Sister-in-law of Thomas Pringle. Obtained a situation in Cape Town as governess, and obtained permission to leave Pringle's party 6th May, 1820.

† Mr. Sydserff, one of the heads of families, had, through the interest of a friend, obtained a special grant of 500 acres in addition to his share of the 1,100 acres general grant. If this is " Chas.," aged 12 below is more likely meant for 21.—Pringle, p. 50.

SETTLER.		WIFE.		CHILDREN.	
*Elliott, William	. 27				
Redgard, Ezra .	. 29	Elizabeth .	. 24	Andrew .	. 2
				Mary Anne	. 1
Erith's Party, Surrey.					
Erith, James Thomas, Dir.	30	Jane .	. 31	Jane .	. 3
				Eleanor	. 2
Robertson, Robert .	. 27	Martha	. 26	Louisa	. 5
				Robert	. 4
				John .	. 2
				Philip	. 1
Kemp, James .	. 24	Hannah .	. 20		
Parkurst, John .	. 20				
Ralph, John	19				
Dry, Thomas .	. 21				
Whittle, Thurston .	. 29				
Hughes, Robert	. 40				
Shepherd, George .	36				
Tailor, John .	. 18				
Gush, Richard .	. 30	Margaret .	. 29	Margaret .	. 6
				Thomas .	. 2
March, Thomas	. 50	Martha	. 50	Sarah .	. 16
				Thomas Wadman	15
				Joseph Pickston	13
				George Duken .	11
				Mary .	. 4
Watkins, John .	. 21	Martha	20		
Brown, George .	. 34			Mary Ann .	. 12
				Luke .	. 6
Urry, Joseph .	. 43	Mary .	. 36	Sarah	. 11
				Martha .	. 9
				Priscilla .	. 8
				Ruddah	. 6
Hogsflesh, Joseph .	. 37	Margaret .	. 21	Hannah	. 3
Jenkinson, George .	. 31	Sarah .	. 31	Hannah	. 11
				Charles	. 5
				Alfred	. 3
				John .	. 1
Tilly, William .	27	Hannah .	. 25		
Beher, George .	. 20	Ann .	. 21		
Colling, John .	25				
Colling, Thomas	18				
Sheppard, William .	. 30			John Wood	. 11
				Sarah .	. 4

* Obtained permission to open a classical and commercial school in Cape Town in conjunction with Mr. A. Duncan, August 28, 1820; afterwards became a missionary of the London Society to the blacks at Paarl.—Pringle's Narrative, p. 20.

SETTLER.		WIFE.		CHILDREN.	
Miller, John	29				
Miller, William	40	Elizabeth	42	Elizabeth	8
				Mary Ann	6
				John	2
Temlett, James	22	Ann	21		
Rayner, William	26	Martha	32	Eliza	2 months
Webb, Christopher	31	Mary	21	Christopher	2
				John	2 days
Wichman, M. W.	40	Catherine	36	Elizabeth	17
Tilmer, John	49	Mary	29	John	11
				Harriet	7
				Ebenezer	5
				Mary	3
				Elizabeth	8 months
Tilmer, Thomas	47	Elizabeth	67		
Jones, Thomas	—				
Watson, Charles	—				
Brag, George	39	Ann	45	Mary	18
(Coachmaker.)				Fanny	13
				Ann	11
				Sarah	6
Muir, William	25	Mary Ann	21	William	1
Gravett, Charles	18				
King, Thomas	39	Sarah	39	Thomas F.	14
				William	6
Pickstock, Richard	45	Frances	35	William Gravett	16
				Charlotte	9
Morton, Thomas	38	Elly	38	Charlotte	2
Hodges, George	32	Mary	30		
Usted, Thomas	40	Susan	28	Sarah	4
				Thomas	2
Searle, Edward	28	Mary	26	Sophia Jane	—
Hood, Thomas J.	20				
Hodges, Samuel	32				

PER "AURORA"
Arrived at Simon's Bay, 1st June, 1820

SETTLER.		WIFE.		CHILDREN.	
Sephton's Party.					
Sephton, Hezekiah, Direc.	43	Jane	43	Hezekiah	12
				Jane	11
				William	2

SETTLER.		WIFE.		CHILDREN.	
Sephton, Thomas	18				
*Campbell, Dr. P.	30	Sarah	—	Margaret and	
		Martha Hill, servant.		Sarah (infants)	
†Shaw, Rev. William	21	Ann	31	Mary Ann (infant)	
Wilmot, Joseph	30	Ann	24	George William	13
Rees, William	47	Ann	41		
Hazett, William	39	Mary	29		
Prior, Richard	44	Sarah	42		
Trotter, William	33	Ann	34	Ann	—
Wetheredge, James	39			Bennetta	13
Howse, James	23				
Patrick, Benjamin	42			Martha	13
				Joel	10
				Sarah	8
				Samuel	6
Lee, William, sen.	39	Ann	38	George	13
				Frederick	11
				Henry	10
				Elisha	9
Lee, William, jun.	18				
Bonnin, Samuel	40	Ann	37	Caroline	16
				Susannah	13
Pratten, William	34				
Cyrus, Samuel	37	Deborah	28	George	9
				Jeremiah	6
				Samuel	4
Owen, Robert	46	Mary	48	Owen	12
				William Smith	
				George Wood (apprentice).	14
Jones, John	25				
Payne, John	33	Sarah	29	Mary	5
Painter, Samuel	37	Harriet	34	Richard Joseph	13
				Mary	5
				Frederick T. 8 mths.	
				Harriet 8 months	
Short, Joseph	33	Mary	30	John	7
				Mary	5
				Penelope	3
				Frederick W. 8 mths.	

* Admitted 14th December, 1809. Since practised in Great Marlborough Street as surgeon, apothecary and accoucheur.

† In December, 1823, left the colony and founded the Mission Station, Wesleyville.—Theal, p. 355.

APPENDIX III 171

SETTLER.		WIFE.		CHILDREN.	
Upcott, Samuel	. 36	Mary .	. 36	Jane .	. 13
Pitt, Robert	. 43	Lucy .	. 39	Robert	. 8
Prynn, William	. 40	Jane .	. 35	William Edward	8
				Elizabeth .	. 6
				Jane Mary	. 2
				Sarah Clark	. 10
Watson, William	. 19	Mary .	. 23		
Watson, Charles	. 13				
Hancock, James	. 43	Ann .	. 29	Mary Ann	. 7
Hancock, Mary (sister)	. 32			Joseph Ebenezer	3
				Thomas .	. 1
				Samuel	1 month
Sargeant, William	. 32	Mary .	. 37	Benjamin .	. 8
				Hester	. 4
				Mary .	. 6
				R. Rawlings	. 15
				J. Rawlings	. 12
Holmes, Thomas	. 34	Mary .	. 34	Mary Ann .	. 12
				Hannah	. 9
				Margaret .	. 5
				Thomas .	. 3
Hall, David	. 32	Ann .	. 24	James	. 2
Wallace, Thomas	. 43	Sarah	. 43	Mary .	. 12
				Henry	. 10
Aldhum, Aaron	. 39	Ida .	. 32	Jane .	. 11
				Aaron	. 4
Harris, William	. 23	Sophia (sister)		Ruth .	. 1
Chandler, Charles	. 32				
Roberts, Daniel	. 37	Harriet	. 33	Mary .	15
				Daniel	13
				Samuel	8
Evans, John	. 27	Ann .	. 25		
Booth, Benjamin	. 32	Margaret .	. 28	Margaret .	. 10
				Sarah	. 7
				Jane .	. 2
Reedman, Samuel	. 28	Ann .	. 18		
Reedman, Benjamin	. 27				
Slater, Thomas	. 43	Sophia	. 42	Harriet .	17
				George .	12
				Henry .	9
				Edward .	7
				John .	5
				Elizabeth .	3
Slater, Charles	. 21				

SETTLER.		WIFE.		CHILDREN.	
Bryant, Thomas	25	Mary Elizabeth	23	James	4
				Thomas	2
Robinson, Thomas	38	Mary Ann	38	Mary Ann	14
				George	13
				William	10
				Charles	7
				Samuel	3
				James	.6 months
Oates, John	31	Elizabeth	35	Mary Ann. (*m.* Dugmore)	3
				Samuel	1
Kidd, James	24	Ann	30	E. Jenkins	13
Wood, Charles	30	Ann	23	Thomas Fred.	3
Wells, Thomas	43	Sarah	42	Elizabeth	18
				George	17
Field, Samuel	26				
Youngs, Thomas	45	Ann	38		
Howe, George	44	Frances	50	Maria	14
Maynard, Levi	44	Sarah	40	Leah	15
Maynard, James	20				
Maynard, Joshua	18				
Edwards, James	24	Ann	23	Daniel	(infant)
Matthews, W. H.	26	Frances	28		
Turpin, Joseph	29	Mary	19		
Sparks, Henry	30	Mary	38	Henry	5
				Francis	2
Croft, Charles	26			Clarissa	2
Fowler, William	23				
Talbot, John	18			Charles	13
Talbot, Priscilla (his mother)	45			Amelia	9
				Henry	7
				Maria	5
				Sophia	2
Penny, Charles	33	Susan	25	Elizabeth	11
				Charles	7
				Edward	1
Clark, George	36	Elizabeth	—	George	8
				Mary Ann	4
				Frances	6
				Catherine	1
Bagshaw, Robert	27	Ursula	20	Robert William	1
Dixie, Robert	30	Elizabeth	27	Elizabeth	5
				Phœbe	1
Penny, William	30	Rosannah	30	Sarah	9
				William	7
Ames, John	44				

PER "BELLE ALLIANCE"
Arrived Table Bay, 2nd June, 1820

SETTLER.		WIFE.		CHILDREN.	
Willson's Party, London.					
*Willson, Thomas, Director	35	Mary Ann .	. 30	Percy Cowell	9
				Douglas .	6
				Thomas .	4
				William Mercer	14
Hagard, Thomas .	. 36	Elizabeth .	. 35	Elizabeth .	. 1
Pawle, Dr. James .	. 30	Jemima .	. 32	James .	. 3
				Henry .	1
Cook, Thomas . .	. 32	Sophia .	. 32	Sophia .	8
				John .	7
				Thomas .	6
				Anne .	4
				Jane .	3
				James	1
Bisset, Lieut. A., R.N., half-pay. . .	. 32	Alicia . .	. 28	Sarah Maria :	6
				Alexander Charles	4
				John Jarvis .	2
Woods, Frederick .	. 21				
Brown, W. J. .	. 20				
Brown, Thomas .	. 40	Jane . .	. 35		
Bond, William . .	. 44	Martha .	. 40	William Henry .	13
				Louisa .	11
				Compure . .	4
†Collis, James . .	. 24				
Piper, Thomas . .	. 36				
Higgins, Barnabas .	. 23				
Gamble, John . .	. 19				
Crawford, James .	. 22	Martha .	. 22	Mary . .	. 1
Currie, Walter, purser R. N., half-pay . .	. 34	Ann .	. 24	Mary Ann .	4
				Walter .	. 1
Lane, Thomas .	21				
Currie, Adam .	24				
Moody, John .	. 49	Sarah . .	. 36	Francis .	. 13
Eales, William . .	23	Sarah . .	. 26		
Bayley, John . .	. 28	Martha .	. 26	Mary .	2

* Formerly in the office of H.R.H. Duke of York. Architect and commercial agent, London.

† Went to Natal in 1830, and in August, 1831, left Graham's Town to establish himself at Natal as a teacher. Killed by an explosion of gunpowder, 1835. "Virtually head of his own party." M.S.

SETTLER.		WIFE.		CHILDREN.	
Mundell, James	24	Catherine	27	Henry	4
				Elizabeth	2
Reynolds, Thomas	28				
Purdon, John	40	Mary	34	William	11
				Henry	9
				Elizabeth	5
				Charles	2
Rowe, Samuel	29	Sarah	26	Edward	6
Dearman, J.	25	Mary	23	Joseph	12
				Osborn	11
				John	9
				James	8
Scrooby, Samuel	31	Ann	33	Richard	7
				George	5
Walker, Thomas	46	Sarah	43		
Walker, Thomas, junior	22	Elizabeth	22	Elizabeth	2
				Sarah	1
Scott, John	39	Frances	38	Eliza	9
				Edmund	6
				Henry	4
				Emma	1
Walkinshaw, Charles	22				
Clarke, Thomas	40	Eleanor	34	E. Maria	13
				Thomas John	12
				Car. Maria	11
				Francis	9
				Sarah Elizabeth	6
				Frederick	4
				Edwin	1
Norton, John	25	Sarah	24	Lewis	4
				Joshua	2
Goadley, Joseph	31	Mary	31		
Lance, James	31	Elizabeth	30		
Austen, Samuel	23	Mary	36		
Carpenter, William	34	Mary	34	Eliza	7
				Maria	4
				Emma	1
Hall, Benjamin	29	Frances	28	Frances	5
				Hannah	4
				Mary	3
Jarman, John	49				
Barrel, William, senior	38			Robert	12
				Charles	10
Perie, Robert	35	Mary	24	Margaret	11
Wheeler, James	39	Harriet	35	Martha	13

APPENDIX III

SETTLER.		WIFE.		CHILDREN.	
				Ann	11
				Harriet	6
				Richard James	2
Barrel, William, junior	19				
Foden, Thomas	40	Mary	36	Catherine	13
				Matilda	6
Pratt, John	38	Ann	37	William	13
Gifford, Theo.	33	Ann	26		
Horn, Robert Hy. Wm.	21	Ann	22		
Kidson, William	34	Ann	32	Frederick	4
				Thomas	1
Lloyd, Henry	36	Alicia	27	Catherine	8
		Mary Delhine		Francisca	6
		(servant)	35	Harry	4
				Samuel	2
Thomas, John	40	Ann	35		
Rathbone, James	22	Susanna	22	Emma	1
Williams, John	38	Ann	35		
Whybrew, John	19				
Phillips, John	19				
Simons, Philip	19			Samuel	10
				Ralph	8
Nelson, Thomas	33	Mary Ann	33	Mary Ann	10
				John Edw.	5
Robertson, John	30	Elizabeth	22		
Palmer, Thomas	32				
Randall, Thomas	40	Maria	21		
Reid, James	36	Ann	30	John William	13
Lucas, Charles John	31	Sarah Ann	27	Charles John	3
				Mary Ann	1
Combley, Dr. William	29	Sarah	27	Ann	1
Smith, John	42	Rebecca	34	John H.	15
				Thomas W.	8
				William	4
Henderson, Thomas	42	Margaret	32	Eliza	12
				Lavinia	10
Bowsher, Charles	21	Elizabeth	21		
Peacock, Richard	34	Maria	28	Eliza	7
				Selina	4
				Emily	4
				Walter	2
Wilmot, James	30	Ann	29		
Wilmot, Benjamin	22				
Wenham, Thomas	28	Elizabeth	26		
Doyle, S.	20				

SETTLER.		WIFE.		CHILDREN.	
Smith, Richard	28				
Lindsey, Robert	36	Isabella	25		
Martin, Thomas	24	Susan	26		
Earle, William J.	19				
Eaton, William Loftie	21	Mary Ann	24		
Griggs, John	20				
Molthy, Frederick	19				
Taylor, Charles	19				
Francis, Thomas	31	Elizabeth	28	Thomas James	9
				Amelia	7
				George	3
Webb, John	35	Mary Ann	34	William	9
				Frederick	7
				John	5
				Maria	3
				Alexandrina	1
Chapman, William	26	Judith		Sarah	
Jolly, John	27	Mary	21	Ann	2
Campion, Thomas	19				
Boardman, Rev. W.	44	Margaret	40	Margaret	17
		Mary (sister)	24	Susannah	16
		Judith „	23	John	13
				Sarah	12
				James	11
				William	8
Goddard, Ralph	26	Sarah	26	George	11
Johnson, Henry	33	Jane	30		
Flogg, William	19				
Dold, John Matthew	22	Sarah	18		
Dold, William Andrew	22	Jane Catherine	18		
Dold, Matthew	50	Jane	46	Ayliff James	13
Scott, George D.	19				
Brown, Thomas Sanders	36	Elizabeth	29	Enos	13
				Elizabeth	10
				Sarah	4
				Joseph	2
Dale, Christopher	31	Elizabeth	29	Elizabeth	7
				Henry	6
Carter, John	28				
Adams, James	30	Harriet	25		
Slee, Charles	26				
Stanton, William	36	Elizabeth	35	William	13
				Sarah	8
				Catherine	5
				Robert	3

APPENDIX III

SETTLER.			WIFE.		CHILDREN.	
Slowman, Moses	.	33	Phillis	24	Mark . .	5
					Rosetta .	3
					Julia . .	2
Donovan, Joseph	.	25	Susannah .	26	Susannah .	8
					Thomas .	7
					William .	4
					George .	2
Pierce, Richard	.	40	Ann .	41	Mary . .	17
					Richard .	11
					Paul . .	10
					Joseph .	9
Jarvis, George .	.	21				
Simons, Benjamin	.	18				

PER "ZOROASTER"

Arrived at Simon's Bay, 30th April, 1820

SETTLER.		WIFE.		CHILDREN.	
Dyason's Party, London.					
Dyason, George, Director	30	Frances .	29	George .	2
				Frances .	1
Dyason, Isaac . .	39	Sarah .	39	Isaac . .	16
				Rodger .	11
				Sarah .	9
				Elizabeth .	8
*Dyason, Joseph .	36	Mary Ann .	25	Joseph .	13
				Ann . .	7
Hudson, Hougham .	26	Elizabeth .	23	William .	10
Ratcliff, Thomas .	27	Elizabeth .	28	John . .	3½
				Mary Ann .	2
				Elizabeth .	1½
Grey, Henry . .	35	Mary .	30	Henry .	3
				Mary . .	2
				Jane . . 7 months	
Maytham, John .	30	Catherine .	30	John . .	15
				Henry .	8
				Elizabeth .	5
				William .	3
				Cornelius . 3 months	

* Quartermaster, Royal Navy, and 6 years Master, Merchant Service. Asked to survey mouth of the Kowie.

SETTLER.		WIFE.		CHILDREN.	
Bennett, Samuel .	39				
Allen, Samuel . .	26	Sarah . . .	30	John . .	1
Wicks, Robert . .	25	Mary . . .	—	Sarah .	6
				Robert . .	4
				Sophia	.6 months
Bear, William . .	26	Sarah . .	22		
Austin, John . .	24	Catherine . .	22	John .	.8 months
Stock, Robert . .	23	Susannah . .	19		
Chandler, William .	29				
Challis, Charles .	20	Amy . . .	20		
Smith, Enos . .	22				
Wright, James . .	29				
Dyason, Robert .	37	Ann . . .	23	Bayley	. 15
				Jassett	. 11
				Jane .	. 8
Marshall, Robert .	21				
McKenzie, Archibald	38	Amelia . .	31	Adam James	. 15
				Marion .	. 6
				John Thomas .	4
				Agnes .	. 3
Wait's Party, Middlesex.†					
Wait, William, Director .	50	Mary Ann . .	30		
Clark, Charles . .	36	Sarah . . .	31	Joshua .	. 8
				Frances .	. 5
				David .	. 1
Clark, Samuel . .	22	Elizabeth . .	19	John .	. 1
Wilkinson, Stephen .	28	Cornelia . .	27	Esther .	. 6
				Joseph	.8 months
Grimsdale, John .	20	Mary . .	20	Maria	.6 months
Rhodes, Robert .	25				
Lofts, Thomas . .	24				
Kirkpatrick, W. .	22	Martha . .	22	Hannah .	. 2
Nibbs, Francis . .	27	Sarah . . .	27	Ellen . .	. 6
Nibbs, Mary (his sister) .	21			James .	. 4
				Jeremiah .	. 1
Keen, Thomas . .	25	Margaret . .	25	Mary . .	6
Badger, John . .	36				
Posser, Robert . .	28				
Kempster, Thomas .	40				
Mayor, John . .	25				
Fowler, Thomas .	24				
Fanner, David . .	24				
Mintoe, William .	20				
Goldswain, Jeremiah	19				

* Specially recommended to Lord Charles Somerset by Duke of Beaufort.

SETTLER.		WIFE.		CHILDREN.	
Webb, Robert	17				
Smith, James	25				
Baster, James Munday	22				
Wilkinson, William	17				
Brown, William	25	Mary	28		
Smith, Joseph	18				
Stephens, Joseph	22				
Herman, James	25				
Wilkinson, John	20				
Barker, Arthur	33	Sarah	30	Sarah	8
				Elizabeth	6
				Samuel	4
				Ann	2
				Richard	1
Uylatt, Henry	38	Lucy	35	Lucy	15
				William	8
				John	7
				Mary	6
				Sarah	4
				Henry	4
				Jane	3
				An infant	2 months
Bradford, John	27				
Smith, William	27	Jane	27		
Covey, William	20				
Crammer, Robert	26				
Moore, William	44	Ann	48	Eleanor	9
Moore, William, jun	25	Margaret	24		
Parcett, Isaac	33	Maria	32	William	11
				Ann	9
				Elizabeth	7

Thornhill's Party.

Thornhill, Chas., Director	47	Dorothy	35	John	15
				Ann	13
				Mary	10
				Christian	8
Gilfillan, Andrew	20				
Brooks, William	31	Ann	30	Elizabeth	12
				William	10
				Ann	9
				Joseph	6
Cannon, Philip	20				

SETTLER.			WIFE.			CHILDREN.		
Dell, Ed. Hunt	.	. 38	Ann	.	. 38	John	.	. 10
						Stephen	.	. 8
						Edward	.	. 6
						Samuel	.	. 3
Bruton, Thomas	.	. 27	Charlotte	.	. 24	Charlotte	8 months	
Annandale, Thomas		. 20						
White, Thomas	.	. 29						
Streak, William	.	. 27	Elizabeth	.	. 22			
Soper, Robert	.	. 24	Alice	.	. 22			
Streak, James	.	. 18						
Mildenhall, Joseph	.	. 28						
Howard, William		. 30	Sarah	.	. 28	Jane	.	. 6
						Michael	.	. 4

PER "SIR GEORGE OSBORNE"
Arrived at St. Simon's Bay, 18th June, 1820

SETTLER.			WIFE.			CHILDREN.		
Mills' Party, London.								
Mills, Daniel, Director	.	. 60	Martha	.	. 40	Martha	.	. 16
						Harriet	.	. 14½
						Daniel	.	. 10
						Maria	.	. 8
						James	.	. 3
						Catherine	.	. 1¾
Potter, William	.	. 29	Hannah		. 27	Mary	.	. 10
						Ann	.	. 6
Hill, Charles	.	. 38	Elizabeth	.	. 45	James	.	. 15
						Jane	.	. 14¼
						Elizabeth	.	. 10
						Charles	.	. 8
						Henry	.	. 6
Carter, James	.	. 34	Sophia	.	. 33	James	.	. 2½
Fischer, Charles	.	. 22	Harriet	.	.			
Curtis, John	.	. 27	Esther	.	. 28			
Jackson, Robert	.	. 22						
Haines, William	.	. 26						
Sampson, Robert	.	. 22						
Turvey's Party, London.								
Turvey, Edward, Director		39	Julia	.	. 39	Benjamin	.	. 17

APPENDIX III

SETTLER.		WIFE.		CHILDREN.	
				Mary	. 14¾
				Eliza	. 11
				Edward	. 9
				Louisa	. 8
				George	. 6
Turvey, John	. 82				
Daniels, Peter	. 46	Eliza	. 38	Peter	. 15
				Isabella	. 14
				Thomas	. 9
				Sampson	. 7
				Eliza	. 4
				Ann	. 2
				Frederick	. 1
Wright, William	. 24	Rosa	. 24	Martha	. 3
				William	. 1
				Sally (servant)	. 14
Daniels, John	. 19				
Keevey, John	. 28	Mary	. 27	Matthew	. 10
				Francis	. 7
				Ann	. 1½
				Mary	. 3 months
Kemp, John	. 35	Mary	. 34	Nancy	. 15
				John	. 14½
				Thomas	. 9
				James	. 6
				William	. 4
				Sophia	. —
				Ann	. —
Burgess, John	. 38	Ellen	. 34	John	. 10
				William	. 8
				Mary	. 6
				Frances	. 4
				Josiah	. 2
				Eliza	. 1
Mulligan, John	. 35	Mary	. 26		
Cartwright, Robert	. 39	Mary	. 36		
Willy, Thomas	. 25				
Holland, Henry	. 26				
Daniels, Sampson	. 32	Mary	. 27	Sophia	. 6
				Eliza	. 5
				Amelia	. 3
				Robert	. 1
				Isabella	. 2 months
Pennell, Thomas	. 17				

SETTLER.	WIFE.	CHILDREN.
Gardner's Party, Warwicks.		
Gardner, Edward, Director 31	Mary . . . 31	
Dugmore, Isaac . . 34	Maria . . . 36	Ann . . . 7
		William . . 6
		Henry . . 4½
		Louisa . . 4
		Caroline . . 2
Abbott, William . . 39		
Roe, Robert . . . 30		
Wright, John . . . 22		
Seal, William . . . 21		
Dudley, John . . . 36	Sarah . . . 21	Matilda . . —
		Frances . . —
		Sarah . . —
Dudley, Edward . . 26		
Bailes, Benjamin . . 24		Robert . . 6
		Henry . . 5
	Mary Haw . . —	
	Sarah Williams . —	
	Ann Mitchley . —	
Lovemore, Henry . . 30	Ann . . . 29	Eliza . . . 15½
		Nancy . . 3½
		Maria . . 2½
		Sophia . . 1½
Colling, Thomas . . 49	Elizabeth . . 36	Ann . . . 16
		Joseph . . 4½
		Eliza . . . 3½
		Charlotte . . 1½
Bowsher, Charles . . 19		

TOTALS.

Male Settlers 1,210
Female Settlers (married) 704
Boys and Youths 816
Girls and Young Women . . . 745

Grand Total . . 3,475

APPENDIX IV

GENERAL CAMPBELL'S SETTLERS

BY the *Mary Ann Sophia.*—Mr. and Mrs. Mead, Mr. and Mrs. Jones, Messrs. Messer, Philipson, Anderson, Stanborough, Sharpe, Talbot, Richards, White, G. Leigh, and one child.

By the *Dowson.*—Mr. and Mrs. Charles Lucas, Mr. Philip and Mrs. Lucas, P. W. Lucas, F. Lucas, Charles and Henry Charles Campbell (the two eldest sons of the General did not come), Henry Campbell, Thomas Angell, A. G. Campbell, H. Leat, William Power, Maurice Garcia, Ely Mills, William Fisher.

By the *Salisbury.*—General and Mrs. Campbell and family, viz., Laurence, John, Frederick, William, Edward, Harriet, Catherine ; Messrs. William Whybone and mother, Thomas Field, Joseph Broadbent and son, Robert Brady, Thomas Norris, James Collett, Aigton, William Cumming.

LIEUTENANT DANIELL'S PARTY.

By the *Duke of Marlborough.*—Rev. Stephen Kay (missionary), and Mrs. Kay, Messrs. Field, J. Beddy, Captain O'Reilly (Madras, N.I.), Surgeon Wentworth, Mrs. A. Stadman, R. Restall, J. and R. Daniell, Mrs. Daniell, three children and one servant, Mr. and Mrs. Handfield, Miss Martin, Miss F. Daniell, R. Daniell, Dickson, Arrowsmith, Graham, Ward, and Hickson, Mr. and Mrs. Nitch (remained in Cape Town), and three sons, Mr. and Mrs. Love, Mrs. Ruthven and three children, Messrs. Young, Moor, Sendle and Board.

APPENDIX V

THE following letter gives a graphic and interesting account of the voyage. It is by Mr. John Mandy, a passenger by the *Nautilus*. It is addressed to his mother at Foot's Cray, Kent :—

"I take the opportunity of writing to you, as we expect in two days to put into St. Jago. I have the pleasure to inform you that we are all well and in good spirits. My letter of 5th December I suppose informed you of our disaster in the Downs; but as I hardly know what I wrote, I will give you more particulars. We left Gravesend on Thursday morning, had a fine wind to the Queen's Channel, where we arrived on the following day in the morning, and dropped anchor. It came on to blow tremendously hard, the sea running mountains high, We could not weigh anchor till Sunday afternoon, when our troubles began, the sea breaking over us in all directions,—tables, chairs, boxes, plates and dishes, men, women and children, all mixed together, tumbling over one another, and all dreadfully sea-sick, except myself and Smith, who was on deck working the ship; I below, basin-holder. In the midst of this the sea broke into our cabin windows, dashed glass and frame in, the things that were below rolling and sliding took to swimming. About three o'clock we had an alarm of fire. I ran into the captain's cabin ; found the fireplace upset, which we soon put out. At half-past eight our pilot informed us we were out of danger. When the ship struck on the sands, all was confusion and dismay; even the sailors seemed panic-struck. Every one only thought of self-safety. We lay in this situation one hour and a half, when a heavy sea set us afloat without much damage. During the time we had a light at the mast-head, and fired guns for assistance. We were much overjoyed at seeing five or six boats come to assist us, not without enduring a heavy sea. One boat's crew came on board, and told us the whole town of Ramsgate was in confusion. We made a subscription of £5 or £6 for them. We passed the Lizard with a fine breeze in two days after, when we had a gale of wind which tossed us much about, but had plenty of sea-room. We have had plenty of amusement at fishing ; saw several whales, one of which came alongside with its back ten or twelve feet out of the water. I shot at it three times with ball. It made a great noise and ran away at the rate of a mile in two minutes when wounded. We had variable winds till we saw Madeira, which we passed on the 29th December. We saw the Peak of Teneriffe, had a good view of it, covered with snow, yet the weather was so hot we were obliged to throw off most of our clothes. On the 5th we had a storm, which lasted three days, the sea running as high as our mast-head, and two of the waves broke over us ; the forepart of the ship had three tons of water in, which swamped almost every person in their beds. Joseph was washed out of his cot. The carpenter scuttled the decks, and pumped the water out. On the 8th we saw Palma, about ten at night, and a sail under land, but could not tell what she was till morning, when, to our great joy, we discovered it to be the *Chapman*—the first time we had seen her since we left the Queen's Channel. At four in the afternoon we spoke her, all well, only lost four children, had nine births. We are now sailing in company, and shall continue to do so till we get to the Cape. We have now just arrived in sight of land—Salt Island, one of the Cape de Verde islands. On the 13th we cast anchor in St. Jago, where we remained four days. Got plenty of refreshment : for an old coat, I bought 200 oranges, a fine goat and kid, and twelve cocoanuts. Mary Anne and the children were never in better health and spirits. We left St. Jago and had calms and contrary winds for a week. Got to the line on 1st February, where we saw a ship from England bound to the Brazils, that kindly offered to bring letters to England. We had a merry day in shaving old Neptune, who came on board over night. I have not time to describe the ceremony, which is not most polite. Please to let Mr. Gower's family know that himself and family are well. Be so good as to let Mr. Whalley's know you have heard from us. We have had fresh beef ever since we left St. Jago. We brought six bullocks on board, which are just gone. I bought a fine sheep for a dollar, and a turkey of 14 lbs. for an old pair of shoes, and which we have killed this day. My goat gives milk for tea night and morning. I conclude in haste, as the boat is going to leave the ship. I hope, mother, to see you and the rest of our family with us in a short time.

"From your affectionate son,
"JOHN MANDY."

The next letter is dated from the Cape of Good Hope, April 13, 1820 :—

"DEAR MOTHER,—I have the pleasure to inform you I have arrived safe at Table Bay, after a long and tedious voyage. After leaving St. Jago on the 14th March, we had variable winds and calms till the 12th April, when we had a heavy gale of wind, which lasted till twelve o'clock at night, when the weather became moderate, and the clouds cleared off, and we saw, to our great joy, the land of promise. Mary Ann, Joseph and myself have been in the best health and spirits. I have the pleasure to inform you that on the 1st March, Mary Ann was put to bed with a fine boy in latitude 18°, longitude 6°. She never had a better getting up in England, and was able to go on deck in a fortnight. When within two miles of Table Bay, it came on a calm, which lasted three hours, when we had, without a moment's notice, one of the Cape gales we hear so much talk of in England, which carried away every sail we had standing. The ship became her own master for a time, which prevented our getting in that day. The next day we saw the *Chapman*, the first time for three weeks, standing in for the Bay, when we weighed anchor, and both got in together.

We were immediately put under quarantine for twenty-four hours, and then only the heads of parties allowed to land, which caused great dissatisfaction among the rest of the settlers. I have been on shore five days, and find it a very pretty place, about as large as Greenwich. The country round about may well be called the garden of the world; the graperies in the greatest perfection, and very cheap. The hedges in many parts are myrtles and geraniums, the aloe in high perfection in full bloom—many thirty feet high. I went into an orange grove; the grandest sight I ever saw. The farmers of the country came to town on hearing of our arrival, to try to get our people to come and live with them. One farmer offered to give Joseph £40 per annum, house, clothes and victuals, or a farming man £20 and sheep. We found mutton and beef cheap,—2*d*. per lb.; fruit in great abundance. We set sail on Sunday night for Algoa Bay, and have had a long and tedious voyage for nearly three weeks. We have this moment got the Bay in sight, which I hope to be to-morrow morning. We have to travel 130 miles by land. We are provided with wagons and camp equipage; the heads of parties a marquee, and a tent to every three families.

Algoa Bay, 26th April, 1820.—I finish my letter in haste. We expect to set off for the country to-day. I have lain in camp eleven days. I landed on Sunday night, to get ready for Mary Ann and the children. When I had got all ready for them, a strong south-east wind set in, and stopped their landing for five days, the surf beating round the shore to the height of ten or twelve feet. They saw me, and could not get at me. Mary Ann and the children came on shore the 19th, very much frightened, the boat three parts full of water. We are now living on the fat of the land,—a fowl for 9*d*., beef 1½*d*. per lb., milk and eggs in great abundance. Joseph is well and in high spirits. Please to send to Gower's and inform them that you have heard from me. They are all well.

"From your affectionate and dutiful son,
"JOHN MANDY."

The following letter will be read with interest as showing how energetically the settlers proceeded in occupying their grants of land, and also giving a vivid description of the country in which they were placed. It is written by General Campbell's precursor, who was nearly sixty years of age, and who had only arrived in Albany a short time before (August, 1820). It is dated,—

"GENERAL CAMPBELL'S LOCATION,
"Albany, 28th January, 1821.

"I like this part of the country very much. It is very pleasant, and capital land; all things seem to thrive well. It is like a gentleman's garden, decorated with clumps of all sorts of flowering shrubs, as if they had been regularly planted, and all parts covered with the finest grass as high as your middle. I never saw in England so much good land together. I have nearly an acre of turnips, which is doing well. My vines are nearly all dead; I shall want five or six thousand next season, as I intend to plant a large vineyard, and some fig, orange and lemon trees. I have plenty of melons, cucumbers and pumpkins, which are coming forward very fast. I have three huts complete, and a well that I sank at the top of the garden, which has plenty of excellent water. I have felled sufficient timber to build General Campbell's house, and the men are digging stones for the walls. I have made a large kraal for cattle; all that have seen it say there is not its equal in the Colony. I am sorry our parties have not come. I think they would have been well satisfied. There is nothing wanted but a good stock of cattle and industry. I wish I had four or five hundred head of cattle, a few quarters of corn, and sufficient rations for one year. I would be better off than with £5,000 sterling in England. I have set fire to more than 500 acres of grass to burn it off the land for the young to spring up. I see nothing of the wild tribe but monkeys and a few springbucks. Near our location we have a wood, I suppose two miles in length, where I fell the timber. I have been in all parts of the wood, but have not seen any snakes. About four miles off, in a wood which I pass through on my way to Bathurst, are elephants, buffaloes, and many other different sorts of animals. I have not as yet met with any curiosities, having been very busy. I believe I have made more progress than most of the settlers. When any more settlers come out for me, I intend to form a town at the 'Reed Fountain River,' as that is a suitable place, and the General will be a good distance from other inhabitants, as it was his desire, and will have a very pleasant place close to a wood, where I can with little trouble cut avenues for him and his family to walk in the shade all day, and will have the river running nearly all round his house. My men have turned out as bad as I expected; they do not earn 8d. each per day; they are too lazy to work. They go to the magistrate at Bathurst, eleven miles distant from home, who gives them encouragement, which causes me to go out of my employ almost every week as well as they. They have already lost fifty-one days at that fun. They are in hopes of getting off next week, as they have been offered two six-dollars per day. They are getting on very fast with the magistrate's house at Bathurst. I shall be obliged to you to ask Captain Chissel for what strawberry roots he can spare, and send them by first conveyance. If Mr. Bouri is not yet gone, he will have the goodness to bring them for me; and if he would likewise be so good as to bring a bushel or two of seed potatoes, for which I will pay him. Please tell Rock to send me five or six thousand vine cuttings, with a dozen of figs in sorts, and two dozen of orange and lemon trees.

"CYPRESS MESSER."

This fine property, which the General called Barville Park, was sold at my grandfather's death, and passed to the Dell family, who are still the owners.

APPENDIX VI
BRITISH SETTLERS OF 1820

Name	Page	Name	Page
Atherstone, John	189	Huntley, Charles Hugh	193
Attwell, Richard L.	204	Jarvis, George	195
,, Richard	204	Keeton, Benjamin	197
,, William	204	Lucas, Philip	198
Ayliff, Rev. John	201	Mahoney, Thomas	194
Biggar, Alexander	190	Mandy, Joseph	222
Bisset, Lieut. Alexander	190	,, John	222
Boardman, Rev. William	194	Maynard, James Mortimer	214
Booth, Benjamin	198	,, Joshua	214
Bowker, Miles	209	McCleland, Rev. Francis	195
Bradfield, John	213	Mills, Daniel	214
Butler, Captain Thomas	191	Moodie	217
Caldecott, Dr. Charles	214	Moorcroft, James	199
Campbell, Capt. Duncan	192	Oates, John	196
,, Dr. A. G.	204	Painter, Samuel	213
,, Dr. Peter	210	Palmer, George	199
,, Major-General Charles	191	Phillipps, Thomas	208
Carlisle, John	212	Pigot, George	198
,, Frederick	213	Pote, Robert	203
Cawood, David	218	Pringle, Thomas	211
Chase, John Centlivres	193	Pullen, Thomas	219
Cock, William	207	Roberts, Dr. Edward	203
Collett, James	212	Scanlen, William	215
Damant, Edward	211	Shaw, Rev. William	197
Dyason, George	207	Shepstone, John	205
,, Isaac	207	Slater, Thomas	215
,, Joseph	207	,, Charles	215
,, Robert	207	Smith	217
Forbes, Alexander	194	Southey, George	212
Garcia, Maurice	192	Stanton, William	204
Glass, Thomas	221	Stringfellow, Thomas	199
Godlonton, Robert	192	Stubbs, John	194
Gray, William	206	Surmon, William Henry	220
Greathead, James	216	Temlett, James	197
Griffith, Charles	205	Trollip, John	213
Hartley, Benjamin	199	,, Joseph	213
,, John	199	,, Stephen	213
,, William	199	,, William	213
Haw, Simon	217	Wedderburn, Christopher	220
Hobson, David	221	White, Lieut. Thomas Charles	189
Holditch, Dr. R.	217	Wood, George	219
Hoole, James	211	Wright, William	195
Hudson, Hougham	196		

White, Thomas Charles, Lieut. in a regiment of Foot, head of White's party from Nottinghamshire. At first he was located with Lieutenant Griffith on the Endless River, which did not answer his expectations. He was subsequently removed to Albany, and the location assigned to him was near Capt. Butler's and Mr. Joseph Latham's, on the Assegai River. The outbreak of the Kafirs in 1834-5 drove him to Graham's Town, where he became Major of the local Volunteers, and Acting Deputy Quartermaster of the burgher forces. During the whole of the campaign he was actively employed in making an accurate topographical survey of the Kafir territory, and in prosecution of this, his favourite object, he had ascended an eminence near the encampment, for the purpose of sketching the surrounding country. Four men of the Cape corps had been ordered to accompany him, and they were posted at different points of the hill to guard against surprise. In spite, however, of this precaution, the wily Kafirs, crouching stealthily in the long grass, succeeded in approaching the spot unobserved, and suddenly springing upon him and the Corporal, despatched them with their assegais before the other men could afford them the slightest assistance or even apprise them of danger. On the first alarm a party proceeded from the camp to the spot where his body was lying with many wounds on the head, loins and back. His remains received a soldier's grave, dug under the shade of a bush with no other implements than the bayonets of his companions. He was of high literary and scientific attainments, considerable property, and a large and successful flockmaster. A memorial tablet in St. George's Cathedral, Graham's Town, erected by public subscription, records the melancholy event of his untoward death in the following terms :—

> Sacred to the Memory of
> THOMAS CHARLES WHITE,
>
> a native of Nottinghamshire, England, Major of the Albany local Volunteers, and Acting Deputy Quartermaster-General to the Burgher forces, formerly Lieutenant in Her Majesty's 25th Regiment of Foot, who, after many years of persevering and successful effort as an agriculturist to promote the welfare of his fellow-settlers and improve the country of his adoption, to which he emigrated in the year 1820, was slain by Kafirs on the 14th May, 1835, on the banks of the Bashee River, whither he had marched with a detachment of the British forces, under the command of Colonel Smith, C.B., to punish the calamitous and unprovoked irruption of the Kafir tribes into this Colony in December, 1834. He thus died as he had lived, in the active service of his country, ætatis xliii.
>
> This tablet is erected by the public as a tribute to those talents and that worth by which he was distinguished alike in social as in public life.

Major White left two sons, who occupy the farms adjoining Graham's Town, viz., Thomas Charles White, Esq., J.P., Table Farm, and George White, Esq., Braak Kloof, married Miss Bliss Atherstone, and are known for their independence and enterprise as sheep-farmers.

Atherstone, John, Surgeon, came with Mr. Edward Damant's party from Fakenham, Norfolk, in the ship *Ocean*. He was married, and brought with him his wife, son, and three daughters. He had been resident house-surgeon at Guy's Hospital, London, before coming to the country. In August, 1820, he applied for and obtained the district surgeoncy of Uitenhage, *vice* Mr. Mann, resigned, where he practised for a year. In 1823, he went overland to Cape Town, where he had the chief practice for several years. In 1828, he accepted the district surgeoncy of Graham's Town, vacant by the resignation of Dr. Cowie, where he remained until his death, which occurred in 1853, the result of a cart accident, aged 62 years. He acquired the farm Nantoo, the original camp of Colonel Graham before he fixed upon the present site of Graham's Town, which he called Table Farm, by which name it is now known, about nine miles distant, where he combined horse-breeding and farming with the practice of his profession. He was twice married: first to Elizabeth, daughter of Castel Damant, Esq., of Fakenham, by whom he had two sons and five daughters; viz., William Guybon, married, in 1839, Catherine, daughter of Edwin Atherstone, the poet. The career of Dr. William Guybon Atherstone was brilliant and interesting. He was only five years of age when his parents arrived in Albany; and after completing his studies under Canon Judge and Dr. Innes, with a view to the medical profession, abandoned that idea and took up survey work. In the Kafir war of 1834-5, he was assistant staff-surgeon to Colonel, afterwards Sir, Harry Smith's division. At the end of the war went home and studied in the Meath Hospital at Paris, and at Heidelberg, where he passed with honours. He returned to England, married, and brought his bride to the Colony, joined his father, and remained in practice till 1887. He is well known throughout South Africa as a scientist, particularly in geology. He was the first to pronounce the opinion that the stone found at Colesberg Kopje, now Kimberley, in 1867, was a veritable diamond weighing $21\frac{1}{4}$ carats, worth £500, which opinion was afterwards confirmed by Messrs. Hunt and Roskell, the crown jewellers in London, to whom it had been sent for inspection, and the stone was bought by Sir P. E. Wodehouse, the Governor of the Colony. In 1883 he was elected a member of the Legislative Council as a representative of the South-East Circle, and sat in Parliament till 1891. He is living in retirement at Graham's Town. Catherine, married to George Cumming, sheep farmer of Hilton, near Graham's Town; Eliza, who died young; Emily, who married John George Franklin, Esq., editor of the *Frontier Times*, Graham's Town; Caroline, married Henry Hutton, Esq., A.D.C. to the Commandant-General, Sir A. Stockenstrom, Bart., *ob.* 21st January, 1896; John, married Anna Bowker, and Bliss 30; Ann, who married George White, Esq., sheep farmer, Braak Kloof, near Graham's Town. The second family consisted of Edwin, a medical practitioner, married to Armeni Girdlestone; Walter Herschel, Acting Surgeon-Superintendent, Port Alfred Asylum; Charles, married to Emily Dickson; and Fanny, married to Hilton Barber, Esq., a noted horse-breeder of the Cradock district.

Biggar, Alexander, retired paymaster of H.M.'s 85th Regiment of Foot, head of a party from Hampshire, in the *Weymouth*. The location assigned to them was in the Kareiga Valley adjoining Major Fraser's farm, and not far from the Theopolis Mission Station. In 1834 he removed to Durban, Natal, where about thirty Englishmen resided, either permanently or in the intervals between hunting excursions. In 1833 he was appointed Landdrost by Mr. Landman, in the name of the "Association of South African Emigrants." He was suffering under great depression of spirits, consequent on the loss of his sons and his entire property, and declined to perform the duties of that office. On the 23rd December, 1838, he was killed in battle with the Zulus. His son Robert was in nominal command of a force from Port Natal against Dingaan, comprising twenty English traders and hunters, twenty Hottentots, about 1,500 blacks, fugitives from Zululand, and succeeded in capturing 3,000 to 7,000 head of cattle, with which they returned to Natal. Soon after this, in command of another expedition against the Zulus, he was killed in battle 17th April, 1838. His other son, George, was murdered by the Zulus in the great massacre of the Boers by Dingaan, 17th February, 1838. His eldest daughter, Margaret Graham Biggar, died unmarried at Graham's Town, 31st May, 1890, at the advanced age of ninety years; his other daughters, Ann, married Charles Maynard, Esq., a merchant at Graham's Town; Mary, married — Kuhr, a merchant at Port Elizabeth; Jane, married H. von Ronn, merchant at Port Elizabeth; and Helen, married N. P. Krohn, merchant at Graham's Town.

Bisset, Alexander, Lieut. on half-pay R.N., was one of Mr. Willson's party from London by the *Belle Alliance*. He brought his wife and three children, all of tender ages. He lived at Fairfax, near the Kowie, and died in 18—, and was buried at Bathurst. Of the three children that came out with him, the eldest, Sarah Maria, married P. W. Lucas, Esq., cashier of the Eastern Province Bank ; Alexander Charles took to farming, which he carried on with varied success, and is still living at East London ; the third, John Jarvis, only two years of age when his parents arrived in Albany, had a distinguished career. He obtained his commission as Ensign and Lieutenant in a battalion of native infantry (medal). He was Field-Adjutant to a division of troops proceeding to Colesberg in December, 1842, to suppress a rebellion of the Boers. He served throughout the Kafir war of 1846-7, at the commencement of which he was appointed Deputy Assistant Quartermaster-General. Was present at the battle of the Gwanga, and all the minor affairs with the Kafirs, and twice slightly wounded. He was repeatedly thanked in general orders by successive General officers, and finally received the brevet of Major for his services during the campaign. At the close of the war he was appointed Brigade-Major of British Kaffraria. On the breaking out of the war, in 1850, he was severely wounded in the first engagement with the enemy at the Boomah Pass in the Amatola Mountains (medal). Was also present in the operations subsequent to June, 1852, C.B. 1867, K.C.M.G. 1877.

Butler, Captain Thomas, of the Dublin Militia, was head of one of the Irish parties. Arrived in the Colony per *Fanny*, and was first located by the Acting-Governor Donkin in the Clanwilliam district. But as that part of the Colony did not suit him, he was removed to Albany. He suffered like the other settlers from failure of crops, the exceptional flood of 1823, and finally from the Kafir irruption of 1834-5. Subsequently he acquired a farm on the main road from Port Elizabeth to Graham's Town, adjoining that of Mr. Pullen. He brought his wife, two sons, and a daughter, the eldest a boy eleven years of age, and the youngest a girl one year old.

Campbell, Major-General Charles, brought out a party of settlers by the *Salisbury* in December, 1820, having previously sent out two other parties, who arrived before him. He was the youngest son of Colonel Charles Campbell, of Barbrick, Argyllshire, Scotland, and had seen active service at home and abroad, his last command being that of Commander of the Forces at Newfoundland. He obtained a grant of land near the Kasonga river, close to the Theopolis Mission Station, which he called Barville Park. He was thrown from his horse whilst riding from Graham's Town to Barville Park, and sustained internal injuries which resulted in his death, May 9, 1822, aged fifty years. He lies buried in the military ground adjoining the Drostdy at Graham's Town, where also his infant daughter Catherine was interred, June 4, 1829, aged eight years and four months. The sons who came to the country with their father and mother were (1) John, who obtained a clerkship in the office of the Protector of Slaves at Graaff Reinet, and by diligence and care rose to various positions of trust and importance, in all of which he earned distinction and the approval of his superiors. In 1847 he obtained leave of absence and visited England, where he married a Miss West. His last appointment was that of Resident Magistrate of Cape Town, from which he was retired on full pay in 1884, after upwards of sixty years' faithful service. He died at Cape Town, August 26, 1888, at the advanced age of eighty-two years, leaving a widow, three sons, all in responsible positions in the public service, and four daughters. (2) Frederick, who served as a Volunteer and afterwards as a Provisional Ensign in the Cape Mounted Riflemen throughout the Kafir campaign of 1835 (medal). In 1844 he proceeded in command of a troop to Port Natal and was engaged against the revolted Zulu chief, Todo. In September, 1848, he commanded three squadrons at Bloemfontein, and advanced to Winburg for the suppression of the Boer rebellion. Served throughout the Kafir war of 1851-3, including the operations in the Amatolas, passage of and operations across the Kei in December, 1852, and other desultory operations. Commanded a squadron with the force under Sir George Cathcart against the Baralong chief, Moshesh, in December, 1852, and January, 1853, which service concluded the war. He received a serious injury whilst actively engaged against the enemy at Buffalo Post, 27th February, 1852, by the dislocation of the right ankle and fracture of the bone of the leg. He retired from the army October 26, 1858, and resided at King William's Town, where he died, December 26, 1884, at the age of seventy-four years. He married late in life, and left three sons. (3) William, who returned to the Colony after completing his education in England, and was for some years manager of the Port Elizabeth Bank, and later a General Agent at Alexandria. He married Miss Jessie Malet Lucas, and died at Graham's Town, 19th December, 1879, at the age of sixty-six years, s. p. (4) Edward Andrews, also completed his education and returned to the Colony. He owned a farm on the Bushman's River, near Sidbury, and was a flockmaster. He married Priscilla, daughter of Lieutenant R. Daniell, R.N., of Sidbury Park, and soon after sold his farm and removed to Graham's Town, where he died of consumption, 26th June, 1857, in his fortieth year, leaving a widow and two daughters, the eldest of whom married Charles A. Dickson, Esq., merchant at Cape Town.

Campbell, Captain Duncan, half-pay officer of the Royal Marines, brought out a party from Hampshire in the *Weymouth*. The Acting-Governor, General Donkin, fearing to pour too many settlers into Albany all at once, located the party at the Endless River, where Captain Campbell tried sheep-farming with the Southdown breed he had brought with him. This locality was quite unsuited to sheep-farming, and Captain Campbell was removed at his own request to Albany, v. a. p. He obtained a grant of the abandoned farm formerly occupied by Philip Botha about three miles to the northeast of Graham's Town, where he lived and died, s. p.

Garcia, Maurice, was one of the settlers introduced by General Campbell, who arrived in the brig *Dowson*, after a protracted voyage of nearly six months. He brought letters of recommendation to the Governor of the Colony, who advised him to purchase the site on which Port Elizabeth has been built; but he obtained from a friend an unfavourable report of the appearance of the place, describing the shores around the port as nothing but bare sand hills. He therefore did not proceed to the Frontier, but succeeded in obtaining a Government appointment at George as Clerk of the Peace, with leave to practise as an Attorney of the Supreme Court. He was well qualified for the position, as he was a gentleman who had received a liberal education in England and France. He studied Dutch in the Colony, and was duly admitted a sworn translator of the Supreme Court. He held the office of Clerk of the Peace until 1861, when it was abolished. He then accepted the magistracy of Richmond, and eventually that of Riversdale, where he died in 1884. He left two sons in the Civil Service, Arthur Garcia, Esq., C.C. and R.M. of Uitenhage, Paymaster-General and Inspector-General of the Colonial Forces during the wars of 1878-81, and at one time Private Secretary to the late General Gordon ; and Egbert Garcia, C.C. and R.M. of Queen's Town.

Godlonton, Robert, one of Mr. Bailie's party from London by the *Chapman*, v. a. p. He married for the second time, Sarah, daughter of Mr. Richard Attwell, of Scott's party. In 1854 he was, with Mr. George Wood, elected a member of the Legislative Council representing the Eastern districts, but he and his colleague resigned that position. In 1862 he was re-elected, and again in 1864, and continued to sit till 1868, when, after the Session, the Council was dissolved with the Assembly. At the general election in 1869 he was again returned, and sat till 1872, when the responsible Government Bill was passed. He died at his residence, Beaufort House, Graham's Town, May 30,

1884, in his ninetieth year, leaving a widow and one son and one daughter. His son, Benjamin Durban Godlonton, is a merchant in London; the daughter married Mr. Benjamin Hoole.

Chase, John Centlivres, formed one of Mr. Bailie's party, arriving by the *Chapman*. He was a married man; his daughter Louisa, an infant child, died in the Bay of Biscay on the passage out. Bailie's party was located at the mouth of the Fish River, and the place was called Cuylerville. Mr. Chase was not cut out for agriculture, and his wife dying at the Kowie, in 1830, leaving four children, he removed to Cape Town, where he practised as a Notary Public, and there married for the second time a daughter of Mr. Korston (of Cradock Place, at one time a Lieutenant in the Dutch Navy) and widow of Commissary General Damant, by whom she had two sons. About 1835 or 36 he returned to the Frontier and continued to practise as a Notary till Sir Henry Young was Lieutenant-Governor (1847) at Graham's Town, where he acted as Secretary to Government till Sir Henry left, when he was appointed C.C. and R.M. to the newly-formed division of Albert. He founded Alcival North, designed and presented its seal, and from there was promoted to Uitenhage as C.C. and R.M., where he remained till he retired on pension, 1855. In 1864 he was elected Member of the House of Assembly for Port Elizabeth, but resigned his seat. At the General Election in 1869 he was elected as a Member of the Legislative Council. He was regarded as an authority on statistics relating to the Colony; author of a continuation of Wilmot's History of the Colony and other volumes descriptive of the Eastern Province; also published Green's Journey to Natal in 1829, with a map of the country traversed by Green and his companion, Dr. Cowie. Mr. Chase was twice married. By his first wife he had two sons—Henry and Frederick—and two daughters. His second wife was a daughter of Mr. Korston, of Cradock Place, near Port Elizabeth (at one time a Lieutenant in the Dutch Navy), and widow of Commissary-General Damant, by whom he had two sons and four daughters. Both sons by the first wife are dead; the sons by the second wife survive, viz., I. C. Chase, auctioneer at Rouxville, O.F.S.; and Frederick Korston Chase, H.M.'s Customs, Port Elizabeth. Mr. Chase died at his residence, Cradock Place, about five miles from Port Elizabeth, his death being hastened by his being thrown from his carriage some time before, December 15, 1876, aged seventy years. The head of the family is Mr. Harry Chase, Attorney-at-Law, Uitenhage.

Huntley, Charles Hugh, son of Captain Huntley, an officer in the Royal African Corps, who fell at the attack on Graham's Town in 1819. He was born soon after the battle in one of the few houses that then existed in the embryo town. He became identified with the settlers by his marriage with Miss Bailie, only daughter of the head of that party, one of the first to land at Algoa Bay by the *Chapman*. At the age of nineteen he entered the public service, and served in the Lieutenant-Governor's office in 1845. He took his share in the war of 1846-7, and was captain of the Graham's Town Volunteers in 1860, commanding the escort to H.R.H. Prince Alfred, when he visited Graham's Town in that year. He filled various offices of importance up to 1869, when he was appointed Civil Commissioner and Resident Magistrate of Graham's Town, which city he did much to improve by tree-planting along the streets and other useful works. He was finally retired on pension after forty-six years of active service. In 1887 he received the distinction of C.M.G. He died in England, August 16, 1889. His wife, by whom he had a large family—six sons and four daughters—predeceased him. His eldest son, Hougham Charles Huntley, obtained a commission in the army, in the 10th North Lincolnshire regiment, September 8, 1863, and is now Lieutenant-Colonel in command of that regiment, stationed at Singapore. His second son, Henry, died at Alcival North, November, 1867; his third son, Hugh Campbell Huntley, took to farming, and is known

O

as an intelligent sheep and ostrich farmer, at Highlands, near Graham's Town; the fourth son, Charles Huntley, was in the public service, and was Acting Civil Commissioner and Resident Magistrate at King William's Town at the time of his death, in December, 1886, at Graham's Town; the fifth son, Gordon Merriman Huntley, entered the public service in 1878, and was appointed accountant to the Administrator of British Bechuanaland in 1885, which appointment he still holds; the sixth son, Douglas Huntley, is employed in the gold mines, Johannesburg. The daughters: (1) Jessie, married Mr. Frederick Holland, a merchant in Graham's Town, and died 3rd January, 1874; (2) Agnes, married Benjamin Herbert Holland, Esq., Registrar of Deeds at Capetown; (3) Amy D'Esterre, married the Hon. Arthur Gilliebrand Hubbard, who died 7th March, 1896; and (4) May, married Owen Dunell, Esq., merchant at Port Elizabeth.

Stubbs, John, one of Dr. William Clarke's party from London by the *Northampton*. He brought a wife and six children. He was killed by the Kafirs at the Clay Pits, near Graham's Town, on the outbreak of the war of 1834-5. His second son, Thomas, was a well-known figure in Graham's Town during the war of 1846-7, being in command of an irregular force called "Stubbs's Rangers," which did good service in scouring the surroundings of the city and clearing it of small parties of marauders. He carried on the business of a saddler and harness maker, and was the first to commence the running of a passenger cart to and from Port Elizabeth, in 1848, at first as often as the conveyance was full, afterwards regularly once a week. His brother, William Stubbs, was a trader at Whittlesea, and did also good service during the war of 1846-7.

Mahoney, Thomas, head of a party who came from London by the *Northampton*. He was a married man with a daughter and a son. He was located on the frontier line of the Zuurveld, with the Fish River Bush just behind him, a situation of great danger in case of an outbreak of the Kafirs. The Komst River bordered the southern extremity of his location, and at the point of his boundary in that direction were the "Clay Pits," a place famous among the Kafir tribes, where they were accustomed to procure the red clay, with which, at certain seasons, they anointed their bodies. The peril of the situation was cruelly experienced by Mr. Mahoney on the irruption of the Kafirs in 1834-5; he and his son, and his son-in-law, Henderson, a merchant at Graham's Town, who was on a visit at the time, were found murdered by the roadside about a mile from their house. Mrs. Mahoney and two grandchildren (having two other grandchildren in Graham's Town with their mother) were in the bush all night, and had walked some twenty miles over a rough and difficult road on their way to Graham's Town, where they were rescued from a cruel death by a search party that had been sent out to the assistance of Mr. Mahoney. Their daughter, Jessie, married Mr. Middleton, a merchant at Port Elizabeth, and later left the Colony. Her mother married Mr. Joseph Smith, a merchant at Port Elizabeth, of the firm of W. & J. Smith, was again left a widow, and afterwards died at sea.

Forbes, Alexander, one of the settlers in Mr. Parker's party, from Cork, Ireland, by the *East Indian*. He was an industrious shoemaker, was, on the breaking out of the war of 1834-5, attacked in open day by Kafirs at his dwelling on Waai Plaats, despatched by numerous assegai wounds, his dwelling fired and reduced to ashes. His wife, with a family of seven young children, fortunately escaped.

Boardman, Rev. William, a clergyman of the Church of England, who came out as chaplain to Mr. Willson's party by the *Belle Alliance*. Of his antecedents nothing is known; but in one of his letters to the Colonial Secretary soon after arrival Mr. Willson describes him as "a most worthy and respectable clergyman of the Church of England."

He was stationed at Bathurst, and there officiated, as well as at Graham's Town and at Cuylerville. He also kept a school at Bathurst, where he finally died, in 1825, aged forty-nine years. He brought with him his wife and six children—three boys and three girls—and two unmarried sisters. A son of his was a farmer at Spijion Kop, district of Albert, where he died somewhere about 1860. One of the sisters married Major John Crause, who was farming near Graaff Reinet, but had no family.

McCleland, Rev. Francis, B.A., T.C.D., came out with the Irish party of which Mr. William Parker was the head. He was then a young married man, and was approved as a properly ordained minister of the United Church of England and Ireland, and as such Earl Bathurst directed that he should be employed, and a salary provided for him by the local Government. He was at first sent by the Acting-Governor, Sir R. S. Donkin, with other immigrants, and located at Jan van Dissel's Vley, district of Clanwilliam, where he remained for about two years. Being thrown almost entirely amongst the Dutch, he acquired the language sufficiently to preach in it, but the pronunciation he never really mastered. "I remember," says his daughter, "being much amused by an old Boer remarking, with more candour than politeness, that he spoke it very 'kromme' (crooked). That situation was quite unsuited to the new comers, and they were finally removed to Albany. Mr. McCleland officiated as Colonial Chaplain at Graham's Town until appointed to the chaplaincy at Port Elizabeth, which he held for over thirty years, where he built St. Mary's Church, and died July 10, 1853. His income for all the years of his pastorate was only £200 per annum, with a trifle for house rent, and some glebe land from which it was expected that he might make something considerable ; but it was rarely tenanted, being barren, worthless ground, and the only addition to his income from that source was a dozen white-handled knives, two pieces of Boer chintz, and an occasional brace of wildfowl. He was allowed to take pupils, and he had a very successful school for boys for some years, most of them well-known names on the Frontier—Chatunds, Pullens, Watsons, Hugh, etc., etc. I can remember but few of the names of the party who came out with my father, but I know there were the Scanlans, one of whose descendants is Sir Thomas, Frans, and Francis, the latter being Collector of Customs for many years in Port Elizabeth, where he died." He had two sons and five daughters. Frank, the eldest son, married in England, and is dead ; George, the other, is supposed to be living somewhere in the Uitenhage district. The eldest daughter, Elizabeth, married Mr. Higgins, a merchant at Port Elizabeth, and is dead ; Anna, the third daughter, married Mr. H. M. Scrivener, attorney of the Supreme Court, in practice at Port Elizabeth, and is also dead ; Adelaide, the fourth daughter, married Mr. W. Fleming, merchant, of Port Elizabeth, and is living in England ; Margaret, the second daughter, and Georgina, the youngest, are unmarried, and living at Wynberg, near Cape Town.

Jarvis, George, one of Mr. Willson's party by *La Belle Alliance*, a young man twenty-one years of age when he arrived. He was a prominent figure in Graham's Town, where he practised as an attorney of the Circuit Court, taking a leading share in the various plans for the improvement of the town and the prosperity of the district. He acquired a farm, which he called Orange Grove, a few miles out of Graham's Town, beyond Howitzon's Poort, which was a pleasant place of resort for himself and his friends. He married a Dutch settler's daughter, by whom he had two children—a son, Frederick, who died at an early age of consumption ; and a daughter, who married Major Charles Hurland Bell, of the Cape Mounted Riflemen, two of whose sons hold important positions under Government in Basutuland.

Wright, William, one of Mr. Mills's party from London, by the *Sir George Osborne*. He was married, and brought his wife, one daughter three years of age, and one son a twelvemonth old. He was chiefly engaged in mercantile pursuits, taking his share in the various political, municipal, and general efforts at improvement of the town and district. In 1855 he was elected member of the House of Assembly for the constituency of Cradock ; and at the same election was returned for the electoral district of Victoria East. He resigned his seat, and represented neither constituency. He died at Graham's Town in 1857, aged sixty-three years and ten months, leaving his wife a widow, who survived him till 1867, when she died, aged seventy-four years, and several daughters, and the son who had come to the country as an infant. The widow, Mrs. Rosa Wright, built and endowed the beautiful church, called Christ's Church, at Oatlands, part of Graham's Town, of which the Rev. M. Norton is the present rector. Mr. Wright's eldest daughter, (1) Martha, married Mr. Charles Henry Caldecott, M.L.C., and died 1892 ; (2) Julia, married James Henry Greathead, Esq., a merchant of Graham's Town, surviving her husband and living at Fairlawn, Graham's Town ; (3) Charlotte, married John Edwin Wood, Esq., M.L.A. ; (4) Emily, married first William Wood and second Joseph Gadd, Esq., who represented Victoria East in the House of Assembly in 1867, and was, with her husband, cruelly murdered by their own servants, October, 1894 ; (5) Eliza, married Dr. Spackman ; (6) Rosa Isabel, who married Frederick Charles Bate, Esq., also a merchant at Graham's Town, who are now living at Queen's Town. His only son, William, married Sophia Rowan, and died 5th March, 1891, aged seventy-one years.

Oates, John, was one of Mr. Sephton's party, arriving by the *Aurora*. He was a married man with wife and two small children—a girl aged three years and a boy aged one year. He was located with the *Salem* party on the Assegai River, where, with others, he carried on farming under difficulties. After being ruined by the three successive Kafir wars, he removed to Graham's Town, where he carried on a baking business in High Street for many years. The daughter, Mary Ann, married — Dugmore, one of Mr. Gardner's party of settlers ; the son was also married, and had a family of seven sons and one daughter. They all migrated from Albany to Griqualand West in 1870, where the old man died on his farm, adjoining Kimberley, in 1870. The grandsons are spread over the country in various directions, one of them being a Wesleyan minister at Cala, Transkei.

Hudson, Hougham, from Canterbury, Kent, by the *Zoroaster*, v. a. p. He was retired from the office of Civil Commissioner and Resident Magistrate of Albany owing to ill-health, 1st October, 1852, and placed on the pension list. In a letter addressed to him by His Excellency Sir George Cathcart, Governor of the Colony, dated 18th September, 1852, this sentence occurs : "I sincerely regret the cause which has induced you to resign an office which you have so long and so ably filled in most difficult times. But it must be satisfactory to you to know that though you are unable to perform service as Civil Commissioner of Albany you contribute to the public service in another generation of your family a Civil Commissioner for the district of Somerset (his eldest son), than whom no officer in that capacity carries on his duties more entirely to my satisfaction." Mr. Hudson had altogether twelve children—nine boys and three girls. His first child was born at Bathurst and died in Graaff Reinet. He died at his son's residence, Hougham Park, Coega, near Port Elizabeth, 5th July, 1860, aged sixty-seven years, leaving the following children : (1) Hougham, who became Civil Commissioner and Resident Magistrate of Graaff Reinet, was retired on pension January, 1890, and is living at Graaff Reinet. He was twice married, first to Helen Maria Currie, sister of Sir Walter Currie, by whom he had six children, two of whom survive ; second, to Fanny Carlisle, widow of Joseph Currie, by whom he has one son, Dr. Hudson, the present district surgeon at Graaff Reinet. (2) Andries, who died at his farm, 1893, s. p. (3)

Charles, who served in the Crimea, and attained the rank of colonel in the army, died in England. (4) Mary, who married Matthew Woodifield, Assistant Colonial Engineer, and died in England ; (5) George, who married a daughter of Mr. Wm. Smith, of Port Elizabeth, and at one time was British Resident at Pretoria, South African Republic, and afterwards head of the detective department at Kimberley, retired on pension January, 1895, and now living in England. And (6) John, who married Dora, daughter of W. Gilfillan, Esq., Civil Commissioner of Cradock; at the time of his death, in 1893, was Civil Commissioner and Resident Magistrate of Oudtshoorn.

Keeton, Benjamin, came as a lad with the Nottingham party, by the *Albury*, being then nineteen years of age. He early took to trading and hunting, which was a great attraction to the young men of the Settlement, and in which pursuit he was successful. He married Miss Ford, a settler's daughter, and, having acquired the farm Lombard's Post, not far from the Kowie, took to farming. He renamed the place Southwell, after his native town in Nottinghamshire. Besides growing oat-hay to supply the troops in garrison at Graham's Town, cattle rearing and horse breeding on a small scale, he cultivated the orange tree, which of late years formed a feature on the estate, a very large quantity of this delicious fruit finding a ready sale at Graham's Town and elsewhere. He was a liberal donor to the English Church, granting to the Bishop of Graham's Town a site for a school and dwelling for a mission station, and subsequently a further grant on which to erect a church for the use of himself, family, and neighbours. He died at a good age, about 1870, leaving two sons, both known as intelligent agriculturists in that part of the Albany district—the eldest, W. Parry Keeton, who lives at Paarde Kraal, and Bucher Keeton, who lives at Southwell.

Shaw, Rev. William, missionary of the Wesleyan Society, came out with the Sephton party by the *Aurora*, who were located on the Assegai River, where they founded the village of Salem, v. a. p. He was General Superintendent of Wesleyan Missions in South East Africa, and returned to England in 1856. He was elected President of the Wesleyan Conference in 1865. He died in London after a long career of usefulness, aged seventy-three years, 4th December, 1872, leaving two sons and two daughters. His eldest son was the Rev. W. Shaw, M.A., Vicar of Zealand Conyers, Cornforth, Lancashire, England, who died in 1890; the second son is Matthew Ben Shaw, who discovered the falls on the 'Tsitsa River in 1843, served during the Kafir war of 1846-47, and was appointed by Governor Sir Harry Smith to act as " mediator between all tribes to whom a British Resident is not nominated." He was also entrusted with various duties of primary importance connected with the Kafirs, representing the Government as British Resident under High Commissioner in Kafirland. His present appointment is that of Magistrate of the Territory of Port St. John's, Pondoland. The eldest daughter married Henry Blaine, Esq., merchant at Graham's Town; the other daughter married the Rev. William Impey, Oatlands, Graham's Town.

Temlett, James, one of Mr. Erith's party from Surrey, which came in the *Brilliant*. He was a young man just married, his eldest son being born in the Bay of Biscay, taking the name of the ship. He engaged in mercantile pursuits, and lived in Graham's Town, on Market Square, where he carried on his business of a general dealer. His eldest son, James Brilliant Temlett, lived at Alice, where he kept a general store ; his second son, John Temlett, carried on his father's business ; and one daughter married Thomas Aylesbury, who kept the roadside house of accommodation on the road to the Kowie. The family were all Baptists, and strong supporters of that sect. The name has died out, neither son having any issue. Mr. Temlett died at Graham's Town, 16th November, 1862, aged sixty-five years.

Pigot, George, head of a party from Berkshire by the transport *Northampton*. He was located with Dr. Dalgairns on a grant of land in the Kowie River Valley, about fifteen miles from Graham's Town. It is presumed he was a widower, as he was then forty-five years of age, and a daughter aged seventeen years accompanied him. He was once a cavalry officer, and he brought with him £5,000 to lay out in improvements among the settlers, besides having several hundred pounds a year of income. He spent a large sum of money in building a fine house and enclosing his cultivated lands—sinking £3,000—which he called Pigot Park, by which name the estate is still known. He was actively engaged with Captain Duncan Campbell, Mr. Phillipps, and others of the most influential among the settlers, in measures against the reversal of Sir R. Donkin's plans, which Lord Charles Somerset did not approve of. He was a great sufferer by the war of 1834-5. He died June 20, 1830, and was buried at Graham's Town, leaving his daughter, Catherine Mary Pigot, executrix of his will, and bequeathing the Pigot Park property in trust in such a way that the executrix was obliged to obtain an Ordinance of the Legislature to enable her to sell and dispose of the landed property and to invest the proceeds thereof in the names of trustees for the purposes provided by his will (Ord. 12 of 1848). Except for this property the name would have died out in Albany. Pigot Park is now owned by Mr. William Wicks.

Booth, Benjamin, was one of Mr. Sephton's party who came by the *Aurora*, and were located on the Assegai River, about sixteen miles from Graham's Town. The village of Salem was founded by this party. He brought a wife and three daughters, all of tender years. He left Salem, and resided at Green Fountain, near the Kowie, a farm now occupied by the family of the late Mr. Richard Walker. He was unsuccessful at farming, and, crops failing, he removed to Graham's Town, where he carried on a general business. Afterwards he retired and lived at Bathurst, where he resided during the war of 1846-7. He died at Graham's Town, April 28, 1862, his wife having predeceased him in June, 1847. He left one son and six daughters, of whom only the son and two youngest daughters are now living. His son, Mr. B. Booth, the present representative of the family, is living at Port Elizabeth, being Superintendent of Natives.

Lucas, Philip, one of the settlers introduced by General Campbell, arriving, with others sent out by the General, in the brig *Dowson*. The vessel had a protracted voyage of nearly six months' duration. She had on board a detachment of the 54th Regiment, commanded by Major Cuyler, and among her other passengers Frank Power, the comedian. Mr. Lucas brought his wife, two sons, and one daughter. General Campbell's premature death no doubt affected his prospects. He carried on farming in an amateur fashion at Eland's Kloof, Reedfontein and in Howitzson's Poort, but not with success. He was very fond of flowers, and whilst at Reedfontein, in the bush in front of the house, had splendid walks cut out, and a maze in which the children could easily lose themselves for a time. His latter days were spent in Graham's Town, where he died October 11, 1855, aged seventy-one years. His eldest son, Philip William Lucas, was first a clerk in Mr. Antonio Chiappini's office in Cape Town, and shortly afterwards entered the business of Mr. Heugh, at Uitenhage. He came to Graham's Town in 1823 or 1824 as Mr. Heugh's confidential clerk, and afterwards became a partner in the mercantile establishment of Heugh and Fleming, at that time the principal establishment on the Frontier. He did not like business, and was glad to accept the agency of the Cape of Good Hope Bank at Graham's Town, which he resigned on being appointed cashier of the Eastern Province Bank, which was established in 1839 at Graham's Town, and which he held till the dissolution of the Bank in 1872. He married a daughter of Commander Bissit, R.N., of Fairfax, Kowie, and died at Graham's Town June 25, 1892, aged ninety-one years, leaving one son, William Tyndal Lucas, who served during the war of 1851-3 as a Volunteer under Mr. Dodds Pringle, and had his horse shot under him in action. Joined the original Frontier Armed Mounted Police as Lieutenant, and was wounded 8th January, 1853. Mr. Lucas's other son, Frederick, married Miss Lamont, daughter of Lieutenant Lamont, of the 2nd Queen's, and was for many years Secretary of the Eastern Province Trust Company at Graham's Town. He died at East London in 1873, leaving a large family, who unfortunately have been unsuccessful in life. The daughter married John Philip Camm, Esq., an officer in the Commissariat Department stationed at Graham's Town.

Moorcroft, James, one of Mr. George Scott's party from Surrey by the *Nautilus*. He was a married man with wife and two children when he arrived. He devoted himself to agricultural pursuits, and after being driven off his location in Lower Albany by the wars of 1834-35 and 1846-47 he removed to the Winter Mountain, beyond Fort Beaufort, where he continued to carry on farming till his death. His son, Mr. Sidney Moorcroft, is a noted horse breeder in the Queen's Town district.

Stringfellow, Thomas, one of Mr. Bailie's party by the *Chapman*. He was a married man with wife and three daughters. He was a printer by trade, and not fitted for agricultural occupation. He had a long and honoured career in the public service, his last appointment being that of Civil Commissioner and Resident Magistrate of Fort Beaufort, where he died in 1860 s.p.

Palmer, George, one of the Nottingham party by the *Albury*. He was driven from his farm at Waai Plaats by the war of 1835, and then took up his residence in Graham's Town, occupying the premises at the corner of Somerset Street and African Street. He was a great horse breeder and patron of the turf. Towards the end of his days he contracted to convey the mails between Graham's Town and Cradock, which service he carried on for some years. His eldest son, Mr. James Palmer, is a farmer at Cypherfontein, a little above Graham's Town, and the younger, who used to ride the race-horse "Clear the Way" at the turf meetings, is farming at Waai Plaats.

Hartley, Benjamin, with wife and two daughters, belonged to Mr. Hazelhurst's party from Lancashire.

Hartley, John, with wife and eight children belonged to the Nottingham party under Dr. Calton by the *Albury*.

Hartley, William, one of Mr. Wainwright's party from Yorkshire by the transport *John*, was forty years of age when he arrived, and not married.

The name of Hartley is to be found scattered over the Colony and beyond it, some engaged in commercial, others in agricultural pursuits. The original settlers did not remain long on the locations assigned to them. The parents soon opened a small business in Bathurst, while the young men started on a life of adventure as hunters and traders on the Kafir border, which latter was forbidden without special permit from the authorities. At that time the Kowie Bush and the Fish River Bush teemed with large game, such as elephants, buffaloes, seacows, etc., and parties of young men left the more peaceful and safer pursuits of agricultural and pastoral life for the rougher and more dangerous but profitable and exhilarating life of hunting and trading. The war of 1835 put a stop to this to a very great extent. Some years before this event the eldest brother, William Hartley, had found his way into and established a home in the country beyond the Fish River boundary then known as the Tarka, where he settled down to a farming life combined with shop-keeping among the Boers in that part. He was fairly successful, and was appointed Field Cornet, and generally acted as Government Agent among the Boers and the Tambookies on the border. When the Boers decided on the "great trek" across the Orange and Vaal Rivers, he declined the offer of a command of some of their party, and shortly after removed to Graham's Town, where he settled until after the war of 1850, when the Tambookies having been driven across the Black Kei, their country, now known as the Queen's Town district, was allotted to farmers, and opened business in the new township. Whilst residing in Graham's Town, he was for some years one of the Municipal Commissioners and took his share of the public duties of a citizen, as he did wherever he resided. He finally followed his children, who had, most of them, settled at the Diamond Fields, and died at Kimberley at the ripe age of ninety years. Some of his children are settled in the Transvaal, the eldest son living, however, is Mr. C. H. Hartley, who edited and published the *Independent* newspaper at Kimberley for about sixteen years, and was the first to start a daily paper on the Diamond Fields, the second or third daily newspaper in South Africa. Thomas Hartley, the next brother, established himself at Bathurst, where he carried on the business of farmer and storekeeper. In the dearth of medical men, he made himself very useful in the surrounding neighbourhood as an unprofessional doctor in simple cases, having studied sufficiently to be able, in cases of emergency, to advise and prescribe until a medical man could be brought from Graham's Town. He also died at a ripe old age. He left a large family, the young men of which removed to Kaffraria on the settlement of that country, and are still farming in the neighbourhood of King William's Town. Jeremiah Hartley went into the Wesleyan ministry and laboured as a missionary amongst the Basutus, Baralongs, etc., in Bechuanaland and Basutuland. He established the important mission station of Thaba 'Nchu, where the chief Moroko finally settled with his tribe. One of the results of his work was shown in the steadfast loyalty to the white man of that chief and his people during all the native disturbances which affected the country. This devoted missionary died at his post, amongst his people, and his grave may be found in the cemetery on the old station. His eldest son was for some years Town Clerk of Cradock, and died at that place while still in office in 1893. Of John Hartley nothing is known beyond that he settled in Graham's Town and died about thirty years ago. Henry Hartley, the youngest, early left civilization behind him and was one of the very few white men who ventured into the dominions of that cruel, bloodthirsty despot Moselikatze, chief of the Matabeles. When that country was more of a *terra incognita* to the civilized world than the "dark" continent is to-day, this adventurous member of the Hartley family hunted elephants and rhinoceri in the far north, bordering on the regions of the Zambesi. Hairy almost as a lion himself physically, he was a terror to the king of beasts, and for about forty years hunted and traded in that country at the proper season of the year. He made a home for himself on one of the slopes of the Magaliesberg, which he called Thorndale, where hunters and travellers were always sure of a hearty welcome and entertainment. He gained the confidence of the cruel tyrant of the Matabeles sufficiently to get permission to hunt in his country, but the guides supplied by the chief had strict instructions not to allow any search for precious minerals, the presence of which in the country was firmly believed in by Mr. Hartley. He died at Magaliesberg somewhere about 1875, having been severely mauled by a rhinoceros about twelve months previously, when he had two or three ribs broken, which no doubt hastened his death. One of his sons died in Matabeleland, having overstayed a few days the proper season in the elephant country. Baines, the traveller, built a tomb and engraved a few lines to keep the memory green of his favourite son Willie, Jewell, a fellow traveller, taking a photo of the little heap of bushes which, under a tree marked J. W. H. 29(5)70, were all that marked the early grave of the gallant boy. "Hartley Hill" was named after Henry Hartley by Baines the traveller as an acknowledgment to him who had first shown him the locality of the Simbo gold reefs (*Gold Regions of South-East Africa*, p. 29), 1,157 miles from Pietermaritzburg). The Hartley family bore their part in the Kafir wars, most of the sons having been on the different commands as volunteers. One of the sisters, Mary, lost a husband murdered by Kafirs, the other sisters married and settled with their families in and about the neighbourhood of Graham's Town and Bathurst.

Ayliff, Rev. John, came to the Colony with the British settlers of 1820 by the *Belle Alliance* as one of Mr. Willson's party. In 1827 he was ordained a Wesleyan missionary, and appointed to Kafirland. He was at Butterworth as missionary to Hintza, the paramount chief of Kaffraria, until the war of 1835 broke out, when, with his family, he had to fly for safety. His dwelling-house and all his property were destroyed. At the close of the war, upon the urgent representations of Mr. Ayliff to the Government, Sir Benjamin D'Urban released the Fingoes from Kafir bondage, and at the desire of the Governor, Mr. Ayliff, led them out, escorted by Colonel, afterwards Sir Harry, Smith, and the missionary had the satisfaction of seeing the vast multitude of Fingoes, numbering 16,000 men, women, and children, with some 20,000 head of cattle, safely settled under British protection in the Peddie district. An Ayliff Memorial Church has, during 1894, been erected by the Fingo tribe at Butterworth, to the memory of this old missionary, costing about £1,700. During 1840 Mr. Ayliff established a mission called Haslope Hills, in the Tarka district, for the emancipated slaves, and laboured there many years. In 1854, at the request of Sir George Grey, then Governor of the Colony, Mr. Ayliff superintended the erection, and established, the Heald Town Native Industrial Institution for the training of Fingo boys and girls. Here he successfully laboured for six years and trained some of the first native ministers, when his health broke down. He shared with other early missionaries the toil and difficulty of translating the Scriptures into the Kafir language, and published a very useful Kafir vocabulary. After forty years spent in benefiting the native tribes of South Africa, he visited England once more, and with her who had been the partner of his toils and labour received honour such as is rarely paid to a missionary from abroad. On returning to his much-loved work his health completely broke down, and he died at Fauresmith, Orange Free State, May 17, 1862, aged sixty-four years, leaving his widow, five sons and three daughters. A short history of the Fingo tribe by Mr. Ayliff, in manuscript, is in the Cape Town library. His eldest son, the Hon. John Ayliff, died at Natal in 1877. He was appointed in 1846 by Governor Sir P. Maitland to raise a body of natives for service in the field during the Kafir war. He acted as Field-Adjutant to Major Sutton's division, was appointed Commandant of Native Levies in the field in the following year, and in 1849 was made interpreter to the High Commissioner of British Kaffraria. During General Cathcart's campaigns across the Kei and against Moshesh he acted as Secretary to the High Commissioner, and in the same capacity to Sir George Grey when he visited Natal in 1855. After holding the appointment of Auditor in Kaffraria for some years he was appointed Treasurer in Natal in 1862; and up to the time of his promotion to be Judge of the newly-constituted Native High Court, in 1876, he continued to discharge the duties of that office, often in conjunction with other officers, as, for instance, when the two somewhat incongruous posts of Postmaster-General and Colonial Treasurer were combined. For some years his health, never very robust, had been failing; yielding at last to necessity, he sought to try the effects of a voyage to Europe. A favourable opportunity presented itself, but the day broke to find he had passed away. The remains were carried by the steamer *Danube* that they might be interred with his friends in the old Colony. Reuben Ayliff, the second son, was employed during the Kafir wars of 1846-47 and 1850-51; during the latter served as Captain Commandant of native lines. Leaving business about 1864 and settling in Graham's Town, became Mayor of the city, and was elected three times to that honourable position. For several years he was one of the representatives in the House of Assembly for the electoral division of Uitenhage. After this he became interpreter of the Eastern Districts Court in the Dutch and Kafir languages, and held the appointment for seventeen years. During the latter years of his life he has devoted much valuable time to the cause of temperance, and for a long time has been a staunch Good Templar. Twice he has been chosen as a delegate to the R. W. Grand Lodge of America, which country he visited in that capacity. For several years successively he held the office in the Colony of G.W.C.T. The Hon. William Ayliff, the third son, has been a successful farmer, and for a long time lived on his farm "Wardens," near to the town and in the district of Fort Beaufort, which electoral division he for many years represented in the House of Assembly. He became Secretary for Native Affairs during the ministry of Sir Gordon Sprigg from 1878 to 1881, and in that capacity rendered valuable service to the Colony. During the long Kafir and Basutu wars, both as Captain of Native Levies as well as Secretary for Native Affairs, he rendered valuable service, and, especially in the latter capacity, was sometimes placed in trying and difficult circumstances. He married the step-daughter of the Hon. Mr. Godlonton, and during late years has resided in Graham's Town, identifying himself with most of its principal institutions. The Hon. Jonathan Ayliff, the fourth son, became an Attorney of the Supreme Court, and practised in Graham's Town, and after the death of Mr. George Jarvis, to whom he had been articled, became one of the leading practitioners in the city. He married the eldest daughter of the Hon. Mr. George Wood. Mrs. Ayliff did not long survive her husband, but died about a year after his death. For many years he was one of the members of the House of Assembly, and was chosen to represent respectively the important constituencies of Queen's Town and Graham's Town. While in the House he was often chosen to sit on Parliamentary Commissions, and was specially selected as one of the members of the Commission on Native Laws and Customs, under the able presidency of His Honour Sir J. D. Berry. Sir Thomas Upington, then in the House of Assembly, being called upon to form a Cabinet, chose Mr. Ayliff to be the Colonial Secretary, an office he held till stricken down by a serious internal complaint which compelled him to give up a position he prized and colleagues he much valued. He died in London at the comparatively early age of fifty-seven years, leaving six children, three boys and three girls, and his valuable services became lost to his family and to the country he loved so well. James Ayliff, the fifth and youngest son, was very early in life appointed by the Governor of the Colony to the office of Superintendent of the Witteberg Native Reserve in 1850, and during the long Kafir war of 1851-52 became Captain commanding the Witteberg Fingo lines, in which capacity he rendered valuable service. He subsequently was appointed Superintendent of the Crown Reserve at Middledrift, Keiskama Hoek, and afterwards, about 1870, was appointed Civil Commissioner and Resident Magistrate of the newly-formed division of Wodehouse, where, at Dordrecht, he performed the duties of the office with satisfaction to Government. In 1873, at the special request of the Native Affairs Department, he was removed to the Transkei, where, as British Resident with the Chief Kreli, he remained some years till the war with the Galekas commenced. During this Galeka and Gaika campaign in 1877 he became Commandant of the Fingo Levies, and after the close of the war he received the war medal. From the Transkei he was removed to the Civil Commissionership of East London, where he remained some time, was transferred to the same office at Cradock, in which important division he continued some years, and was then promoted to the first-class Commissionership of Graaff Reinet, where he continued till his retirement on his well-earned pension. His present residence is at Uitenhage. Besides the five sons above mentioned the Rev. Mr. Ayliff left three daughters, two of whom have not married ; but the youngest, Elizabeth, married the Rev. C. F. Overton M.A., a gifted clergyman of the Church of England, who, after some twenty years of a happy married life, died in Graham's Town. The three daughters, now all living in Graham's Town, are actively engaged in all good works of charity and benevolence.

Pote, Robert, was one of Mr. Scanlan's party who were included in Mr. Parker's, or the Irish, party, as they were called. He was the eldest son of Edward Ephraim Pote, who was in the East India Company's service and became Governor of Patna twice, and then returned to England after having amassed a large fortune. Robert was educated at Eton to become eventually a priest in the Roman Catholic Church, and on his marrying a Miss Grant, of Edinburgh, where his children were born, his father " cut him off with a shilling," which led to his embarking on board the vessel *East Indiaman*, on his way to India to join his brothers, where he was induced by this party of settlers to change his mind and remain at the Cape, which he did, and regretted it ever afterwards, as he was quite unfit for the rough life of the settlers, having been brought up in luxury. He was, with other settlers, brought out by Mr. Parker, sent to join Van Dusel's Vley, district of Clanwilliam, but that locality was altogether unsuited to them, and Mr. Pote removed to the Frontier, where he joined Norman's party on the Assegai River, which he left before the war of 1835 broke out, and brought his family into Graham's Town ; so they escaped all the troubles and trials which the other settlers had to endure. Here he opened a school. The work was distasteful to him, although doing well, and his wife's health failing, they were ordered to Port Elizabeth, where he died in 1826. His son, Charles Pote, was then sixteen years of age, and left with the burden of a large family of seven children to look after besides his mother, who died in Cape Town in 1856. He had the management of Messrs. Thomson & Watson's business in Port Elizabeth and Graham's Town, and was obliged to live for a certain portion of the year in each place. He struggled on, gaining the confidence of his employers, and, working industriously, he was enabled to marry a Miss Wathall in 1837, when he had comfortable means and was fairly wealthy, which wealth he afterwards lost through his brother's folly. He finally settled at Graham's Town, where he carried on a large business as auctioneer and appraiser. He became a member of the House of Assembly for the electoral division of Graham's Town in 1854, but resigned his seat. At the general election in 1859 he was returned as a member of the Legislative Council for the term of ten years, and re-elected for a similar period in 1864. He carried on a very extensive auctioneering business in Graham's Town, in which his strict integrity was conspicuous, and took an active part in all political, social and municipal movements for the advancement of the town and country. He was also a zealous Freemason, and elected W.M. of the Albany Lodge 389, 1847 to 1849, and for six years afterwards. Misfortune followed him towards the close of his life, his ruin being caused by a man whom he had trusted too implicitly, and he died at his residence, Oakville, Graham's Town, October 4, 1882, aged seventy-two years, his wife having predeceased him in 1876, leaving five sons and seven daughters. Robert Pote, the second son, took to farming and was fairly successful. He and his wife died at their farm, Hopewell, district of Somerset East, in June and July, 1894. Peter, the third and youngest son, succeeded to his brother Charles's auctioneering business in Graham's Town, and resided in that city. He was twice married : (1) Miss Wathall, by whom he had two daughters and one son ; (2) Miss Velling, by whom he had eight children, two boys and six girls. He died at Graham's Town, July, 1895, aged seventy years.

Roberts, Doctor Edward, one of Mr. Bailie's party of settlers from London, which arrived in the *Chapman*. There were two surgeons and a physician among these settlers, viz., Dr. Roberts and Dr. Walker of the former, and Dr. O'Flynn the latter, the party numbering one hundred and one families. Soon after arrival at Cuylerville, at the mouth of the Fish River, where Mr. Bailie's location was fixed, these gentlemen found there was no scope for the pursuit of their profession. They accordingly obtained permission to remove from Albany—two to the Western Province, the other, Dr. O'Flynn, being appointed provisional medical officer at Uitenhage. Dr. Roberts married Louisa, eldest daughter of Mr. Simon Biddulph, who was a fellow passenger in the same vessel, and settled at Cape Town, where he practised successfully his profession until his death in 1830. He left a family of four sons, one of whom is Alfred Biddulph Roberts, Esq., Landdrost of Fauresmith, O.F.S.; another, Richard Miles Roberts, Esq., J.P., secretary to the Mining Boards at Du Toits Pan and Bultfontein.

Campbell, Doctor Ambrose George, fourth son of General Campbell, was a passenger by the *Dowson*, which brought twelve others sent out by the General. He had lately been admitted to practise his profession, and for a short time set up in Pimlico, at that time a suburb of London. He gave up his prospects there, married, and came to the country as one of his father's party. He fixed his residence at Graham's Town and there practised his profession, acquiring an extensive practice over the enormous districts of Uitenhage and Somerset as well as Albany. His quick perception and prompt decison made him eminently successful in the treatment of his cases, while his skill in operations was marked in several cases of delicacy and difficulty. During the time that Graham's Town was a garrison town his house was noted for his hospitality, which was extended with generous liberality as well to travellers and others passing through the town. After a residence of forty years he made a voyage to England, and after a short stay there, finding the climate unsuited to him, he returned to the Colony, and shortly after died at Port Elizabeth, 12th December, 1884, at the age of eighty-five years. The doctor was twice married, first to Rose, daughter of Thomas Ainswick, Esq., merchant, of London, having by her one son—Lionel Donald Williams Campbell, now at Johannesburg,—and two daughters; the eldest, Janet Isabella Suffield Campbell, married Herbert Penderell Longlander, Esq., M.A., Oxon, now at Maritzburg, Natal; the youngest, Ambrosina Georgina van der Dupen Campbell, who married William Henry Daniell, Esq., of Sidbury. His second wife was Johanna Sophia van der Reit, daughter of F. van der Reit, Esq., C.C. and R.M. of Uitenhage, by whom he had one son, who died in infancy.

Attwell, Richard, wife and four children, Edwin, Sarah, James and Brooke,—
Attwell, William,—
Attwell, Richard L.,—
all settlers of Mr. George Scott's party from Surrey, by the *Nautilus*. They occupied the location assigned to the party near the mouth of the Fish River, where they remained till driven away by the irruption of the Kafirs, 1834-35, when Mr. Attwell came to Graham's Town, where he died in 1846, leaving three sons and one daughter, Sarah, who married the Hon. Mr. Godlonton. Richard L. Attwell married a Miss Whiley, and removed to Cape Town, where he became the founder of the now celebrated Attwell Baking Company; James Attwell married a niece of Mr. Robert Hart, of Glen Avon, Somerset East, and took to farming; Brooke Attwell, who was only 9 years of age when he arrived, followed the trade of a boot and shoemaker in Bathurst Street, Graham's Town, having married a Miss Booth, until he was appointed Market Master of the Graham's Town municipality, which office he held for the long period of twenty-five years. He died in Graham's Town at the advanced age of eighty-one years in 1892. His eldest son is Mr. Benjamin Booth Attwell, J.P., practising in Graham's Town as an Accountant and Financial Agent.

Stanton, William, one of Mr. Willson's party by the *Belle Alliance*, with wife and four children—William, Sarah, Catherine, and Robert. He was driven from the location by the war of 1834-5, came to Graham's Town and settled there, pursuing the occupation of a wagon builder. He was for many years Field Cornet of Graham's Town. Died in 1855, at the patriarchal age of seventy-two years. His son, William, only thirteen years of age when the family arrived, was returned as member of the House of Assembly for the electoral division of Fort Beaufort, in 1859, but was declared disqualified. He was, however, elected for the constituency of Victoria East in 1869. He lived at the drift of the Kat River, on the north side of the town of Fort Beaufort, where he carried on the business of a soap boiler and trader. His other son, Robert, who was only three years of age on coming to the country, lived in Graham's Town, where he carried on the wagon-making business, which has made the name famous in that speciality. He died in Graham's Town, December 11, 1894, at the advanced age of seventy-seven years and ten months. The sons, descendants of the foregoing, are numerous, and for the most part engaged in the same line of business.

Shepstone, John, one of Mr. Holder's party of settlers from Gloucestershire, who came in the *Hennersley Castle*. He was a married man and had one son three years of age on arrival. The family is known chiefly through the distinguished services of this son, Theophilus Shepstone, who early became identified with the history of the settlers. Shortly after the beginning of the war of 1835 he acted as guide to a party of volunteers from Port Elizabeth to Wesleyville, to rescue white people, to the number of one hundred, who had taken refuge at that Wesleyan Mission Station in Tatsu's country. After serving as interpreter during the war, he was appointed clerk to Mr. Hougham Hudson, who had been created Agent-General of the new province of Adelaide, stationed at Graham's Town. In December, 1836, he acted as interpreter for Lieutenant-Governor Stockenstrom, when that officer concluded treaties with the Kafir and Fingo chiefs. In November, 1838, he was attached to the military force sent by General Napier to occupy Port Natal as interpreter. In February, 1839, he succeeded Mr. J. M. Bowker as Diplomatic Agent with the Fingoes, and was stationed at Fort Peddie, and marched in 1843 with a Fingo contingent to support Lieutenant-Colonel Somerset in an attack against Sandilli, and in the same year assisted in an unsuccessful expedition against a Kafir chief, Tola. In November, 1844, he was sent to Butterworth to obtain Kreli's signature to a treaty concluded with that chief by Sir P. Maitland in October previous; and after to Pondoland, to obtain Faku's signature to that treaty, acknowledging him paramount chief over the whole country between the Umtata and Umzimkulu Rivers; and 13th November, 1845, when Mr. Martin West was appointed Lieutenant-Governor of Natal, he was appointed Agent for Natives. By his wise management the Colony of Natal escaped the horrors of an invasion. Up to 1879 the Zulus were always peaceably disposed towards the colonists, and previous to the war which broke out in that year, Theophilus Shepstone was entrusted with the crowning of Cetewayo as King of Zululand. He was deputed by the Imperial Government to annex the Transvaal in 1877, when the attempt at autonomous existence as a Boer Republic proved a miserable failure. This delicate business he accomplished without even the semblance of resistance. Unfortunately, he was not retained as Administrator of the Transvaal territory, or possibly the after occurrences ending in the retrocession of that country to the Boers would have been avoided. For his distinguished and long service he was made a K.C.M.G. He died in Natal in 1893.

Griffith, Charles, a retired First Lieutenant of the Royal Marines, was head of a party from Cardiganshire, Wales, arrived in the *Stentor*, and landed at Cape Town, 19th April, 1820. He was accompanied by two brothers and three sisters. The brothers were (1) Valentine Griffith, also a retired officer of the Royal Marines, and John Griffith, a doctor. The Acting-Governor of the Colony, Sir R. S. Donkin, fearing to pour too many settlers into Albany all at once, located Mr. Griffith at the Endless River in the district of Caledon, where he first started sheep-farming. After spending some time on a farm at Groen Kloof, and finding the locality unsuited to his purpose, he was removed, at his own request, to Graham's Town, where he held the appointment of Barrack Master at Fort England until after the war of 1835, when he again turned sheep-farmer, and lived near Graham's Town at Burnt Kraal, being with Lieutenant Daniell of Sidbury, the first to introduce the merino breed of sheep. Here he remained till 1843, when he gave up sheep-farming and moved to Cape Town and Port Elizabeth, where he resided till 1849, when he was appointed Clerk of the Peace at Cradock, which appointment he held until his death in 1855. In or about 1826, Mr. Griffith married at Cape Town the widow of Lieutenant James Fichat, also of the Royal Marines, and by her had four children, namely, Anna Elizabeth, who married the Rev. E. P. Green, M.A., rector of Queen's Town, and now vicar of St. Simon Zelotes, Bethnal Green, London, E. (2) Charles Duncan Griffith, who married Dorothea Mounsey Gilfillan, fourth daughter of William Gilfillan, Esq., Civil Commissioner and Resident Magistrate of Cradock. (3) John Valentine Griffith, who went to Tasmania, in 1851 married and settled there. And (4) Mary, who married Colonel E. C. Saunders, of Her Majesty Commissariat Department. The brothers: Valentine Griffith only remained a short time in the Colony, and then went to and settled in Tasmania, where he died leaving a family; John Griffith, the doctor, lived a few years in Cape Town, where he died. The three sisters lived and died in Cape Town. The son of the above, Charles Duncan Griffith, distinguished himself in the Kafir irruptions, notably in the capture of the chief Vandauna during the war of 1846-47, for which service he received the distinction of C.M.G. (1887). He held various appointments in the public service, the duties of which he performed with uniform care and credit, which led to his being selected for the delicate and onerous position of Chief Magistrate and Governor's Agent in Basutuland, which responsible office he held till that territory was taken over by the Imperial authorities in 1883, when he was retired on pension. He represented the native constituency of Tembuland in the House of Assembly from the date of its creation as an electoral division of the Colony in 1891 to 1894. He lives at East London.

Gray, William, one of Mr. Bailie's party from London, who came in the ship *Chapman*. He was then nineteen years of age. He was first in the employ of Mr. Ford, surveyor and farmer, grandfather of the Fords now living near to Highlands railway station, on the Graham's Town and Port Elizabeth line. Afterwards he became the senior partner of the firm of Gray & Harper, farmers and contractors for oat-hay, etc., who also had a business as jewellers, etc., in Howard's party, Kowie Valley, about seven or eight miles from Graham's Town. He was a grantee of a small farm between Graham's Town and Bathurst, which, however, he never occupied. He also possessed property near the Fish River mouth. He married Elizabeth, daughter of Mr. George Marsden, one of Mr. Dixon's party of settlers. Eventually he bought the farm Walsingham, near Southwell, from Captain Crause, who gave the name to the farm. Here he carried on agriculture extensively, being with the Dells and other settlers in that neighbourhood, a contractor for the supply of oat-hay to the Commissariat for the military garrison at Graham's Town. He was Field Cornet of the ward Southwell during the sudden defection of the Hottentots of the Theopolis mission station near by in 1848. His house, stacks of forage, wheat, etc., etc., were burnt down and stock all taken in the two successive Kafir wars of 1835 and 1846. He was Commandant of the Levies which went from Graham's Town to attack the rebel Hottentots of Theopolis, when he lost his life, being shot dead by one of the rebels on the 2nd June, 1850, in a dense bush called the Gorah, where the villains had formed a camp. A memorial window was erected in the church of Southwell to his memory by the inhabitants of Southwell, and the Government granted to his widow a Captain's pension for life. He left three sons ; viz., (1) George Gray, now a wealthy sheep farmer in the Komzha district ; (2) William Marsden Gray, farmer in Lower Albany; and (3) James Wakelyn Gray, farmer and scab inspector near Lady Frere, district of Queen's Town ; also several daughters, one of whom married the Rev. William Henry Turpin, missionary of the English Church in charge of St. Philip's Church and Mission Schools in the Kafir location, Graham's Town, related to the Baronets Coningham and Plunket of Ireland, from the latter of whom the present Archbishop of Dublin is descended.

Cock, William, head of Cock's party, which came in the *Weymouth*, and were located near the mouth of the Kowie River, v. a. p.

He died at Graham's Town in 1876, at the advanced age of eighty-three years, leaving three sons and five daughters. The sons were all engaged in agricultural pursuits, but also took an active part in the wars of 1835 and 1846. When the war of 1835 broke out, the boys were at school on Sir Richard Southey's farm, and had a narrow escape, Sir Richard's brother-in-law, John Shaw, being killed by the Kafirs. The eldest son, William Frederick Cock, married Miss Lucy Netherton, and died in 1884, leaving three sons. Cornelius Cock, the second son, did a great deal of active service, particularly in the war of 1846 ; was engaged in a big fight at Kowie West defending his father's cattle, some six hundred head, which were swept off; again at Wolf's Craig, under General Somerset. Was Captain in Meurant's levy under Colonel Armstrong, and subsequently in charge of the Commissariat from Waterloo Bay to the Kei under General Somerset's division. In the war of 1851 served under Sir Walter Currie, clearing the Blackwater's point on the Fish River, and in the Amatolas under Colonel Percival and Colonel Eyre. Was personally thanked for his services by Sir George Cathcart, and at the request of the Magistrate of the district made a J.P., which honour he has held for forty-four years. He was twice married, first to Miss Letitia Smith, by whom he had three sons and two daughters. She died in 1860, and in 1870 he married Miss Edith Jaffray, by whom he has six sons and one daughter. He is now living at Lessendrum, district of Peddie. The third son, Nathaniel Cock, also did good service during the wars, particularly at the surprise of Hans Bunder, a notorious Hottentot, and his party, when he captured sixteen guns in one batch. He married Miss Mary Bacher, and had a family—three daughters, all married—who now live in Bechuanaland. He died at Johannesburg, February 14, 1895, aged sixty-five years.

Dyason, Isaac, wife and four children ;

,, **Joseph,** wife and two children ;

,, **George,** wife and two children ;

,, **Robert,** wife and three children ;

came with sixteen others as Dyason's party by the *Zoroaster*, and were located between Mr. Willson's party and the Nottingham party. Mr. Joseph Dyason had been a Quartermaster in the Royal Navy, and six years master in the Mercantile Navy. He was employed by Government to survey the mouth of the Kowie River, to determine whether it was navigable. Mr. George Dyason became Resident Magistrate at Bathurst, and finally Civil Commissioner and Resident Magistrate at Graaff Reinet. A survivor of the family writes : "I can just remember living on our farm, Rokeby Park, joining Mr. Currie's, between Graham's Town and Bathurst. The old chief Pato lived near, and when he came to see my father would say, 'Kill sheep,' for his councillors. He himself used to drive with my father sometimes. He always wore, I have heard, a black tail coat and a bell-topper. Another circumstance I have heard my father speak of was, when they lived at Lushington Valley, how the elephants rubbed themselves against the corner of the house, which was made of wattle and daub, and how terrified the inmates were to go out. There some vines were planted—the very first; also the first merino sheep my father got from England. During one of the wars, I don't remember which, my father was magistrate at Bathurst; my mother would not leave him and go to Graham's Town with all of us, so we were for three months barricaded in the church, each family having a pew. We had the vestry, being the principal people, and the Ayliffs had the inside of the communion rails. We used to have stumped mealies with them one night, and the next they would come and have what we had. Provisions were becoming scarce, when, luckily, a schooner put into the Kowie, and my father paid £5 for a bag of fine flour. There was no kind of communication with Graham's Town until the 73rd Regiment came to our help from Mauritius. A very dear brother, George, was killed by Kafirs on his way from the Fish River farms with wool for Graham's Town merchants, 15th June, 1851. The bodies of three Kafirs were found near his body whom he had shot. Commandant Currie, who went to the rescue, found the rebels had cut the bales of wool off the wagons to make a kind of scherm. The Hottentot drivers and leaders had run away. Another of the family, William Dyason, was shot by Kafirs while on duty under Commandant McTaggart in the islands of the Orange River, 10th April, 1879. From Bathurst my father was sent to Graaff Reinet as Civil Commissioner and Resident Magistrate. We had a party of soldiers sent from Graham's Town to protect us through the Kowie Bush, as we had to go in ox-wagons to Port Elizabeth, and so to Graaff Reinet." Mr. George Dyason was retired from the service in 1855, after having served thirty-five years. He died at his residence at Port Elizabeth, August 7, 1862, aged seventy-one years. Field-Adjutant Dyason was killed in an engagement with the Korannas, on the Orange River, April, 1879.

The Dyason family is represented by Durban Dyason, Esq., attorney-at-law, Port Elizabeth.

Phillipps, Thomas, head of a party from Pembrokeshire, Wales; arrived by the *Hennersley Castle.* He was a man of opulence, had been a banker at Haverfordwest, and was in middle life. He brought his wife, seven children, and three female servants. His location was towards the coast, with Mr. Greathead and Mr. Southey as immediate neighbours. Here he applied himself to the cultivation of the land, and the erection of his dwelling-house. Mr. George Thompson, who travelled through the Settlement in January, 1821, and again in May, 1823, gives a pleasing description of the progress made by the settlers, their cheerful homes and their anticipations of prosperity. He gives a vignette of Mr. Phillipps's house, "Glendour," at p. 146 vol. ii., and refers to him as one of the leading inhabitants in industry and enterprise. All prospects of future happiness were ruthlessly destroyed by the irruption of the Kafirs in 1835, when his house was consumed by fire, his crops destroyed, and his cattle and other properties carried off. He was all at once entirely ruined, and thankful that he and his family escaped with their lives to Graham's Town. Adversity followed him through the rest of his life. His eldest son Edward removed to Natal, and there settled. His eldest daughter Catherine married Mr. John Carlisle, and left issue; the next daughter, Charlotte, married Mr. Temple Nourse, and left two sons and two daughters; Sophie, the third daughter, was the only one who survived her father, and died at Graham's Town, 1892, at the age of eighty-four years. Frederick, the second son, married Miss Mary Ann Currie, and was killed by lightning on his farm near Bedford, leaving one son, Edward, and a daughter, who married Mr. Frederick Carlisle. This son Edward left two daughters only, so there is no male representative of the family. Singularly, Edward, walking behind his cart up the Katberg was struck by lightning, and about the same time his sister, travelling by wagon, had a narrow escape, six or eight of the oxen being killed and the wagon also struck. John, the youngest son, died in Cradock in 1852. Mr. Phillipps was a staunch Freemason, and, by his efforts and those of Dr. Peter Campbell and others, obtained a charter from the Grand Lodge of England, granted by H.R.H. the Duke of Sussex, K.G., 3rd January, 1828, as the Albany Lodge, No. 817, then 584 in 1832, and in closing up the numbers in 1863 was renumbered 389. The first officers for this Lodge, the oldest but one in all South Africa, the British at Cape Town being the premier, for 1828-29 were—Bro. Thomas Phillips, W.M.; Bro. R. M. Whitnal, I.W.; Bro. Peter Campbell, S.W.; Bro. W. E. Smith, Treasurer; Bro. G. F. Stokes, Secretary. Bro. Phillipps was re-elected W.M., 1829-30.

Bowker, Miles, head of a party from Wiltshire, who came in the *Weymouth*. He was of gentle birth, a scholar, and a good botanist. His first residence was at Oliveburn, near the coast, and subsequently at Tharfield, on the Lynedoch or Kleinemond River. He was appointed, with Captain Duncan Campbell, Heemeraad of Albany for many years, but resigned office, preferring the cultivation of his farms to politics. He died early in the year 1839, in the seventy-fifth year of his age, and was buried at Tharfield. He brought with him from England eight sons and two daughters. His youngest son was born at Oliveburn, making nine sons in all. Their names are well known in the Frontier districts and Colony. They all followed in their father's footsteps as farmers and agriculturists, and all took an active share in the numerous Kafir engagements, giving their services for the benefit of their country. (1) William Monkhouse Bowker, J.P., M.L.A., Commandant of Burghers, Eastern District, served in the Fikani Expedition in 1828, was Commandant of the Bathurst Corp of Guides during the war of 1835-36, served in the Kei patrol under Sir Benjamin D'Urban, and through the war of 1846-47. He was the first to raise the Somerset Volunteers in the war of 1851-52, and go to the rescue of families in the Winterberg, and was in command of burghers at the battle of Balfour and taking of Fort Armstrong. (2) Miles Brabbin Bowker, served throughout the wars of 1835-36, 1846-47, and 1851-52. (3) John Mitford Bowker, J.P., Commandant of Burghers, served on the Fikani commando in 1828, in the war of 1835-36, and was wounded. He was Commandant under Sir A. Stockenstrom during the war of 1846-47. He died in 1847. (4) Thomas Holden Bowker, J.P., M.L.A., served on the Fikani expedition in 1828, served as an officer in the Graham's Town Native Infantry in the war of 1835-36, and served through that of 1846-47, commanding old Kafir Drift post until close of the war. After Resident Magistrate of Kat River, defended Whittlesea during the greater part of the war of 1851-52. He drew up a plan for the defence of the Frontier, which he submitted to His Excellency Sir George Cathcart, Governor, and was partly carried out in the formation of the district of Queen's Town, which town he founded, preventing Kafir incursions for many years. He was further engaged in the greater part of the action taken along the upper Kei border against Kreli, and was in 1872 appointed member and Secretary of the Land Commission on the Diamond Fields. He was many years in Parliament, representing the electoral districts of Albany, Victoria East, and Queen's Town. (5) Bertram Egerton Bowker, J.P., a farmer, lived on the eastern Frontier of the Colony since 1820. In 1827 he was commandeered by Captain John Crause against marauding Kafirs; in 1828 commandeered under Major Dundas to put down marauding Zulus under Matawani their leader, served eight weeks, together with commando and Tambookie army, retook 50,000 head of cattle; in 1834 commandeered on Christmas Day, remaining in active service until peace was proclaimed, after which had charge of 6,014 head of Government cattle; in 1846 had command of a camp with fifteen English and Dutch families, patrolling the neighbourhood till the end of the war; in 1851 again had charge of a large camp, doing good service in constantly patrolling; in 1873, when the police were dead beaten at the Ibeka, volunteered for active service, when Kreli's house and kraal were burnt and his tribe

P

driven over the Umtata. On returning from the Transkei was put in command of East London district. Was on active service when Tainton and Brown were murdered; caught two of the murderers, who were hanged. The Government offered a reward of £200 for the capture of the leader; caught the leader, who died in gaol, but never received the reward. During the last skirmish with the rebels had two men killed, one wounded, and two horses shot. In 1876 was returned as a member of the Legislative Council for East London. (6) Robert Mitford Bowker, J.P., M.L.A. and M.L.C., served with the Corps of Guides during the war of 1835-36; was at the taking of Murray's Kranz and other engagements until close of the war. Served in the Zuurberg and other points during the war of 1846-47. Volunteered for the rescue of Winterberg families in 1851, was at Balfour and taking of Fort Armstrong, carried out a wounded comrade under close fire. Elected member of the House of Assembly for division of Somerset East in 1854, and served in Parliament for over thirty-six years. (7) Septimus Bourchier Bowker, J.P., served throughout the wars of 1835-36, 1846-47, and 1851-52. (8) Octavius Bowker, served during war of 1835-36, and during that of 1846-47 in the Zuurberg. In 1851 accompanied his brother, W. M. Bowker, and was at the battle of Balfour and taking of Fort Armstrong. Served with the Free State forces during the Basutu war, and engaged in various affairs up to annexation of Basutuland in 1868. (9) James Henry Bowker, J.P., F.L.S., F.Z.S., F.R.G.S., F.S.S., gold medalist, served in the war of 1846-47 and in that of 1851-52, was at the suppression of the Kat River rebellion and capture of Fort Armstrong (medal and clasp) in 1846-47. Inspector of the Frontier Armed and Mounted Police, 1855; served in the Transkei Expedition, 1858, and remained in Transkei until withdrawal in 1865. Associated with Sir Walter Currie in locating Fingoes in Transkei; served in expedition to Basutuland, 1868, and appointed High Commissioner's Agent for that territory; engaged also in settling the boundaries and formation of the different districts. Commandant Frontier Armed and Mounted Police, 1870. Commanded expedition to the Diamond Fields for annexation to the Cape Colony; appointed one of the three commissioners, and for some time Chief Commissioner of the Diamond Fields; commanded expedition for annexation of Tembuland, carried it out, and also selected site for present town of Umtata; planned expedition which led to the suppression of Langalabellila outbreak and capture of that chief, thanked by Secretary of State. Reappointed Governor's Agent, Basutuland; retired in 1878 with the honorary rank of Colonel; appointed one of the Commissioners for Natal, Indian and Colonial extradition; was twice thanked by Secretary of State for service done; is a Justice of the Peace for the Cape Colony, Natal, and under William IV. to 24th degree of south latitude; also under Victoria, ditto.

Campbell, Dr. Peter, was one of the Salem party under Mr. Hezekiah Sephton by the *Aurora*. He brought his wife, two infant daughters, and a female servant with him. He was of Scottish descent, but born at Omagh, County Tyrone, Ireland. He studied medicine, and took his diplomas from the Royal College of Surgeons, Dublin, December 14, 1809. He practised his profession in Great Marlborough Street, London, as a surgeon, apothecary and accoucheur, up to the time of his embarkation for the Colony. He settled in Graham's Town, lived in Bathurst Street, and continued in practice till his death, 31st July, 1837. He was a Freemason, and owing to his exertions the first lodge on the Frontier was built in Graham's Town, viz., the Albany Lodge 389, in January, 1828. He was elected Senior Warden, and in 1831 Worshipful Master thereof. In 1832-33, on his retiring, was presented with a past-master's jewel; and in August, 1837, the Lodge went into mourning for Dr. Campbell. Dr. Campbell was twice married. First in England to Miss Sarah Sanderson, of Cutland, Cumberland, a cousin of Captain Cook, the navigator. By her he had two daughters: (1) Margaret Ann, the eldest, born December, 1817, married Thomas Bailie, had three children, two sons and one daughter, is still living in Potchefstroom with her second son, John Crause Bailie. The daughter and eldest son are both dead. (2) Sarah Lucy Cecilia, born July 2nd, 1819, never married, and is still living at Alice. These were the two children who came in the *Aurora*. Their mother died 21st July, 1825, after the birth of twins—a boy and a girl—who died in infancy. On the 28th July, 1826, the doctor married Mary Anne Cumming, eldest daughter of Thomas Cumming an officer, who had served with his regiment—the Rifle Brigade—through the Peninsular War, and had come to Africa to join the Royal African Corps, which, on arrival, he found was disbanded. Of this marriage only two children lived, viz., Alexander Cumming Campbell, born July 9, 1827, who married a Miss Martha Nel, now dead, has a family of five sons and four daughters, and is living in Tembuland; and Rosina Jane, born 17th May, 1834, married Mr. Richard Harris Blakeway, youngest son of John Blakeway, formerly in the 21st Light Dragoons, and later Adjutant in the Cape Mounted Rifles; had four sons and three daughters. In 1870 Richard Harris Blakeway was murdered by a Kafir at Gounbie, and in 1880 his eldest son, William John Blakeway, was killed in action against the Tembus.

Damant, Edward, head of a party from Norfolk, by the *Ocean*. The Damant family originally came from Ghent and Antwerp after the revocation of the Edict of Nantes. Doctor John Atherstone had married a sister of Commissary General John Damant, who married Miss Korsten, of Cradock Place, near Port Elizabeth, and it was this circumstance which led to the Damants and Atherstones coming to settle in the Colony. Lieutenant Edward Damant, above named, formerly of the 38th Regiment of Foot, came from Fakenham, Norfolk, and brought his wife and two daughters with him. He had been in Sir Thomas Willshire's company at the storming of Badajos, and led the company over the walls, coming out with only four men. He died at Table Farm, near Graham's Town, at an advanced age, his elder brother, John, who was one of the party, having died there in 1846. The only son of Mr. Edward Damant is Mr. Hugh Damant, who has long resided at Kimberley, and has a large family.

Hoole, James, one of Mr. Bailie's party from London by the *Chapman*. He brought his wife and three children, the eldest of whom was only eight years of age. Nothing is known about the parent, but the two sons were prominent figures in the wars of 1835 and 1846. They were both engaged in mercantile pursuits, and James Cotterell Hoole was one of those elected in 1866 to represent the Eastern Districts in the Legislative Council, and took his seat till 1869, when the Council and House of Assembly were dissolved. In 1870 he was re-elected, and sat till the Responsible Government Bill was passed in 1872. The other brother, Abel Hoole, was a trader at Whittlesea. Of the family the only members now living are Mrs. Dick and Mrs. George Wood, jun.; also Mr. Benjamin Hoole and Mr. T. T. Hoole, son of Mr. James Hoole, jun., and two Miss Powells, daughters of the late Mrs. James Powell, sister of Mrs. George Wood, jun.

Pringle, Thomas, head of a small party from Scotland, who were located on the Baboon's River, beyond Albany. After successively planting his little band of relatives and followers in this remote corner of the Frontier, he removed to Cape Town, where he intended to devote himself to literature. He was appointed librarian to the Public Library, Cape Town, and with the assistance of his friend and fellow-countryman, James Fairbairn, whom he induced to come to the Colony and join him, projected and commenced the publication of a newspaper, which, however, owing to the narrow-minded fears of the Governor, Lord Charles Somerset, that it might become an engine of evil, was suppressed. After years of appeal to the authorities in England, and by his personal influence and that of his friends, he succeeded in overcoming all obstacles to the publication, and left it in the hands of his colleague, Fairbairn, to become a power in the land in the direction of public thought and liberty of speech and action. He returned to Scotland and then died, December 5, 1834. He wrote an account of the settlement of the British immigrants, and a volume of poems, which are prized for their simplicity and description of African scenery.

Southey, George, head of a party from Somersetshire by the *Hennersley Castle*. He was a married man, and besides his wife brought four sons, two daughters and two servants. His location was the east corner of Mr. Willson's, along the edge of the plains of Mount Donkin, or the Roundhill, a striking landmark showing where the Zuurberg range gradually sinks into the plain near the coast. A signal station, now disused, was formerly erected there. Richard, the second son, was, for five years, clerk in the firm of Heugh & Co. He left this situation to join his brothers who purchased the farm on the Kap River, about half way between Graham's Town and the mouth of the Fish River. They had nearly completed the erection of commodious and extensive farm premises when the war of 1835 broke out. The Kafirs drove off 800 head of their cattle, and waylaid and murdered a young man named John Shaw, a near relative, who had quitted Graham's Town to their assistance. The sons, William, Richard and George, did good service during that war, as members of the Corps of Guides. Richard, as Captain under Mr. William Bowker, as Commandant of the Bathurst Corps of Guides, assisting the military operations by their intimate knowledge of the country and of the Kafir language and character. It was George Southey who helped to track the chief Hintza, and pursued him through the defiles of the Fish River bush, when Colonel, afterwards Sir Harry, Smith was engaged in his capture, and who, at a critical moment, when that Kafir chief had already thrown his assegai at Colonel Smith, and would certainly have killed him, shot him dead. After the war, the brothers removed to Graaff Reinet, where they engaged in farming and trade. On his return to the Colony as Governor, Sir Harry Smith remembered Richard Southey, and employed him in various capacities, of which an account is given in a previous part of this volume, v. p. William Southey, the elder brother, acquired influence among the Boers of the Graaff Reinet district, and was returned as a member of the Legislative Council in 1858, and after the dissolution of both Houses was re-elected in 1859, but declared disqualified.

Collett, James, was one of the settlers brought out by General Campbell, who arrived with others in the brig *Salisbury*. He was a man fairly well educated, intelligent, and cautious. He made his way into the Cradock district, where he commenced sheep farming. After a few years he acquired by purchase the farm Green Fountain, about three miles beyond the town of Cradock, and married a daughter of Mr. Joseph Trollip, a settler of Hyman's party, who had also removed to Cradock to pursue sheep farming. This union of families has been fruitful to a degree, the names of Collett and Trollip being found all over that large district. In 1834, James Collett was returned as a member of the House of Assembly for the electoral division of Cradock, but forfeited his seat, preferring his pastoral pursuits to the toil of a long and tedious journey to Cape Town, and the distractions of a parliamentary session.

Carlisle, John, head of a party bearing his name from Staffordshire, arriving by the *Chapman*. He was a young man and unmarried. He was a terrible sufferer by the Kafir irruptions, his house and buildings being destroyed by fire, his stock swept off, and his crops unreaped. He lived at his farm called Belmont, in the Kowie Valley, about four miles beyond Graham's Town. He married Catherine, the eldest daughter of Thomas Phillipps, Esq., and dying left three sons. Robert, a farmer, who married a Miss Botha; Sydney, an attorney of the Supreme Court, who married a daughter of

General Sir John Bissit, died s. p. ; and Edmond, a farmer, who married a daughter of Dr. Eddie, of the C.M.R.

Carlisle, Frederick, brother of the foregoing, and one of the same party. He lived in Graham's Town after being driven from his location by the Kafirs, and was for many years Deputy-Sheriff of Albany, Bathurst, and Victoria East. He married a daughter of Mr. Frederick Phillipps ; died and left two sons, the younger of whom, William Montagu, survives, and who served in Basutuland and Transkei, 1872 to 1884, as clerk to the Resident Magistrates, and also as lieutenant in the Mafeking native contingent during the Basutu rebellion, and is now in the public service at Kimberley.

Bradfield, John, a settler by the *Albury*, in the Nottingham party, of which Dr. Thomas Carlton was the head. He brought a wife and four children with him, and was accompanied by Edward Bradfield, John Bradfield, and John Bradfield, jun. The location assigned to the Nottingham party was near Bathurst, through which the Torrens, formerly the Brak, River flows, to which the name of Clumber was given in honour of their patron, the Duke of Newcastle. There are at this day many of the name of Bradfield living at Clumber, engaged in agriculture. One of this family emigrated to Dordrecht, in the Wodehouse division, carrying on trading and farming there, is well known as a successful and enterprising colonist, who represents the electoral circle of the Eastern Province,—the Hon. John Linden Bradfield, M.H.L., Dordrecht.

Painter, Samuel, one of Sephton's party who came in the *Aurora*. He had a wife and four children. His eldest son, Richard Joseph Painter, settled in the Fort Beaufort district, where he acquired property and influence. He was elected member of the House of Assembly for that division in 1854. He is described by "Limner" in his Pen and Ink Sketches in Parliament, like a man who had borne the heat and burthen of the day, and the scenes of blood and devastation that he had interpreted as having a powerful impression on his mind. He was re-elected for the same constituency in 1859, but resigned his seat. Again, in 1864, he was elected to represent the electoral division of Port Elizabeth, but resigned that seat also. In 1866, when the members of both Houses were augmented by annexation of British Kaffraria by the Act 3 of 1865, he was returned as a member of the Legislative Council, but at the General Election in 1869 did not offer himself for re-election.

Holditch, Dr. Robert, was one of Mr. Scanlan's party from Ireland by the *East Indian*. He, with others of the Irish party, was sent to Clanwilliam, where he was appointed Provisional Medical Officer to the Deputy Drostdy of Clanwilliam, which appointment, however, he resigned 31st December, 1820. He subsequently met his death by drowning, as per letter of the Landdrost, of Stillenbosch, dated 25th December, 1822.

Trollip, Joseph, with wife and six children,—

Trollip, William, with wife and infant child,—

Trollip, John, young married man, and

Trollip, Stephen, also a young married man,—
were all of Mr. Hyman's party from Wiltshire, who came by the transport *Weymouth*. Hyman's party were located between Bathurst and the mouth of the Lynedoch River. The war of 1835 dispersed the unfortunate settlers, and the Trollips migrated into the Cradock district, where they are now numerous, and flourish as sheep farmers. The descendants of the original settlers of this name are, next to the Cawood family, the most

numerous of all the others. The senior representative of the name is Mr. Joseph Trollip, sheep farmer, of Mount Pleasant, Dagga Boer's Nek, district of Cradock.

Mills, Daniel, head of a small party from London by the transport *Sir George Osborne.* He was sixty years of age when he arrived, and brought his wife and six children—Martha, Harriet, Daniel, Maria, James, and Catherine. His location was on the Kasonga River, on which there was an abandoned house which had been occupied by the Boer who had previously lived there. He was quite unsuited to farming, his tastes being literary. He soon found farming in Albany beyond his powers, and obtained permission to remove with his family to Graaff Reinet. Here his daughters, two accomplished young ladies, set up an academy, and he having nothing to do, and being fond of books, was glad to accept the post of Librarian to the Public Library just then formed. His income was miserably small, and as he saw better prospects in Cape Town, he proceeded thither with his family.

Caldecott, Doctor Charles, came as surgeon in charge of the emigrants by the *Brilliant.* He brought his family with him, and settled at Port Elizabeth. Pringle, who came out in the same ship, describes him as "a little dogmatic, anabaptist surgeon," who used to preach on board ship. He died, soon after arrival, from drinking cold water when overheated, having walked to Bethelsdorp Mission Station, nine miles from Port Elizabeth, which produced acute indigestion, followed by inflammation of the bowels. His third son, Charles Henry Caldecott, married Martha, eldest daughter of William Wright, Esq., merchant of Graham's Town. He was driven from the farm Prospect, district of Toroka, by the irruption of the Kafirs in 1846, and came to Cradock, where he established himself in business. In 1857 he retired from business and removed to Graham's Town. He took an active part in all the political, social, and municipal movements for the improvement and development of the town and districts. He was twice returned to Parliament as member of the House of Assembly for the electoral division of Cradock, in 1857, and again in 1859, but resigned his seat in the latter year. In 1868 he was returned as a member of the Legislative Council. He was also Mayor of Graham's Town in 1860. He died at Kimberley in July, 1879, his wife having predeceased him, leaving seven sons and six daughters; viz., (1) the Rev. William Shaw Caldecott, Wesleyan Minister at T'Somo, Transkei, married to a daughter of Mr. J. B. Hillier; (2) Charles Henry, married Elizabeth Booth, daughter of Mr. J. Williams; (3) Harry Stratford, attorney of the Supreme Court, married Joanna, daughter of Mr. J. J. Sauer, of Aliwal North, in practice at Johannesburg; (4) Robert Torkington, died by drowning in the river Severn, near Wick St. Lawrence, Somersetshire, 27th July, 1868; (5) Frederick Horatio, died at Cradock, 27th August, 1856; (6) Alfred Edward, Attorney of the Supreme Court, married Ella, daughter of Commissary-General Sir William Drake, died at Salisbury, Mashonaland, where he held the appointment of Crown Solicitor, 5th July, 1894; (7) Frederick Reginald, married Fanny, daughter of Mr. Warren, of Bleak House, Kei Road. The daughters were (1) Emily, who married Mr. Selby Coryndon, an attorney of the Supreme Court, who predeceased her, and died at Kimberley, 5th July, 1889; (2) Charlotte Isabella, died at Cradock, 27th October, 1850; (3) Jessie Lucretia Baldwyn, died at Port Elizabeth, 11th January, 1852; (4) Rosa Wright, married 14th October, 1872, John E. A. Dick-Lauder, Esq., second son of Sir John Dick-Lauder, Bart., of Grange and Fountain Hall, Scotland; (5) Alice Annie Martha, died 25th July, 1863; and (6) Maud Isabella who died at Queen's Town, 8th June, 1881.

Maynard, James Mortimer,—

  „   **Joshua,—**
were two brothers who came with Mr. Sephton's party by the *Aurora.* They did not

long remain with the Salem party, but obtained leave to remove to Cape Town, where they settled and worked as sawyers. From this humble beginning, by patient industry they soon acquired wealth, and by lending small sums of money at high interest to needy men both laid the foundations of their fortunes. James, the elder brother, was by far the most shrewd, and the fortune he amassed was immense. He purchased land, had miles of forests at Wynberg and Newlands, and held mortgages on properties in Cape Town, it is said, to the extent of £300,000. He held a large number of shares in the Wynberg railway, had a good deal to do with its construction, and was a director. He sat in Parliament as one of the members for Cape Town at the opening of Parliament by Lieutenant-Governor Darling in 1854 and for several successive years, but did not offer himself for re-election. He died September 9, 1874, having two or three years previously been seized with a serious fit, aged seventy-four years. He was a very liberal donor to the Wesleyan Society, of which he was a member, as well as to other charitable institutions. He left his enormous wealth to his nephew, Mr. William Maynard Farmer, merchant at Port Elizabeth.

Slater, Thomas, one of Mr. Sephton's party, the *Aurora*, a married man with wife and six children. His eldest son George was a well-known farmer and post contractor when he lived at Quagga's Flat, on the main road between Graham's Town and Port Elizabeth. He was member for Albany in the House of Assembly in 1866 and 1869. He had several daughters, one of whom married Mr. William Haw, hardware merchant, Graham's Town; another, Mr. Thomas C. Strut, a farmer near Sidbury. A son, John, was an agriculturist on the Bushman's River.

Slater, Charles, a brother of Thomas, came in the same ship. He carried on business in Beaufort Street, Graham's Town, as a tallow and soap maker. He was an estimable person and much respected. He represented Albany in the House of Assembly previous to the introduction of responsible government in 1856, 1859, and 1870.

Scanlen, William, head of a subsidiary party that came out with Mr. William Parker, of Cork, Ireland, in the *East Indian*. Mr. Scanlen came from Longford, and brought with him a wife and five children. His location was between the Assegai and Nazaar Rivers, adjoining that of Captain Butler, also one of the Irish party. Mr. Scanlen was a man of mature age, not fitted to endure the rough life and usage of the first Settlement, and he removed to Graham's Town before the outbreak of the Kafirs in 1835, where he died about 1854 at the age of eighty-four years. Of his four sons, (1) William died about 1839 at Port Elizabeth, leaving one son, now in the Transvaal, and a daughter; (2) John died about 1834; (3) Charles lived on the farm Waay Plaats, near the Fish River. "In my earlier years," says a descendant who has obligingly supplied the particulars of family history given, "I have often heard him tell the events of that Christmas (1834). Late in the afternoon of that day he saw from his front door a neighbour named Forbes running with a gun towards some horses in the valley separating their houses. He went in the direction of Forbes to see what was amiss, and when about a couple of hundred yards off, saw some Kafirs rush from the corn in the valley and stab Forbes to death. He turned to reach his own house, and was under the shelter of a stone wall round a bend for some distance. Reaching his house, my mother handed him at the door the only weapon at hand, a musket with a defective lock. During the previous week he had visited Graham's Town and left for repair his double-barrelled fowling piece. The Kafirs halted about a hundred yards or so from the house upon his pointing the musket at them; and while they were apparently deliberating upon the course of attack, a horseman appeared at a distance upon the brow of the hill. The Kafirs rushed off after this man, whose fate I do not remember. While they were in pursuit, a fog came over the rise between the house and the party of Kafirs. Taking advantage of this, my father concealed in a cattle kraal a writing desk containing papers, the only thing he saved. My father and mother, carrying myself, fled to a kloof in the opposite direction to that in which the body of Kafirs had gone, and they had not been there long before the lurid glare in the sky indicated that their house and the house of Forbes were in flames. They remained in the bush that night, and the next morning my father, under cover of the bush, got on to the highest ground he could reach to look out. He descried a party of horsemen approaching from the direction of Bathurst, and from the glint of the guns in the sunlight concluded that they were friends. Using his shirt as a flag, he attracted their attention, and when they galloped up found that upon the news of the inroad reaching Bathurst the previous night, the party had been sent out to bury the dead! Under care of this escort they reached Bathurst, and subsequently went on to Graham's Town." Charles Scanlen joined the Corps of Guides got up under the auspices of Colonel, afterwards Sir, Henry Smith, and proceeded to the front under Captain Southey, now Sir Richard Southey, and served during the war, being near the spot where Eno, the Kafir chief, was shot, but not actually witnessing the event. After the war of 1835 he went to Cradock, and carried on a mercantile business there for some years. He served as a volunteer during the war of 1846, and was present at the attacks on Farmerfield during that year. In 1850 he was out with the Cradock Volunteers, was present when Thackwray shot a native chief during the attack on Shiloh, and in one of those skirmishes a bullet struck his watch in his pocket. That watch, with the dent caused by the bullet, is still in possession of his son, Sir Thomas C. Scanlen. His mercantile business suffered by this war, and after that he carried on a general agency business. On the granting of the present constitution he declined a requisition to go to Parliament, Mr. J. Collett and Mr. W. T. Gilfillan being the elected (1854). Subsequently he was elected a member of the House of Assembly, and represented Cradock until his health failed in 1869. He died in 1870, at the age of sixty-four. (4) The youngest son of the original William Scanlen, Thomas Ross Scanlen, was wounded in an action near Fort Broner, and died of his wounds in 1851 at Graham's Town, aged thirty-six years. The only daughter, Hannah, was married to Mr. Samuel Roberts, who had a boot and shoe warehouse in Church Square, Graham's Town. Both are dead. Their eldest son, Mr. Samuel Henry Roberts, is the Native Location Inspector, who did good service in that capacity in Albany, and is now stationed at Queen's Town. Thus the only descendant of this family is the son of Mr. Charles Scanlen, born in July, 1834, near Cawood's Post, Fish River, who became an attorney of the Supreme Court of the Colony, and by industry and natural talent raised himself to the distinguished position of Premier of the third Ministry under responsible government in 1881, representing the constituency of Cradock in the House of Assembly from 1870 to the present time. In May, 1881, he was created a K.C.M.G., and is now Solicitor-General to the British South Africa Company at Salisbury in Mashonaland.

Greathead, James, head of a small party from Worcestershire by the *Hennersley Castle*. His location was about half way between Graham's Town and the coast, with Messrs. Erith, Southey, Phillipps, and Scanlen for neighbours. He was a surveyor by profession, and built a house at Bathurst, where he resided. He died of sunstroke about 1830, leaving a widow and one child, a son ten years of age. After some years the widow married Mr. William Smith, a land surveyor, and died in Graham's Town in 1843. The son, James Henry, was actively engaged in mercantile pursuits, and became senior partner of a large firm in Graham's Town. He married Julia, daughter of Mr. William Wright, by whom he had twelve children, all except one, who died in England, surviving him. He died in 1864. The sons are (1) William Wright, formerly living at Aliwal North, superintending the working of a mill on his late father's estate, subsequently a successful farmer in the Orange Free State, married Miss Emilie Halse ; (2)

James Henry, an engineer of repute in connection with the subterranean works under the river Thames, in England, now a member of the Council of Civil Engineers, married Blanche Coryndon ; (3) Herbert Harding, a farmer in the district of Fort Beaufort, married Miss E. F. Halse ; (4) D. C. R. Greathead, merchant and miller at Aliwal North, Mayor of that town for some years, married Miss E. Burnet ; (5) John Baldwin, M.B. Edin., M.R.C.S. Lond., living in Graham's Town, enjoying an extensive practice, married (i.) Esther Louisa Merriman, (ii.) Miss E. Bubb ; (6) Walter Horatio, Civil Engineer and Surveyor, who surveyed most of Griqualand West, now living in England, or working there, unmarried ; (7) Octavius Ernest, for some time in the Mounted Police at Aliwal North, and fought in Basutuland, married Miss Philips, subsequently retired and went to Johannesburg, where he was killed by the falling of a building (Roode Porte) ; (8) George Alfred, surveyor practising in the Transvaal, formerly in the Colonial Civil Service, unmarried. The daughters are Rosa, unmarried ; and Julia Emily, married Hon. C. T. Smith, a judge of the Supreme Court of the Colony.

Moodie, ——. There were three of that name identified with the eastern part of the Colony, viz., Benjamin Moodie, who, in June, 1817, brought out about 200 Scotch families, and who subsequently obtained a grant of land on the Beka River from the Acting-Governor of the Colony, Sir R. S. Donkin, which grant was cancelled by Lord Charles Somerset, as not being Crown land within the Colony, and who, in consequence, left the Colony and settled in Upper Canada, where he died in 1835. (2) Lieutenant J. W. D. Moodie, 21st Fusiliers, who arrived in 1819, and after a residence and struggle of ten years abandoned the Colony. And (3) Lieutenant Donald Moodie, R.N., who followed his brothers, and arrived about the time of the British settlers. He was appointed by Lord Charles Somerset Provisional Magistrate at Port Frances (now called Port Alfred), in 1823. After the breaking up of that establishment he was appointed Clerk of the Peace and Protector of Slaves in 1834, which appointment he held till 1836, when he was entrusted with the task of compiling the records regarding intercourse between the Colonists and the various native tribes of South Africa. On 13th November, 1845, he was appointed Secretary to the Government of Natal. He was afterwards Speaker of the first Legislative Council, and died at Maritzburg, August 27, 1861.

Haw, Simon, a settler of Mr. Dalgairn's party from London, who came in the *Northampton*. He was married, with a wife and one child. He resided in Graham's Town, where he carried on the business of a money-lender to his brother settlers. He died about 1860, at the age of seventy-seven years, leaving a numerous family. His eldest son, Charles, had an honourable career in the public service in various capacities, was Civil Commissioner and Resident Magistrate of Victoria East. A son died prematurely at Cradock. The third son, William, was a hardware merchant at Graham's Town, who married a daughter of Mr. George Slater, M.L.A., farmer, at Quagga's Flats ; and Edward, who practised for many years as a general law agent at Graham's Town and who survives.

Smith, ——. There were many of this name among the settlers. Two of the parties were headed by persons of this patronymic—Mr. George Smith's party from Manchester, and Mr. William Smith's party from London. The former had been an officer in the 95th Rifle Brigade, and his location was along the coast between the Lynedoch and Kowie Rivers ; Mr. William Smith's was on the northern border of the Settlement on the road to Trompetter's Drift, adjoining Mr. William Clark's, an exposed situation in close proximity to the Fish River Bush. Both were driven from their locations by the irruption of the Kafirs in 1835, escaping with their lives. To distinguish one Smith from another, they were known by epithets indicating their personal appearance. Thus there was "long-armed" Smith, "short-armed" Smith, "punchey" Smith, "boatswain"

Smith, etc., etc., otherwise it would have been difficult to identify the particular individual intended. Mr. William Smith, head of the party from London, married the widow of Mr. James Greathead, and practised in Graham's Town as a land surveyor, where he died leaving a family. His son, Mr. William Benstead Smith, served in the Imperial Commissariat Department during the wars of 1846-47 and 1850-53. During the latter war he was in charge of the transport, and received the Kafir war medal. He was for many years Secretary to the Kowie Harbour Improvement Board, and, finally, Registrar of Mines on the Diamond Fields, where he died in 1892. A daughter married Mr. Skeleton Wimble, a merchant, at Graaff Reinet. Another of the name, Mr. John Hancorn Smith, one of Mr. Willson's party of settlers who arrived by the *Belle Alliance*, devoted himself to agriculture, and owned one of the largest and most beautiful farms in Lower Albany. Owing to the successive Kafir wars, he became greatly impoverished, and having a family of ten children, all small, to support, the outlook after the last war was more hopeless, and it was a struggle for existence to the last. Latterly, he lived at Assegai Bush, a farm about sixteen miles from Graham's Town, on the main road to Port Elizabeth, where he died in 1857, aged seventy-nine years, leaving a wife and ten children. He married a Miss Stringfellow, and she died at Kimberley in 1862, aged eighty-six years. His three sons: John Hancorn was killed by lightning in 1874, Thomas W. died at Kimberley in 1872, and William, who had explored the interior far beyond the Zambesi, was attacked by the prevailing fever, carried in a palanquin by natives 200 miles trying to reach the coast, but died three days beyond Senna in 1885. He was buried at Senna, the particulars being sent to his wife with his diary by the British Consul at that place. Five of the daughters married: (1) Captain Nicolson, of the 27th Regiment, late of H.M.'s Cape Mounted Riflemen; (2) Colonel Lyons, Royal Artillery; (3) Sir Drummond M. Dunbar, Bart.; (4) George Harding, Esq.; (5) the Rev. C. F. Taberer, missionary of the English Church in charge of the important Kafir Industrial Establishment at Keiskama Stock, near King William's Town; and (6) Mary, who remains unmarried.

Cawood, David, was one of Mr. Hazelhurst's party, whose location was on the north-east of the Nottingham party. He was accompanied by six sons—James, William, John, Joshua, Samuel and Joseph—and three daughters. The Cawoods were descended from a Yorkshire family, many of whom, according to the chronicles of Cawood and Cawood Castle, held important positions and offices as far back as 1201. David Cawood and his family settled on the farm known as "Cawood's Post," in Albany, but no long time elapsed before the sons, young and enterprising, moved off, the war of 1835 scattering many others also who never returned to their locations, finding more satisfactory openings for their energy elsewhere. Previous to this period the young Cawoods went through Kafirland to Natal—no ordinary feat in those days—on a hunting and trading expedition. They penetrated as far as Dingaan's Kraal, and were received and entertained by that chief for ten days. Although well treated while at the kraal, after they had left, Dinghaan sent an impi after them with orders to kill them and take their property. Providentially the party took the route along the coast, whereas the impi took the inland road and so missed them. James, the eldest son, was the senior partner in the firm of Cawood Brothers, consisting of William, Samuel and Joseph, who for many years carried on a large mercantile business in Graham's Town with several country branches, and they were army contractors for some years. They took a prominent part in pubic matters as Municipal Commissioners, etc., James, Joshua, Samuel and Joseph having been returned to the Legislative Council and House of Assembly respectively, where they ably represented Eastern Province interests. William Cawood served in Southey's Corps of Guides, when the forces entered Kafirland and brought the Fingo tribe out of slavery. He was present at the death of Hintza, the great paramount chief of those times. These men have left a name for courage, enterprise and honesty, second to none, and their descendants are to be found throughout the Cape Colony, Natal and neighbouring States, possibly more numerous than any of the immigrants of 1820. The Rev. H. H. Dugmore, in his Jubilee lecture delivered at Graham's Town in 1870, gives the united generations then living as 356, the original family comprising nine, of whom Mrs. Stuart and Mrs. Gradwell are the only survivors.

Wood, George, came out as an apprentice to Mr. William Smith Owen, with the Sephton party in the *Aurora*, being then fourteen years of age. After completing his term of engagement with Mr. Owen, and after with Mr. W. Thackwray, he struck out for himself and set up on his own account in a modest way in Bathurst Street, Graham's Town, where he kept a shop and supplied all sorts of necessaries and useful articles (v. a. p.). He married Susannah Garbett, step-daughter of Mr. Joseph Donovan, one of Mr. Willson's party of settlers, by whom he had a numerous family—eight sons and five daughters. He died at his residence, Woodville, Beaufort Street, Graham's Town, 1st November, 1884, aged eighty years, his wife following him in 1890, aged eighty-one years. His eldest son, George Samuel, was admitted as a partner in his father's business in 1851. He was the first Mayor of Graham's Town, and was elected to the same office twice afterwards. He represented the City of Graham's Town in the House of Assembly from 1864 to 1868. He married Fanny, daughter of the Hon. J. C. Hoole, and died in Graham's Town in 1884, aged fifty-six years. (2) John Edwin, also became a partner in his father's business in 1851. He, like his brothers, took an active part in all the institutions established for the advancement of the town, was second Mayor of Graham's Town, and represented the constituency of Albany in the House of Assembly from 1864 to 1866, and was returned to represent the City of Graham's Town in 1887, and continues to hold that seat. He married Charlotte, daughter of Mr. William Wright. (3) William died in Cradock, 8th January, 1856, aged twenty-four years and six months. (4) Joseph Garbett, engaged in farming pursuits at Summer Hill, near Bathurst. He represented the Albany constituency in the House of Assembly from 1884 to 1887. He died at Graham's Town, 25th September, 1892, aged fifty-nine years. (5) Henry Richard joined his brothers in business about 1863, from which time it has been continued under the style of Wood Brothers. He is a director of several joint-stock companies, and also Deputy Sheriff for Albany. (6) Ben Horace, also joined his brothers in business in 1863, but retired from the firm in 1870, going to Natal, where he is engaged with his large estate known as Clairmont. (7) Alfred Jesse is now in London, where he is practising his profession of an artist, having for several years been under the tuition of Sir — Firth, Royal Academy. (8) Garbett, the youngest son, died at the age of seventeen years. The daughters (1) Susannah, married Mr. Jonathan Ayliff; (2) Eleanor, married Mr. George McKiell; (3) Harriet, married Mr. G. N. H. Curzen; (4) Elizabeth, married Commissary-General Sir W. H. Drake; (5) Lydia, married Mr. George W. Impey.

Pullen, Thomas, came out with Mr. Thomas Owen's party by the *Nautilus*. He brought his wife, twelve children, and a female servant. Two daughters and one son were born to him after his arrival. Owen's party were located near the mouth of the Fish River, between the locations of Mr. Charles Crause and Mr. Thomas Rowles. The family remained in Port Elizabeth, the father and three sons only going on to the location. They got back to Port Elizabeth before the war of 1835 broke out. The eldest son, Thomas, died ; the second son, Edward, served in the expedition against the Fitcani in 1828, afterwards married widow Plackett and took to farming, near Uitenhage ; Tendall, the third son, married a Miss Maritz, and also took to farming. The fourth son, William Turner, served with the auxiliary forces in the three Kafir wars of 1835, 1845 and 1850, is still alive, living near Pretoria with his sons, aged eighty-three years and nine months. The fifth son, Charles, died young ; the sixth and youngest, engaged in farming, married Miss Raymond, and died at his residence, Cuton Park, near Port Elizabeth, in 1892. The nine daughters married severally : (1) Dorothy, John Anthony Chaband, attorney-at-law, Port Elizabeth ; (2) Adelaide, Captain Walton, who died and left a son farming near Sandflats ; (3) Augusta, Mr. William Metelerkamp, of Zuurbron, division of Humansdorp, and died October, 1894, aged ninety-one years ; (4) Julia, Mr. Joseph Butler, farmer, of the Kei Road division of Komzha ; (5) Ellen, Mr. Sievwright, farmer, near King William's Town ; (6) Harriet died young ; (7) Lavinia, Mr. Leonard Bean, farmer, Uitenhage district ; (8) Octavia, Mr. John Smith, also a farmer, near East London ; and (9) Emily, Mr. Dewes, farmer, near Addo Bush, division of Alexandria. All the sons and daughters are remarkable for large families, and the descendants of Mr. Thomas Pullen are to be found in most parts of the Frontier districts and in the Transvaal.

Surmon, William Henry, came in the *Nautilus* with Mr. Thomas Knowles's party. He was a married man, with one child, a boy a year old, also named William Henry. He settled in Albany, and worked at his trade as a master carpenter in Graham's Town. He died in 1836, leaving five sons, namely, William Henry, James, John, Thomas, and Henry, and four daughters.
(1) William Henry was also a master carpenter in Graham's Town, and followed his trade till appointed Inspector Frontier Armed Mounted Police. He was wounded in the Kafir war of 1852, died of Bright's disease in 1866. He was married, and left five sons : William Henry, James Edward, George Thomas, Edward, and Walter, and four daughters. (2) James worked at his trade of a carpenter in Graham's Town till he joined the Frontier Armed Mounted Police, in which force he rose to the rank of Inspector, afterwards Captain, when the name of the corps was changed to C.M.R. He was shot at the head of his troop in first attack on Morosi's mountain, April, 1879. He married, but his wife predeceased him, leaving two daughters, who were granted a pension of £50 each by the Cape Government. (3) John, also a carpenter, now farming on the Fish River, near Graham's Town, married, and has four sons, all farmers. (4) Thomas, a carpenter, working at his trade in Johannesburg, has two sons, who are working with him. (5) Henry, who at Johannesburg has several sons and daughters. The grandson of the original William Henry Surmon is the present Assistant Commissioner at Gaberones, Bechuanaland Protectorate, who was educated at St. Andrew's College, Graham's Town, has had various service in Basutuland as Magistrate, Assistant Commssioner, Captain in the Basutu Contingent, in the Morosi Campaign, and as Commandant of Mohali's Hoek Contingent in the Basutu War of 1880-81. He was present at the relief of Mohali's Hoek and Mafeteng, and took part in most of the fights during the war, and was mentioned in dispatches. He is married, and has four sons and three daughters.

Wedderburn, Christopher, with wife, two sons and three daughters, were among the settlers brought out by Mr. George Smith, late of 95th Rifle Brigade. They came from Manchester, and sailed from Liverpool in the transport *Stentor*. The voyage occupied three months, and they arrived in Algoa Bay in April, 1820. From there they proceeded by ox-wagon to Green Fountain, Albany, where they were located. Christopher and his son William received grants of land in the location assigned to Mr. Smith, about three miles from Port Alfred, near Kubane's River. Christopher became a successful farmer until the cruel Kafir war of 1835, when the Kafirs carried off all his cattle and destroyed all the homesteads. He, with the other settlers, sought refuge in Graham's Town, as all lower Albany was overrun by the savages, who murdered all the white inhabitants they caught. For eight months the settlers were driven from their homes, when peace was again restored. In 1845 they bought a farm near Salem, on the Assegai River, where George and his father carried on farming, and, with a good market in Graham's Town, being noted for their excellent cheese, butter and oat-hay, obtained good prices and did well. Another drawback was experienced when the war of 1846 broke out. This time the farmers banded themselves together, and by sheer pluck defeated the Kafirs at the Kareiga River, who had stolen all the cattle from the encampment. After several hours' fighting all the cattle were recaptured and the Kafirs gave the Salemites a wide berth, George Wedderburn being conspicuous with others for his bravery. Peace was again restored until Christmas day, 1850, when, with the help of rebellious Hottentots, the Kafirs again invaded the Colony, murdering right and left, George Wedderburn being among the fallen. He lingered some months, and died of his wounds, leaving a widow and five small children to battle with the world. The father and mother passed away previous to this war, only William and Esther remaining of the original stock. William early left the location and started business in Graham's Town as a tailor, married Martha Patrick, also a settler, had thirteen children, four of whom survive. He had six sons, and died October 27, 1894, aged sixty-five years, John and Christopher being his two male representatives. John is well known in Graham's Town as a successful wagon builder, whose vehicles are in demand all over the Eastern districts, on the Diamond Fields, Bechuanaland, and the Interior. The first white lady who penetrated to the Zambesi was conveyed in a wagon built by John Wedderburn.

Glass, Thomas, was one of Mr. George Southey's party which came out in the *Hennersley Castle.* He was married, and brought his wife and six children, four sons and two daughters, two more sons and one daughter being born to him in this country. He took to farming, and acquired a property near Graham's Town, which he called Coldstream, where he successfully pursued his operations till his death in 1849, at the age of sixty-five years. Of his six sons, John and James became carpenters and builders at Graham's Town, John eventually migrating to the district of Peddie, where he died about 1871. James went to the Diamond Fields soon after they were discovered, and attracted a large population in 1872, and followed his trade at Kimberley until his death, which occurred in 1874. Both John and James left a numerous family. Thomas and Benjamin (who was born in Albany) were both masons. Thomas met with his death by a fall from a scaffold to a house he was building; Benjamin is still alive, and at present on the farm Coldstream. Daniel and William followed in their father's footsteps and became farmers. Daniel acquired land near Driver's Bush, a little beyond Graham's Town, and farmed it till he met his death about 1874, a young cow having gored him, from which he died in a few hours. William went into the Victoria East (Alice) district and acquired farms there. He too met with an untimely death. While placing a tarpaulin over a load of grain on his wagon, he fell over and broke his neck. A son of James Glass served in the Zulu war, and was present at the battle of Ulundi; and a son of Benjamin's who was a member of the Yeomanry Corps was killed during the Basutu war.

Hobson, David, was one of Mr. William Smith's party by the *Northampton.* He was quite a young man, being twenty-two years of age, and was accompanied by his brother Carey Hobson, aged fourteen years. The brothers began sheep farming in Albany, on the farms Salem and Cottesbrook, but lost everything during the three successive Kafir wars, in which they took an active part, being noted as dead shots. During the war of 1835 David accepted service in the Commissariat department. In 1842 the brothers left Albany for the Karroo—Carey first, David following, bringing with them a few merino sheep, up to that time unknown in the Graaff Reinet district, the Boers there farming only with the Cape sheep and common goats. They settled down in-the neighbourhood of Lot's Kloof, being then the only English farmers in that large district. By dint of undaunted perseverance they became the owners of many square miles of land, and were fairly prosperous. David married Mary Anne Robinson, and had four sons and five daughters. He died at his farm Wellfound, aged seventy-three years. Carey married Susan Bonin—two sons and two daughters. He died at Graham's Town. At the present day the descendants are numerous, and among the influential inhabitants of the Graaff Reinet. The oldest of the name alive is Mr. D. E. Hobson, who has been a member of the Licensing Court and Divisional Council of Joannesville from the time that Joannesville was made a seat of magistracy. The two brothers, David and Carey Hobson, were nephews of Dr. Carey, of the Serampore Mission. Carey Hobson was a J.P. for Graaff Reinet and Uitenhage, and after him his son, Samuel Bonin Hobson, and after his death Jonathan Hobson.

Mandy, John, head of a small party who came with others by the *Nautilus*. He came from Foot's Cray, Kent, was a married man with two sons, John Wilkinson and Stephen Day, aged respectively six and five years. On the voyage another son was born to him named William. The location assigned to him was at the mouth of the Fish River, near Shaw Park, next to that of Mr. Rowles. From this he was driven by the irruption of the Kafirs in 1835, and took refuge in Graham's Town, where he resided till his death, May 25, 1848, aged sixty-one years, his wife having predeceased him, 15th February, 1823, aged thirty-five years. The sons established themselves in business in Graham's Town, where they took a leading part in promoting the prosperity of the town and district. Stephen Day carried on a large wholesale and retail wine and spirit business at the corner of Bathurst Street and High Street. He was a bank director and a member of the Graham's Town municipality. His brother John Wilkinson was in the business, and he died at Graham's Town 23rd June, 1853, at the age of thirty-nine years. Stephen Day retired from business and went to reside in England, where he died 4th June, 1869, aged fifty-four years. William settled on the farm, Lushington Valley, near Bathurst, which afterwards became his own. Experience gained in former Kafir wars secured him the post of Commandant of Burghers in the war of 1850-53, in which he and his followers did good service to Lower Albany. After the war of 1850 the late Sir Walter Currie organized his famous Frontier Armed Mounted Police Corps, and selected William Mandy as one of the first to take command of one of its troops, which trust he refused. Sir Walter knowing what he was made of, insisted upon his joining, which he eventually did, and served for several years as sub-inspector at Cawood's Post and Waai Plaats. But the wear and tear of active service proved too much for his health. He retired to his farm against the wishes of his friends in arms, who offered him several good appointments, and died there 20th January, 1887, aged sixty-seven years.

Mandy, Joseph, a younger brother of the above John Mandy, by trade a coach-maker, was also a passenger by the *Nautilus*, and then unmarried. He settled in the Orange Free State district of Harrismith, but little is known of him. His son Francis Mandy was a very successful farmer in that district, and he died in August, 1892.

Butler & Tanner, The Selwood Printing Works, Frome, and London.

NEWLY PUBLISHED.

The Naval Pocket Book for 1897. By W. LAIRD CLOWES. Containing particulars of all the Navies of the World, corrected up to December 1st, 1896. Cloth, gilt edges, 16mo, 878 pages, price 5s. nett.

The Daily Chronicle says:—" The second year of this handy and admirable work is in many respects an improvement on the first issue, excellent as we thought that. This classification is of vast value, if only for the saving of time, even to experts, while to the ordinary man taking an interest in the Navy it is an additional recommendation of a little work which, though it has grown since last year, is still pocketable. The plates are excellent, and the information on ordnance is well put together and very useful. Nor can we omit calling attention to the fulness of the index by which the references to any war vessel in the world may be found instantly."

The Morning Post says:—" The 'Naval Pocket Book' was favourably received when first issued last year, and this year is more complete and accurate."

The Westminster Gazette says:—" We know of no work in which such a mass of information is given in such a compact and handy form,—or, indeed, in any form. We are glad that the first issue was so very favourably received, and are sure that the present, more complete as it is, will also be a success. The Pocket Book is printed on thin paper, and is altogether neatly got up."

The Scotsman says:—" This valuable, concise, and well-packed book gives its matter in a form considerably improved from that of the original issue last year; and the Editor of the work, Mr. W. Laird Clowes, is to be congratulated on the skill with which he has brought the many figures and facts in the book up to date. The arrangement of the matter for purposes of reference is admirable, and the Pocket Book cannot but continue to grow in the estimation of those for whom it is designed."

Lord Rosebery's Speeches (1874-1896). Compiled by A. T. CAMDEN PRATT. Crown 8vo, 471 pages, price 6s.

" The selection represents many sides of Lord Rosebery's political interests."—*Morning Post.*
" The volume will be immensely useful."—*Birmingham Daily Post.*
" Much might be said of them; they have already been so widely read and so freely commented on that no purpose would be served here by a discussion of the matters they deal with, and their importance does not need to be signalised. Even if they are regarded from a literary point of view, as pieces of accomplished oratory, the time is happily not yet come when their value is of so remote a kind as to be appropriately subjected to any academical analysis. The volume will be welcome to many readers as useful to refer to and interesting to read. While its scope is not by any means restricted to political questions, it has its most essential character and value as being representative of the best aspects of contemporary statemanship."—*Scotsman.*

Rottenness. A Study of America and England. By ROGER POCOCK, Author of " The Rules of the Game," " The Dragon Slayer," " The Blackguard," etc. Crown 8vo, cloth, price 2s. 6d.

" His description of the frauds and villainies practised in America both in public and private life is indeed lurid."—*Literary World.*
" Such a title requires a subtitle, and 'Rottenness' has one. We would fain hold it back, but it glides from our unwilling pen. . . . There is nothing to be done but for the two nations to cable their blushes to each other."—*Globe.*
" At one time we deplore that we are English, until cheered by the wickedness of our American cousin."—*Pall Mall Gazette.*
RICHARD LE GALLIENNE in the *Statist* says:—" Mr. Pocock writes with much ability, has a considerable gift of fierce sarcasm, and has evidently studied observantly the questions with which he deals."

The Novel of the Hour.

Rose of Dutcher's Coolly. By HAMLIN GARLAND. Cloth, 6s.

" The author of 'Rose of Dutcher's Coolly' scores a marked success, chiefly, as it seems to us, because he has written his book to please himself, and with no attention to rigid rules of form or to conventions of modern fiction. The book is the spontaneous outcome of a man's mind, a thing much more rare now than in the days when the novelist's art was in its infancy. . . . The outcome of this and of his talent is a book, striking, original, and throughout distinguished above the ordinary. . . . We wish the book the success it deserves, and in congratulating the author on his achievement, we desire to add a word of congratulation to the publishers; for the get-up of the book is as excellent as its matter."—*Pall Mall Gazette.*
" In some points she is peculiar; not so much modest as prudish, and although avowedly averse from marriage, concerning herself very much more about the relations between the sexes than is wholesome in young persons of her age and sex. The whole story seems, indeed, to be the answer to the question whether this gifted being shall devote herself to art and culture or condescend to devote herself to the vulgar duties of a wife and mother."—*Times.*
" Some may object to the extreme outspokenness on subjects of sex. There is, perhaps a little too much of it; but one can see the necessity for it in most instances, and the general tone of the book is by no means objectionable, though subjects are now and then touched upon which even contemporary fiction usually avoids."—*Saturday Review.*
" A novel of more than ordinary merit."—*Lady*
" The character of Rose is well and strongly drawn."—*Dundee Courier.*
I. ZANGWILL, in the *Pall Mall Magazine*, says:—" Mason is a creature worthy to stand beside Langham, the one memorable figure in 'Robert Elsmere.' . . . Mr. Garland belongs to the few novelists who do not write second-hand books."

NEVILLE BEEMAN, LIMITED, 6, BELL'S BUILDINGS,
SALISBURY SQUARE, LONDON, E.C.

Exciting Tales of the Battles of To-morrow.
Price 6s. each.

The Captain of the "Mary Rose" (Seventh Edition). By W. LAIRD CLOWES, compiler of the "Naval Pocket-Book." Illustrated by the CHEVALIER DE MARTINO and FRED. T. JANE.

"Deserves something more than a passing notice."—*Times*.
"The most notable book of the season."—*Standard*.
"We read the book at a sitting."—*Pall Mall Gazette*.

Blake of the "Rattlesnake"; or, The Man who Saved England. By FRED T. JANE, Author of "Life on Board a Torpedo Catcher," "The Incubated Girl," etc., etc. With Illustrations by the Author.

Novels of Note. Cloth, 6s.

The Incubated Girl. By FRED T. JANE, Author of "Blake of the *Rattlesnake*," etc., etc.

"A most remarkable book."

The City of Gold. By E. MARKWICK. With Eight Illustrations by H. PIFFARD.

"It is really interesting and exciting."—*Daily Telegraph*.
"A thrilling compound of strange and perilous adventures."—*Globe*.
"The marvels discovered rival the 'Arabian Nights.'"—*Scotsman*.

Merlin. A Piratical Love Study. By Mr. M——.

"Of all weird stories this is surely the most startling."—*Dundee Advertiser*.
"Beggars description. . . . Two of the most remarkable persons that ever novelist created."—*Scotsman*.
"Sensational and powerful writing . . . the mysterious region of the China seas."—*Lloyd's*.

A Woman's Courier. A Tale of the Famous Forty Conspiracy of 1696. By W. J. YEOMAN, Author of "King William III.," etc., etc. With Eight Illustrations by H. PIFFARD.

"An entertaining and even exciting romance. Mr. Yeoman has proved his ability to produce a stirring and readable tale from the materials supplied by English history, and his own fertile imagination."—*Literary World*.

The New Vagabond Library. Cloth, 2s.; Paper, 1s. 6d.

Vol. I. GASCOIGNE'S GHOST. By G. B. Burgin.
 „ II. THE CHEST OF OPIUM. By Mr. M——.
 „ III. IRRALIE'S BUSHRANGER. By E. W. Hornung.
 „ IV. THE BLACKGUARD. By Roger Pocock.
 „ V. HIS DAUGHTER. By W. L. Alden.

General Literature.

Unknown London: Its Romance and Tragedy. By A. T. CAMDEN PRATT. 276 pages, price 3s. 6d.

"Mr. Pratt's acquaintance with the metropolis is both extensive and peculiar."—*Daily Telegraph*.
"Supplements our knowledge in an unexpected and charming manner. . . . The ancient times seem to throb with the atmosphere of reality."—*Morning Leader*.

Indian Gup; or, Stories Untold of the Indian Mutiny. By an Indian Chaplain. 354 pages, price 6s.

"Thoroughly readable."—*Dundee Advertiser*.
"The book will be read with interest by all classes of Anglo-Indians."—*Scotsman*.
"Full of pleasant anecdotes and interesting descriptions of India."—*St. James' Gazette*.
"An interesting book of reminiscences."—*Globe*.
"Such an unvarnished account of India by a religious man of the world has higher merits than literary finish. Mr. Baldwin went out to India just as the Mutiny was being suppressed, and worked in several provinces, seeing a good deal of life, official and native. It is interesting, in view of a recent controversy, to examine the view he takes of missionary effort."—*Yorkshire Post*.

JUST OUT:

Light Thrown on a Hideous Empire. By an ORIENTAL WIDOW. A Vivid Portraiture of Russian Life. Crown 8vo, cloth, price 2s.

LONDON: NEVILLE BEEMAN, LIMITED, 6 BELL'S BUILDINGS, SALISBURY SQUARE, E.C.

www.ingramcontent.com/pod-product-compliance
Lightning Source LLC
Chambersburg PA
CBHW021822230426
43669CB00008B/842